Soviet Asia

About the Book and Author

Soviet Asia constitutes three-quarters of the USSR's territory, an area exceeding the size of Brazil and Australia combined. However, most of this vast hinterland is weakly and unevenly integrated into the country's economy and its political and cultural life. The regions of Soviet Asia play very different roles in the Soviet spatial system and are affected by different policy choices at the national level. Dr. Dienes examines the geographic position of Soviet Asia in relation to the economy of the USSR and analyzes the impact of major national policy issues on the development and prospects of Soviet Asia, arguing that national economic priorities are inevitably defined in terms of the needs of the European USSR, where 80 percent of the Slavic population and more than 75 percent of the state's economic power are concentrated. Economic priorities, however, may be greatly modified, even overridden, by strategic interests and concerns about the cohesion and internal security of the multinational Soviet state; these concerns especially influence the relationship of Soviet Asia to the country's economic heartland.

Leslie Dienes is professor of geography at the University of Kansas.

Soviet Asia

Economic Development and National Policy Choices

Leslie Dienes

Westview Press / Boulder and London

Westview Special Studies on the Soviet Union and Eastern Europe

Published in 1987 in the United States of America by Westview Press, Inc.;
Frederick A. Praeger, Publisher; 5500 Central Avenue, Boulder, Colorado 80301

Library of Congress Cataloging-in-Publication Data
Dienes, Leslie.
   Soviet Asia.
   (Westview special studies on the Soviet Union
and Eastern Europe)
   Includes index.
   1. Siberia (R.S.F.S.R.)--Economic policy. 2. Siberia
planning--Siberia (R.S.F.S.R.) 4. Soviet Central Asia--
Economic conditions. 6. Regional planning--Soviet
Central Asia. I. Title. II. Series.
HC336.9.S53D53   1987   338.957   87-8331
ISBN 0-8133-7437-5

Composition for this book was provided by the author.

Printed and bound in the United States of America

 The paper used in this publication meets the requirements of the
American National Standard for Permanence of Paper for Printed
Library Materials Z39.48-1984.

6   5   4   3   2   1

To the memory of
Ted Shabad

Contents

Tables and Figures

FIGURES

Preface

This work examines the geographic position of Soviet Asia in the overall economy of the USSR and analyzes the impact of major national policy issues on its development and prospects. The Asian USSR constitutes three-fourths of the country's territory, an area exceeding the size of Brazil and Australia combined. Its acquisition was the result of Russian expansion and conquest in the past 400 years. This vast territory is still hinterland to the European USSR, weakly and unevenly integrated into the country's economic and societal mainstream. Moreover, the Asian USSR is hardly uniform, culturally or otherwise. Its regions play very different roles in the Soviet spatial system and are affected by different policy choices on the national level. On the one hand, there are striking contrasts between Moslem Central Asia and Siberia (including the Far East). On the other hand, the Siberian regions are also assigned different economic and strategic roles according to their resource endowment, their links to the economic power centers in the European USSR (partly a function of their east-west and north-south positions) and their strategic vulnerability or importance.

In any country, the economic profiles and prospects of regions are a result of interaction between extraregional and local, regional impulses. In the centrally managed USSR, regional development is inexorably linked to and may indeed be fully determined by national policy choices and priorities. These priorities are decided by the center of political and economic power in the European USSR, where over 70 percent of the population, 80 percent of the dominant Slavic population and three-fourths of the Soviet state's economic potential are concentrated. Naturally, even here, policy decisions are in the hands of a narrow political elite.

Such strictly economic priorities, however, may be substantially modified, even overridden, by two additional concerns especially manifest along the far-flung periphery of the vast Asian hinterland. This necessarily means that strategic interests, perceptions, and fears significantly affect investment and development policy east of the Urals. The distant borderlands of Soviet Asia project into two of the world's major geopolitical regions: the East Asian and Pacific rimland and the Moslem Middle East. The second concern pertains to the cohesion and internal security of the multinational Soviet state. Whereas the Siberian-Far Eastern hinterland is fully part of the Russian ethno-cultural domain and is populated overwhelmingly by Slavs, Central Asia remains a distinct, separate realm, despite a century of Russian-Soviet rule. Its large, rapidly growing Moslem population culturally and linguistically still belongs to the Turko-Iranian world flanking the southern frontier. Central Asia accounts for most of the population growth of the USSR and represents not only a problem of development, but one of social and political stability.

The book is organized in three parts. Part I presents the framework for the analysis, sketching the problem of integration (with a focus on economic integration) between the European USSR and both the Siberian and Central Asian hinterlands. It then explains the regional scheme. Part II examines the relationship between economic development in the Asian USSR and major national policy issues that most affect the economic structure, growth, and prospect of macroregions in Soviet Asia. Separate chapters deal with Siberia, the Far East and Central Asia--Southern Kazakhstan. Part III treats manpower, settlement policy, and regional planning in the harsh environment of Siberia, the Far East, and Kazakhstan. Economic development takes place not in abstract space but through a concrete settlement network, both urban and rural. One chapter shows how the harsh environment and the vast, roadless expanses magnify the difficulties of employment and of human and economic interaction through the far-flung settlement hierarchy. Another chapter examines the problem of regional planning in the centrally managed economy of the USSR. It relates that problem to the need to develop Siberia more efficiently and to reconcile regional, ministerial, and national interests. Finally, a conclusion summarizes the issues analyzed in the book and makes some judgment about the future of Soviet Asia under Mikhail Gorbachev.

This book follows the transliteration system of the

Library of Congress, with four exceptions. In the text, the words Yakut (and its derivatives), Yamal, Yamburg, and Yuzhno-Sakhalinsk are transliterated as shown, instead of Iakut, Iamal, Iamburg, and Iuzhno-Sakhalinsk, spellings that are required by this system. The spelling used here (following that of the Board of Geographic Names) is the one commonly encountered in the Western press and is more familiar. In the Russian footnotes, the transliteration conforms to the system of the Library of Congress without exception.

Leslie Dienes

Acknowledgments

I express my sincere appreciation to the Earhart Foundation for its financial support. The International Research and Exchanges Board (IREX) provided funds for a month-long, useful stay in Moscow and Novosibirsk and battled red tape to arrange my visit. I am grateful for its assistance. I also thank my Soviet colleagues at the Institute of Economics and Organization of Industrial Production (IEOPP), Novosibirsk, for the professional courtesies and help extended to me at their institute. Parts of this book were written during my stay as a visiting scholar at the Slavic Research Center of Hokkaido University, Japan. The support of the Center is gratefully acknowledged. I am indebted to the Cartographic Service of the Department of Geography at the University of Kansas for the three maps and to the Research Committee of the university's Faculty Senate, which provided funds for them. I also thank Victor Merkin for his help with hard-to-obtain Russian research material and John Dreiling for typing the numerous tables. I am also much indebted to Barbara Ellington and others at Westview Press for painstaking and conscientious editorial work. Finally, I wish to express my deep gratitude to my wife, Jennie, who typed and retyped the various drafts, prepared the final copy, and unfailingly assisted me throughout the work.

Chapter 4 of this book is an updated, slightly modified version of an earlier article on the Soviet Far East, which appeared in the April-June 1985 issue of Soviet Economy. Chapters 6 and 7 incorporate another article from the October 1985 issue of Soviet Geography and small portions from the April 1982 issue. I thank the editors of these journals for permission to use this material. This is also an appropriate place to acknowledge the invaluable service of the late Ted Shabad, editor of <u>Soviet Geography</u>, as a tireless monitor and incisive analyst of geographical developments in the USSR. I have benefited greatly from the abundance of authoritative material provided by that journal and from the generous advice of its editor. This book is dedicated to Ted Shabad's memory.

Leslie Dienes

PART ONE

Soviet Asia:
A Framework for Analysis

1

Introduction:
Hinterland and Metropolis—
The Problem of Integration

Geographic space is a cardinal factor in economic development, but only if integrative forces are present to cement the diverse parts of that expanse into a structurally and functionally cohesive whole. Political and social integration of the area is clearly a necessary condition for a steady, long-run economic advance--a process which then further binds the geographic fragments into an interdependent system. For any regionally diverse country, however, this process of integration is a lengthy one. At any particular time, some regions will have become more integrated in all three respects (political, social, economic) than others.[1] Physical obstacles and great distances tend to slow and may block the process; so does linguistic, ethnic, or cultural diversity. To a considerable degree, the first can be conquered by technology and capital; more subtle and subconscious human adjustments are needed to compensate for the diversity.

The progress of integration in all three dimensions can be clearly observed through Russian-Soviet history, as can the strenuous efforts to overcome the barriers of physical geography and distance and moderate those of ethno-cultural plus linguistic diversity, which resulted from expansion and conquest. The process, however, is far from complete and may never be fully completed. To this day, the USSR exhibits a strong dichotomy between core and periphery with regard to both sparsely settled hinterlands and regions populated by substantial non-European nationalities linked to the Slavic core in a quasi-colonial dependency. Siberia, with adjoining Northern Kazakhstan, constitute the first type of this periphery; Moslem Central Asia-Southern Kazakhstan and, to a degree, Transcaucasia--represent the second type. (Because Transcaucasia can be

3

regarded economically as much an extension of the European core area as part of the Asian periphery, it will not be treated in this work. Nor will we treat the Baltic Republics, a sliver of Scandinavia and Central Europe inside the USSR. They present a different issue of integration altogether, but their small size and population keep them from being a major regional issue, despite their strategic significance.)

This book examines the success of the Soviet regime in developing the Asian periphery and integrating its diverse regions into the country's economic mainstream. Given the size of this landmass, these disparate parts play very different roles in the Soviet spatial system and are affected by different policy choices and issues on the national level. In any large state, of course, the economic configuration of regions is a product not only of the local ethos but of principal structural trends acting on these units from the nation (and even the world) at large. The future prospects of these regions are the product of that interplay. In the USSR, a state which is managed centrally through the vertical hierarchies of the Party and the federal ministries, regional performance and direction are particularly strongly affected by major national policy choices. The development and prospect of macroregions in the Asian USSR are intimately tied to such policy decisions (Figure 1).

National energy policy choices have been and remain most critical for West and East Siberia. These choices are closely intertwined with questions concerning the structure and regional dimension of the Soviet economy as a whole, particularly its energy and material-intensive branches. Contrasting mobility and economic priority among the available energy sources, inertia of industrial structure, and the spatial configuration of that structure combine to produce different linkages between energy policy and regional development within the huge territory from the Urals to the Far East. For the latter area, strategic priorities, Soviet ocean policy, and relations between the USSR and Japan and China are decisive. Although prospects for easing Sino-Soviet tensions are important conditioning factors, developments vis-à-vis Japan and in Soviet strategic position in the Pacific are proving to be the most important national factors for the economic fortunes of the Far East. As for Central Asia and Southern Kazakhstan, its course will be charted by decisions on basically new patterns of investment allocation, industrialization, and ethnic relations. For all these macroregions, choices

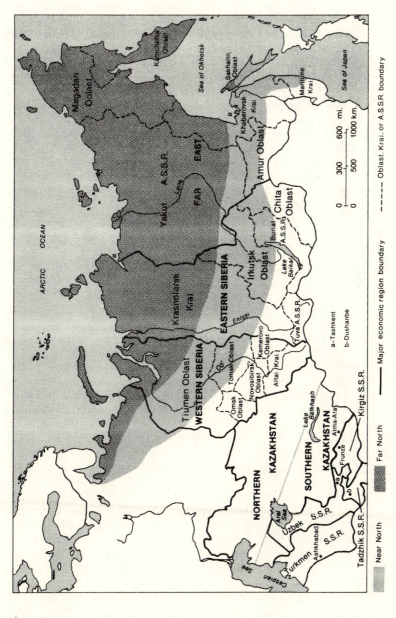

FIGURE 1 Macroregions of the Asian USSR.

foregone and decisions not made will have an impact as important as choices made.

Both the Siberian and the Central Asian peripheries present distinct problems for the Soviet leadership. Politically, both are securely tied to Moscow through the highly centralized Party and Government hierarchies. The pioneer hinterland from the Urals to the Pacific is part of the Russian ethno-cultural domain and thus fully shares the values of a body politic dominated by the Great Russians. The weak and dispersed Paleo-Asian and Turkic nationalities put no real strain on internal cohesion and legitimacy in the political and social spheres. The threat comes from the outside due to strategic vulnerability and to distance of supply lines that becomes pronounced east of Lake Baikal. In contrast, the socio-political integration of the southern, non-European periphery, especially of Central Asia, is still somewhat tenuous. The peoples of Central Asia are poorly represented in the highest echelons of political life and, for the most part, are constrained in exercising power even within their own territory. And in their mores and value systems, these nationalities, as do all traditional societies in the process of modernization, exhibit a considerable degree of schism and social strain.

In the economic sphere, incomplete integration is the rule both in the pioneer hinterland and in Central Asia. This is evident from the unbalanced, narrow profiles of their economies and linkages to the central core of economic power in the European USSR, which I shall call here the metropolis. Again, there are significant differences in that relationship not only between Siberia and Central Asia but within Siberia (including North Kazakhstan and the Far East) as well. Siberia today is overwhelmingly an energy, mineral, and timber source for the European USSR. Central Asia, on the other hand, despite vital mineral exports, is more a "plantation economy" in its relationship to the metropolis. This difference has important implications for the industrial structures of Siberia and Central Asia such as capital-labor ratios and production functions throughout their economies, in both the static and dynamic senses. Within Siberia, orientation, type of linkages, and the degree of economic integration vary according to accessibility to the established core and the priority of their resources for the national economy. Finally, the relationship of Siberian regions with the metropolis, just as those of Central Asia, vary by the degree of their strategic importance and vulnerability.

Geographically and economically, Kazakhstan presents a

serious problem to the analyst. The northern two-thirds of this republic (north of Lake Balkhash and the Aral Sea) is clearly part of that resource-rich frontier zone that stretches from the Urals to the Pacific. At the same time, it is today mostly a part of the Slavic ethno-cultural realm, with Russians, Ukrainians, and Belorussians constituting over 55 percent of the population in 1979 and, with Germans, other European migrants, and deportees as much as 63.1 percent. By contrast, its five southern oblasts (provinces) belong to the Central Asian oasis world where, outside the capital Alma-Ata, the autochthonous nationality dominates.[2]

These five oblasts of Southern Kazakhstan accounted for 22.6 percent of the industrial fixed assets and 21.4 percent of the industrial labor force of the Kazakh Republic in 1980, shares that grew only modestly since the mid-1960s.[3] In contrast to industry, the relative importance of Southern Kazakhstan in the agriculture of this republic rose sharply over the past two decades, as measured by both employment and fixed capital. As the former Virgin Lands of North Kazakhstan, with their largely Slavic population, have experienced increasing rural outmigration, agricultural employment in the native-dominated south has continued to rise. At the same time, heavy investment in irrigation greatly augmented the share of Southern Kazakhstan in agricultural fixed assets. In 1980, the five southern oblasts claimed over 36 percent of agricultural labor force and almost 30 percent of fixed agricultural capital in that republic, 7.3 and 11.5 percentage points higher respectively than 15 years earlier.[4] In other words, the economic trend in the northern two-thirds of Kazakhstan followed that in West Siberia, and in the southern third it followed that in neighboring Central Asia. If one adds the significant differences in industrial structure, especially the overwhelming concentration of coal, electric power, and metallurgical industries north of the Aral Sea and Lake Balkhash, the splitting of Kazakhstan between the Siberian and Central Asian realms for the purpose of analysis is still more supportable.[5] Yet, for some economic data, Kazakhstan will have to be treated as a unit, considered separately, or assigned either to Siberia or Central Asia.

Economic integration means the radical transformation, if not outright destruction, of traditional, largely self-contained and fragmented production and consumption units, be it the village community or the tribe. The system, as a whole, becomes the cementing and organizing force of

economic behavior. In this process, indigenous traditional
cultures may be entirely destroyed or, at best, absorbed by
the metropolitan economy into a state of dependency. This
has been the case in Russian and Soviet history as well.
Again, different parts of the Asian periphery show great
variations in the interaction of their original inhabitants
with the commanding core, in their role and function within
the enlarged spatial system, and the degree they may shape
economic relations with the center.

In the case of Siberia, the impact of the expanding,
colonizing metropolis on traditional societies has been as
one-sided as in North America and, at least through the
tsarist era, as universally disastrous. Although, in this
respect, the Soviet regime has had a better record, the
integration of that vast hinterland with the European core
is proceeding entirely according to the needs and desires
of the metropolis. Concern for the welfare and future of
weak native societies and their role in the modernizing
Soviet state has been purely incidental. It is otherwise in
Central Asia. The dominance of the metropolis in economic
power relations (just as in the political sphere) is, of
course, without question. Nor has the native production
system and economic relations escaped radical transformation and destruction. Indeed, during the collectivi-
zation campaign that impact was as brutal as elsewhere in
the USSR. Yet, the relatively large size of the Central
Asian nationalities, combined with their demographic
vitality, their strategic location, and their place in the
world Islamic community have meant that metropolitan
dominance cannot be arbitrary. Economic and social policy
is not to be decided solely according to the needs of
Moscow. The role of the Central Asian populations in the
spatial economy of the USSR is far from incidental; with
demographic stagnation in most other areas of the country,
their relative importance can only increase.

Related to this concept is the interplay of external
and internal factors in regional growth. Again, despite
some similarities, the two parts of the Trans-Ural periphery have diverged in the dynamics of that interplay. In
the future, they will diverge even more. Siberia's
development throughout history has always hinged on factors
and forces external to the region itself. Overwhelmingly,
these were forces which issued from or were controlled by
the commanding economic and political centers of the state.
It has been the economic and military requirements of the
metropolis which governed the rate, sequence, and strategy
of development in that resource-rich hinterland. (Except

for select areas and brief periods during the tsarist era, world market and outside influences played a role mostly indirectly.) In contrast to developmental impulses originating outside the region, internal initiatives (local demand, enterpreneurship, innovation and capital) achieved sufficient importance only towards the end of the nineteenth century. These local impulses were quickly quenched in the Soviet era by the overriding national priorities set in motion in the Five-Year Plans. Despite some relaxation after the mid-1950s, the decisive control of national priorities on Siberian regional growth has continued.[6] At the same time, the population of this vast land has remained too small and scattered even to cope with priority projects of national significance, let alone to broaden local industries and the social infrastructure essential for a more advanced and mature economic profile. Given the demographic stagnation of the Slavic population throughout the USSR and the improbability of massive population shifts, internal factors will not be significant for the economic development of Siberia in the future.

Metropolitan priorities have dominated the development of Central Asia and Kazakhstan as well. Before the Revolution, Russia's need for cotton and land for colonization had already transformed much of the native economy.[7] Yet traditional agriculture and handicraft industries based on local technology and initiative continued to show considerable vigor. In the Soviet era, that economic transformation imposed from the center was completed. It culminated in the Virgin Land Campaign in Kazakhstan and the huge expansion of cotton growing at the expense of food crops, agricultural processing, and consumer industries. Cotton today represents almost two-thirds of the value of all agricultural output in Central Asia as a whole, while over one-third of all industrial production is also immediately tied to the processing of that crop.[8] This has made the region a large importer of foodstuffs and most necessities (in addition to capital goods) from the Slavic belt to the north.[9] The fact that gas, gold, uranium, and other critical minerals are shipped to the Slavic core further shows the latter's dominance. The area now is more strongly tied to the metropolis in a state of economic dependency than ever in its history.

Yet external factors are not so overriding as in Siberia and will be still less so in the future. The regional market is large, manpower reserves are plentiful, if not yet adequately trained. Import substitution policies and the greater processing of local materials to

provide employment and add value to interregional exports
have long been a goal of the increasingly sophisticated and
vocal native elite. As one-tenth of the area of Siberia,
Central Asia boasts a population equally large but growing
more than twice as fast as in the former region, and some
70 percent of that population is under 30 years of age.[10]
The degree to which the vast cohort of mostly rural youth
can acquire skills, and enter and integrate itself into the
economy will be of fundamental importance to the region's
future and, indeed, to the future of the USSR. Investment
from the Center (for which, at any rate, there are mounting
claims from all over the country) alone will not solve the
problem. Considerable reliance on local efforts and a
combination of traditional cottage industries and skills
with modern production methods will be necessary for
development in the years ahead. Indeed, this is now
admitted in Soviet writings. In addition, the semilegal
and bazaar economy has always been vigorous in the region,
providing a sizable share of personal income. With rising
population pressure, it can be expected to increase in
importance.

The improvement of transport links is an essential
precondition for the integration of the periphery into the
economic mainstream. In pioneer hinterlands, the search
for transport routes tends to dominate early economic
history. Enhancing the capacity of existing routes and,
more important, the construction of new modes of transport
underpin the history of later periods, whether in Russia,
North America, or elsewhere. The sequence of resource
exploitation is greatly influenced by the transportability
and per ton value of commodities needed. The extraction
and cultivation of bulky, relatively low-value commodities
must wait for the coming of mass freight, which in continental interiors mean chiefly the railway and, more
recently, the pipeline. Distance, intervening and alternative opportunities, and the relative transportability of
the resource, however, remain crucial in developmental
priorities even after that. And just as new transport
technology allows the development of more remote resources,
with innovations, and improvements in production techniques, attention may turn back to abandoned but better
located deposits, overcut forests, or the intensive
cultivation of older agricultural land. In a similar vein,
conservation, recycling, and structural change in the
economy of the metropolis and outside industrial centers
may retard or stop the growth of demand for resources from
frontier areas.

In the case of Russia and the USSR, history records several "waves of resource exploitation," spreading out from the European core in rough conformity with this model.[11] High-value precious metals and tin have long been mined in northeast Siberia for the markets of Russia and Europe, while rich coal reserves remain untouched and hydrocarbon potentials east of the Enisei are barely scratched. In the much better located and less forbidding southern belt of Siberia-North Kazakhstan, on the other hand, coal has long been extensively produced and hauled to the European USSR in growing quantities from as far east as the Kuzbas. However, it is the feverish development of oil and gas reserves in the wilderness of Tiumen' Oblast (province), almost all for the needs of the European USSR and for export, which most exemplifies the interplay of these factors. Intense national needs, the relative ease in moving hydrocarbon fuels over distances because of current technology, and the lack (or at least very low probability) of alternative combinations to satisfy the energy and hard currency export demands of the metropolis all combine to accord this province the highest priority in Soviet resource exploitation today. It is this combination which has made the construction of the gigantic pipeline network from Tiumen' not only the biggest energy transport project in the world, but the single largest construction undertaking in the USSR.[12] The most visible tranport links between Siberia and the European core consist of such massive, largely one-way funnels for the outshipment of bulky resources. But regions generating the raw material and energy flows also require supplies which, while still relatively small compared to the volume of outflow, have been rapidly growing. In addition, especially in the northern regions of Siberia, "there is only a partial overlap between the transport modes used for raw material-energy exports and those used for supplies" into these remote areas. Finally, the crucial role of transport in Siberian development is further enhanced by the great distances between production centers east of the Urals and the rising quantity of freight flowing between them.[13]

The return from remote areas to resources nearer to or within the economic core, a move spurred by innovation or improvement in production technologies, is exemplified by locational changes in the geographic growth points of Russian and Soviet ferrous metallurgy--from the Urals back to the European core. In the latter part of the nineteenth century, this shift produced the heavy industrial citadel of the eastern Ukraine, in the last twenty years the ore

and steel producing centers in the Central Black Earth
region of the RSFSR (Russian Republic). Agriculture intensification in the European USSR, the Non-Chernozem Program,
and potentially greater reliance on reforested timberland
with sustained yield west of the Urals are other examples.
Potentially, too, the tapping of numerous very promising
but deep-lying structures (at 5,000 to 7,000 meters) of the
Caspian Lowland, for which technology is as yet unequal,
could return the hub of the Soviet oil and gas industry to
the edge of the European USSR.

Improvements in transportation have also been crucial
for Central Asia, as shown conclusively by Taaffe.[14] In
several oases, the expansion of cotton cultivation was
predicated on the creation or radical improvement of
transport links (the railway from Chardzhou to the Amu
Dar'ia delta is a good example) and these have been
similarly vital for the exploitation of mineral deposits.
Significantly, from the late 1960s to the late 1970s, when
overtaken by the pipeline system from West Siberia, the
pipeline "bridges" for natural gas from Central Asia to the
Urals and the Moscow region were the largest anywhere in
the world. As already mentioned, despite such mineral
exports, however, the economic relations of Central Asia to
the metropolis is more that of a plantation province than
of a mining and energy frontier. That implies the outshipment of relatively high-value commodities and the inshipment of much basic bulk freight besides those of machinery
and finished products. Indeed, unlike Siberia west of Lake
Baikal, inshipment by railways to Central Asia exceeds
outshipment by a considerable margin. The 1970s witnessed
a very rapid growth of inshipment into the region,[15] which
no doubt was further augmented by military freight following the invasion of Afghanistan. In addition, as Soviet
economists themselves forecast (both those from the region
and those based in Moscow), Central Asia during the 1990s
should cease to be a net fuel exporter, while population
pressure dictates the faster growth of local industries.[16]
Therefore commodity movement and the pattern of circulation
(both inside the region and between it and the economic
heartland), which already differ significantly from that
characterizing Siberia, may diverge still more in the
future.

The economic and cultural environment of peripheral
regions and their functional relationship with the metropolis also affect the settlement network through which
economic space is organized. In a frontier hinterland,
permanent habitations of sparse native groups are few and

far between. The settlement network is established by colonists from the metropolis or abroad, and it is through this network that economic (and political) power from the controlling center is exercised. By contrast, where European conquest absorbed more advanced and organized native societies a well-developed mesh of rural and urban places are likely to have existed prior to colonial rule. In the course of development and integration with the metropolis, the settlement network and its internal economy undergoes substantial change, given sufficient time and interest on the part of the metropolitan administration.

These generalizations apply to the Asian periphery of the USSR. Virtually all Siberian cities (just as most villages) were founded by Russians, first as forts, then as administrative, and later as industrial centers. The same is true in Kazakhstan and in those parts of Central Asia where the autochthonous population was mostly nomadic, even if numerically far stronger than in Siberia. On the other hand, the cultivated oases and rich, loess-covered piedmont of Turkestan could boast cities and well-developed rural settlements for millennia. These native settlements remained virtually untouched by Slavic migrants before the Revolution but a few of them experienced substantial inflow during the Soviet era. Nevertheless, economic development and industrialization, directed by the metropolis, are producing significant changes in the settlement network, its economic function, and social ecology in both of these peripheries.

In Siberia, where four-fifths of all social infra-structure is found in urban areas,[17] the concentration of population in major cities at the expense of small and middle-size towns is both more pronounced and is proceeding faster than elsewhere in the country. This leads to enhanced spatial disparities on the subregional level. Twenty-one cities, each with more than 200,000 persons, contain almost a third of the total population today.[18] At the same time, as Chapter 6 will show, a much higher share of towns are stagnating than elsewhere in the Russian Republic. Economic development proceeds largely through the creation of new towns and the growth of the largest urban centers. Yet, to a very large extent, both of these are fed not by migration into Siberia, but by outmigration from small and medium-size cities and the rural areas within the region. The outflow from the farm belt of West Siberia may have abated in recent years, but elsewhere, such as in the Nazarovo Basin (Krasnoiarsk Krai), it has accelerated. The liquidation of villages continues apace:

in West Siberia, one-third of those of under 500 persons disappeared during the 1970s. Further consolidation is underway, although this policy is now questioned and may be tempered.[19]

In Central Asia, small towns and villages make up a much more important part of the settlement hierarchy and account for a far larger portion of the population than in Siberia. Today almost three-fifths of the population in the four republics is still rural and over 70 percent live in settlements with less than 50,000 persons. With overwhelming native majorities, these settlements show great demographic vigor and contributed some two-thirds of all population growth since the 1959 census.[20] During the 1970s, the rural areas of Uzbekistan alone contributed two-thirds of all persons reaching working age in this republic, and with those from small towns added, this share must have been around three-fourths.[21] Yet, up till now, they have received little of industrial and infrastructural investment, which has been flowing mostly to cities where Slavic immigrants compose a large part of the population.[22] The demand for small town and rural industrialization in the region, therefore, is particularly urgent, but for such a strategy the Soviet type of economic management is not very appropriate, and Soviet planners are neither experienced nor skillful. The ministries "are still building large plants and still building them in large cities."[23]

However, even in these large cities, with their Russian cultural milieu, demographic realities seem to be changing the social ecology and may even alter economic power relations between the Slavs and the autochthonous population in the future. The share of indigenous nationalities has risen appreciably in Central Asia's main urban centers, especially the republic capitals. During the 1970s, the proportion of Kirghizes and Tadzhiks in their respective capitals increased by 40 and by 20 percent; those of Uzbeks and Turkmens by 10 percent each.[24] There is also evidence of the beginning of outmigration by some of the Slavs in contrast to the 1960s which witnessed the net influx into Central Asia of almost half a million persons. In the long run, a closer resemblance to Transcaucasia, where the titular nationalities have long dominated economic, even political, life and which experienced a 56,000 absolute decline in its Russian minority since 1970 is at least conceivable.[25]

Soviet planners have long been more explicitly involved with issues of regional development and policy than decision makers in market economies. First, because

of immense size and the uneven distribution of population
and resources, the variables of geography play a more
influential if not decisive role in economic development
for the USSR than in nearly all other nations. Second, the
Soviet state is multinational, with ethnic groups of
different cultural background inherited from the colonial
conquests of Imperial Russia. The questions of regional
growth and levels of economic development, investment, and
project allocation cannot be isolated from the ethnic
issue. Finally, the regional and ethnic problem, its
historic role and resolution, are imbued with a deeply
ideological meaning. It is associated with Lenin's contribution to the theory of economic relations along territorial, ethnic lines. Under capitalism, according to this
view, the unevenness of economic development engenders not
only class antagonism and struggle, but equally sharp
inequalities, exploitation, and eventual confrontation
between "metropolis" and "colony," developed and underdeveloped areas and their inhabitants. Such inequalities
develop both on a world scale and within multinational
empires. In the evolution of this theory, much of the
stigma attached to the metropolis--colonial dichotomy was
even attributed to the core-periphery division between
developed regions with complex economic structure and
sparsely inhabited, pioneering areas with nearly exclusive
roles of resource exploitation and raw material supplies.

In addition to such ideological motives, strategic
considerations have also forced Soviet leaders to pay
sustained attention to regional issues. Indeed, these
strategic concerns can often be traced back to Imperial
times, magnified greatly for Soviet leaders by the searing
experience of the Civil War, foreign intervention and,
still more, World War II. The USSR, like the Russia of the
tsars, is the only military power with land frontiers in
three of the great geopolitical and cultural world regions,
Europe, East Asia, and the Middle East. Such a position
forces the Soviet state to defend itself on all these
fronts but also allows it to project its power into all
three geopolitical theaters from within its own territory.
In the last twenty years, however, new military developments represented by the nuclear submarine and the SLBM
(submarine-launched ballistic missiles) resulted in the
need to balance land and naval forces both for defense and
for the more effective projection of that power. In this
geopolitical context, the regional significance of the Far
East and Soviet Central Asia is greatly enhanced by the
tremendous growth of the economic capacity of East Asia and

16

the new pivotal role of the Persian Gulf states in world
oil reserves and supplies. The Pacific provinces today
also play a key role in Soviet maritime strategy (both
commercial and military) well beyond the East Asian
theater. The contribution of the Pacific fleet to Soviet
commercial and, still more, naval strength many times
exceed the puny share of the Far East in Soviet national
income.[26]

To summarize: the diverse regions of the vast Asian
USSR represent distinct problems to the Soviet leadership,
mainly because their degree of integration with the
metropolis in the political, social, and economic realm,
and the mix of these components differ greatly. Regional
development everywhere has been dominated by metropolitan
priorities. The nature of the relationship with the
controlling center of economic and political power has
strongly influenced migration, the evolution of the settlement hierarchy, transport linkages, economic profiles, and
the transformation of indigenous societies. While national
policy decisions will continue to dominate the fortunes of
Soviet Asia, internal factors are destined to increase in
significance for the Moslem periphery as opposed to Siberia
and the Far East.

NOTES

1. John Friedman, "Integration of the Social System:
An Approach to the Study of Economic Growth," Diogenes,
Spring, 1961, pp. 75-97.
2. Tsentral'noe statisticheskoe upravlenie SSSR
(TsSU), Chislennost' i sostav naseleniia SSSR (Moscow:
Finansy i statistika, 1984), pp. 116-123.
3. N.K. Kuzembaev, Regional'nye problemy formirovaniia
territorial'nykh ekonomicheskikh proportsii i ikh sovershenstvovaniia (Alma-Ata: Kazakhstan, 1985), p. 187.
4. Ibid., p. 191.
5. Essentially all coal and 83 percent of electricity
in Kazakhstan is produced north of the Aral Sea and Lake
Balkhash, and the northern two-thirds of the republic also
accounts for about nine-tenths of Kazakh ferrous and nonferrous metallurgy as well. Ibid., pp. 18-19, 78-79 and 80-
81.
6. Robert R. North, Transport in Western Siberia:
Tsarist and Soviet Development (Vancouver: University of

British Columbia Press, 1971).

7. V.P. Semenov-Tien-Shanski, ed., Rossiia. Polnoe geograficheskoe opisanie, Vol. XIX. Turkestanskii krai (St. Petersburg, 1913) and Violet Conolly, Beyond the Urals (London: Oxford University Press, 1967), pp. 34-39.

8. M.A. Abdusaliamov, Problemy ekonomicheskoi integratsii Srednei Azii i Sibiri (Tashkent: Fan, 1982), p. 41. In Uzbekistan, concentrating three-fifths of Central Asia's national income, cotton growing and processing accounted for 58 percent of the republic's economy according to the 1972 interindustry balances. The "cotton complex" composed 56.5 percent of industry and 74 percent of agriculture (82 percent of crop farming) during that year. Moreover, compared to the 1966 balances, there was a sharp increase in the contribution of cotton to all branches of the economy. While in 1966 only 8 percent of the value of construction was devoted to the cotton complex, by 1972, 41.7 percent of the output of that branch was directly or indirectly so devoted. T.D. Nurullaev, Mezhotraslevye sviazi khlopkovogo kompleksa Uzbekistana (Tashkent: Fan, 1977), pp. 81-82. Uzbek and Central Asian national income produced in 1972 was taken from U.S. Department of Commerce, Foreign Economic Report No. 19, The Reconstructed 1972 Input-Output Tables for Eight Soviet Republics (Washington, D.C.: U.S. Government Printing Office, December 1982), p. 84. See also Hervé Gicquiau, "Développement et dépendance économique de l'Asie Centrale soviétique," Le Courriers des pays de l'Est, 1983, October, pp. 3-34.

9. Products of the food industry today make up 38 percent and products of the light industry 34.4 percent of all industrial shipment into Uzbekistan, while they represent only a negligible portion of exports. The republic processes only a little more than 5 percent of the cotton grown on its soil into cotton cloth. R.N. Khakimov, Effektivnost' sovershenstvovaniia proportsii promyshlennosti v soiuznoi respublike (Tashkent: Uzbekistan, 1982), p. 91. About 70 percent of the cotton fabrics consumed in Uzbekistan are imported from elsewhere in the USSR, overwhelmingly from the Russian Republic, although Uzbekistan produces 65 percent of all Soviet cotton and Central Asia-Southern Kazakhstan, as a whole, 91 percent. Referativnyi zhurnal. Geografiia, 1980, No. 3, 07E and Narodnoe khoziaistvo SSSR v 1985 godu (Moscow: Finansy i statistika, 1985), p. 210. (Soviet yearbook. Published annually. Henceforth cited without place, publisher and date.)

10. Data refers to Uzbekistan. The other republics,

18

however, have very similar age structures. R.A. Ubaidullaeva, ed., Sotsial'no-ekonomicheskie problemy ispol'zovaniia truda molodezhi v Uzbekistane (Tashkent: Fan, 1982),
pp. 3 and 12.
    11. Robert N. North, "The Development of Soviet Asia,"
Current History, Vol. 73, No. 430 (October), 1977, p. 126.
    12. Soviet sources report either that West Siberian
oil and gas development and the necessary pipelines to the
European USSR require more investment than the contruction
of BAM (Baikal-Amur Mainline), the Kama and Toliatti
automotive plants and Atommash (the huge factory for serial
production of pressurized water nuclear reactors) combined,
or that investment in the Tiumen' oil and gas complex
exceeds that channeled into any of the above several times.
S.N. Starovoitov, ed., Problemy razvitiia Zapadno-
Sibirskogo Neftegazovogo Kompleksa (Novosibirsk: Nauka,
1983), p. 8 and A.D. Khaitun, Ekspeditsionno-vakhtovoe
stroitel'stvo v Zapadnoi Sibiri (Leningrad: Stroiizdat,
1982), p. 6.
    13. Robert N. North, "Transport in Siberia: Problems
and Perspectives," in Boris Chichlo, ed., Sibérie I.
Questions sibériennes. Economie, écologie, stratégie,
colonisation, développement et perspectives (Paris:
Institut d'Etudes Slaves, 1985), pp. 265-285. Citation on
p. 268.
    14. Robert N. Taaffe, Rail Transportation and the
Economic Development of Soviet Central Asia (Chicago: The
University of Chicago, Department of Geography, Research
Paper No. 64, 1960).
    15. S.K. Ziiadullaev, "Sredniaia Aziia: Sovremennoe
industrial'no-agrarnoe khoziaistvo," Ekonomika i organizatsiia promyshlennogo proizvodstva (EKO), 1982, No. 12, p.
86 and Iu.V. Lasis and I.N. Nikiforova, "Tendentsii razvitiia mezhraionnykh sviazei i territorial'nogo razdeleniia
truda v SSSR," in Gosplan Kazakhskoi SSR, Vsesoiuznaia
konferentsiia po transportno-ekonomicheskim sviaziam i
razmeshchenie proizvodstva. Tezisy dokladov. Tom. 1 (Alma-
Ata, 1983), p. 38. In Uzbekistan alone, inshipment by
tonnage exceeds outshipment by about two times. M. Abdusaliamov, "Mezhraionnye aspekty dolgosrochnogo razvitiia
Uzbekistana," Obshchestvennye nauki v Uzbekistane, 1981,
No. 1, p. 77.
    16. L.A. Melent'ev and A.A. Makarov, eds., Energeti-
cheskii kompleks SSSR (Moscow: Ekonomika, 1983), pp. 194-
195; M. Abdusaliamov, "Mezhraionnye aspekty" Obshchestvennye nauki v Uzbekistane, 1981, No. 1, p. 78; P.
Savchenko and A.R. Khodzhaev, Toplivno-energeticheskii

kompleks Sredneaziatskogo ekonomicheskogo raiona (Tashkent: Uzbekistan, 1974), pp. 176–177; K.M. Kim, Sovershenstvovanie struktury toplivno-energeticheskogo balansa Srednei Azii (Tashkent: Fan, 1973), pp. 197–198, and 208–209.

17. V.T. Barinov, "Gorodskaia infrastruktura (voprosy teorii i problemy razvitiia)" in M.B. Mazanova, ed., Rasselenie naseleniia i razmeshchenie proizvodstva (Moscow: Nauka, 1982), p. 185.

18. Narodnoe khoziaistvo SSSR v 1985 godu, pp. 12–23. One of the twenty-one had a population of 199,000 as of January 1, 1986 and must, therefore, be over 200,000 today.

19. T.I. Zaslavskaia and L.V. Korel', "Migratsiia mezhdu gorodom i selom," Sotsiologicheskie issledovaniia, 1981, No. 3, p. 48; V.V. Vorob'ev and L.M. Korytnyi, eds., Priroda i khoziaistvo raiona pervoocherednogo formirovaniia KATEKa (Novosibirsk: Nauka, 1983), p. 162; E.E. Goriachenko, Sotsial'nye problemy razvitiia malykh sel'skikh poselenii. Preprint (Novosibirsk: AN SSSR, SO, IEOPP, 1986), pp. 20–21 and A.A. Vershinin, ed., Napravleniia razvitiia prodovol'stvennogo kompleksa Sibiri (Novosibirsk: Akademiia sel'skokhoziaistvennykh nauk, Sib. otdel and Sibirskii nauchno-issledovatel'skii institut ekonomiki sel'skogo khoziaistva, 1985), p. 29.

20. Calculated from Narodnoe khoziaistvo SSSR v 1982 godu, pp. 15–16 and B.S. Khorev and G.P. Kiselev, eds., Urbanizatsiia i demograficheskie protsessy (Moscow: Finansy i statistika, 1982), p. 37. In Central Asia, particularly Uzbekistan, small cities under 50,000 inhabitants actually grew faster than the urban population as a whole, with the growth rate of these towns accelerating after 1970. Khorev and Kiselev, Urbanizatsiia, pp. 37 and 42 and E. Akhimedov, "Razvitie malykh i srednikh gorodov Uzbekistana," Kommunist Uzbekistana, 1984, No. 1, p. 38.

21. Ubaidullaeva, ed., Sotsial'no-ekonomicheskie problemy, p. 45.

22. Only 30 percent of total capital investment in Central Asia during the 1976–1980 Plan was allocated to the development of small towns. G. Kopanev et al., "Segodnia i budushcheie," Ekonomika i zhizn', 1982, No. 2, pp. 23–24.

23. Pravda, June 18, 1984, p. 2.

24. L.L. Tybakovskii and N.V. Tarasova, "Vzaimodeistvie migratsionnykh i etnicheskikh protsessov," Sotsiologicheskie issledovaniia, 1982, No. 4, p. 31.

25. TsSU SSSR, Chislennost' i sostav, pp. 126–135 and TsSU, Itogi vsesoiuznoi perepisi naseleniia 1970 goda (Moscow: Statistika, 1973), Tom 4, pp. 253, 263 and 303.

26. The Pacific coast accounts for about one-fifth of

the tonnage of the Soviet commercial fleet. It is the home
base for two-fifths of Soviet ballistic missile submarines
and almost a third of surface combatants (the small,
isolated Caspian flotilla excluded). By contrast, the
Soviet Far East contributes a mere 3 percent to national
income and all of Siberia and the Far East combined
contributes only 12.5 percent. V.P. Mozhin, ed., Ekonomicheskoe razvitie Sibiri i Dal'nego Vostoka (Moscow:
Mysl', 1980), p. 78; V.I. Ivanov and K.V. Malakhovskii,
eds., Tikhookeanskii regionalizm. Kontseptsii i real'nost'
(Moscow: Nauka, 1983), p. 243; Jane's Defence Weekly, 1985,
April 14, pp. 560 and Soviet Military Power, 1986
(Washington, D.C.: U.S. Government Printing Office, 1986),
pp. 12-13 and 29.

2

The Regional Setting

The Asiatic USSR composes three-fourths of the country's territory. These acquisitions east of the Urals and the Caspian Sea, the result of Russian expansion in the last 400 years, exceed the area of Brazil and Australia combined and are almost as large as all of South America. Most of this enormous land, however, is unsuitable for large-scale, permanent settlement, so its 77 million people are very unevenly distributed. Almost half of this population (ca. 37 million persons) live south of the Aral Sea and Lake Balkhash on only 15 percent of the territory of the Asiatic USSR.[1] The regional setting of this Central Asian portion will be sketched first. The Siberian hinterland between the Urals and the Pacific, including the northern two-thirds of Kazakhstan, is not only very much larger, but itself must be divided into several macro-regions according to geographic orientation, stages of development, and integration with the metropolis and strategic importance.

CENTRAL ASIA

Central Asia and Southern Kazakhstan form a region quite distinct from the rest of Soviet Asia. Its deserts, scorching summers, and mild winters (with average January temperatures ranging from 0° to only -8°C everywhere except the high altitudes of the Tien Shan) clearly mark it off climatically from the Siberian realm to the north and northeast.[2] Outside small areas in Transcaucasia, Central Asia is the only region of the country with the requisite thermal regime for the cultivation of cotton and certain exotic fruits. The scanty rainfall comes entirely in winter and spring, in contrast to the world of steppe and forests north of the Kazakh desert, where year-round precipitation exists but a summer maximum prevails. Along the southern flank, the formidable mountains of the Tien Shan and the Pamir wring significant moisture from the westerly winds in winter, when the circulation system shifts further south. In addition, their snowcapped peaks and glaciers provide water for dozens of streams flowing north towards the deserts. Their northern foothills and basins are covered with thick loess, fertile and easily cultivated. It is in this piedmont zone, varying in width from 80 to 320 kilometers, that most of the population has always been found. Farming depends on irrigation everywhere; settlements and economic life are heavily concentrated in oases, cultivated for millennia, where rural population densities today reach up to 500 per square kilometer.[3] In the deserts, semideserts and along mountain valleys, large herds of animals have traditionally been driven over long distances following seasonal pastures. The nomadic way of life is now a thing of the past, but the extensive pasturing of animals has continued to the present.[4]

Although it is this agricultural oasis and desert way of life which gives the region its clearest economic stamp, its geology and mineral riches have also assumed great importance in recent decades. The Kopet Dag trough from the Pamirs westward through the central Caspian, part of the great Eurasian geosyncline, represents one of the major deep sedimentary accumulations in the USSR, in some areas almost 18 kilometers in depth.[5] Until the construction of the mammoth pipeline system from Tiumen' Oblast (West Siberia), it had been the largest supplier of gas to the European core. Elsewhere in the region, complex metamorphic rocks are a rich source of uranium, nonferrous, rare and precious metals, of which gold, with possibly the largest deposits anywhere in the Soviet Union, is perhaps the most significant.[6] Finally, the torrential, glacier-fed rivers of the Tien Shan provide parts of the region with the largest hydroeletric potential in the USSR outside East Siberia and the Far East.

This is an ancient world, valued enough by Alexander to conquer, Tamerlane to choose for the center of his ephemeral empire, and civilized enough for Omar Khayyam to call one of its cities his home. The region has been part of Russia and the USSR for not much more than a century and remains ethnically non-Russian and non-Slav. The latter

represent less than 16 percent of the population today
(14.2 percent in Central Asia alone, without southern
Kazakhstan in 1979).[7] These shares are appreciably smaller
than ten or twenty years ago, a decline explained by the
virtual cessation of net Slavic immigration and the very
high natural increase of the indigenous nationalities. The
overwhelmingly Moslem population has barely begun to limit
its birthrate, which still averaged (weighted average) 30.8
per 1,000 among the five major autochthonous nationalities
of Central Asia-Kazakhstan during the 1970s.[8] Given the
massive size of young cohorts reaching reproductive age,
the rapid population growth of the indigenous nationalities
is destined to continue for the rest of the century. The
share of the Slavic colons overall will be reduced to
insignificance and may fade even in the few large cities,
where most of them are found.

SIBERIA (INCLUDING FAR EAST)--NORTH KAZAKHSTAN

In contrast to the ancient oasis world, virtually all
of the vast expanse of Siberia-North Kazakhstan has stayed
beyond the edge of settled civilization until recently. It
is to this day a raw, pioneer land, Russia's America beyond
the Urals. Except for the Kazakh steppes and the southeast
corner along the Amur, it was conquered and firmly attached
to European Russia for over 300 years, but barely touched
until much later. Accelerated development began only from
the era of the Five-Year Plans. Today Siberia accounts for
all or most of the increments and very large shares of a
range of resources supplied to the Soviet economy. Because
of an immediate and large multiplier effect on the entire
GNP, some Soviet scholars calculate that the optimum rate
of expansion for the region, that which maximizes national
growth, lies between 1.2 and 1.4 times the national rate.[9]
Environmental harshness, however, has always presented
a truly formidable obstacle to economic exploitation even
with conscript labor, tsarist or Soviet. Over the bulk of
the Siberian landmass, such exploitation, in fact, has
become possible only in the last few decades through modern
science and technology. Low insolation and even lower
effective insolation (incoming solar energy left over after
the melting of snow and vaporization of the melt water),
low temperatures made extreme by continentality and wind
chill, and the world's most extensive area of permafrost
are the prime variables in that environmental harshness and
the physical obstacles to development. In over two-thirds

of Siberia, and 60 percent of Siberia including North
Kazakhstan, mean daily temperatures stay below freezing for
more than 200 days. Rugged topography east of the Enisei,
especially in the Pacific provinces, high seismic activity
over a large part of the trans-Baikal territory, volcanoes,
landslides, and avalanches add to the physical constraints.
Because of the low effective insolation, the boreal forest
and tundra are distinguished by very low production and
carrying capacities of biomass.[10] This rules out farming
in all but a small area of Siberia, where currently only
2.5 percent of the land is arable. Three-fifths of this
arable land is located in the southwest corner of Siberia,
merging with the still more extensive farm belt of North
Kazakhstan, the primary location of the Virgin Lands.[11]
Here, the share of cultivated land does reach half of the
land area in a few oblasts, but the average is lower, 13 to
14 percent in the whole of Northern Kazakhstan, where the
chief limitation to agriculture is no longer temperature
but moisture.[12] In the Far East, which alone composes some
45 percent of that vast frontier between the Urals and the
Pacific, large stretches of arable land are found only in
the Amur-Ussuri Valleys.

Most of this frontier hinterland, therefore, can never
be densely populated. A Soviet specialist on medical
geography and conditions east of the Urals has recently
stated that, in his opinion, there are no territories with
comfortable conditions in Siberia.[13] In particular, the
vast Northland, which covers some three-fourths of the
region and two-thirds with North Kazakhstan added, is home
for less than 5,000,000 people and has an average density
of under 0.5 persons per square kilometer. The bulk of
this territory belongs, in Soviet parlance, to the Far
North[14] (Figure 1), where population densities are even
lower and where the percentage of economically opened or
developed land (osvoennaia territoriya) reaches a mere 7
percent of the total area.[15] In this region of "extreme
discomfort," permanent settlement of immigrants from mid-
latitude climatic zones is both unlikely and inadvisable.
A number of illnesses, both physical and mental, affect
residents of the Far North much more frequently than those
of the mid-latitudes. Soviet medical investigations, for
example, show that in Yakutsk children of under fourteen
years are 50 to 100 percent more prone to sickness and
disorders of the endocrinal system than those in mid-
latitude cities, three times more prone to illnesses
afflicting the nervous system, and suffer much more from
blood deficiencies. Soviet sources attribute these higher

risks to the physical environment itself, though poorer
nutrition and the inadequacy of preventive medical services
must be a contributing factor.[16] At any rate, from the
medical-geographic point of view, the length of stay of
immigrants should be limited to a three-to-five year period
according to specialists.[17]

The southern belt of Siberia and most of North
Kazakhstan, on the other hand, are certainly suitable for
permanent settlement for people from the mid-latitudes,
though even here the rigors of the climate do take their
toll. Some 35 million persons live here, in contrast to
the 5 to 6 million of the Trans-Ural North.[18] The western
portion of this much more habitable zone is over 700 miles
wide in meridional extent, though aridity sharply reduces
densities in the center of Kazakhstan. Owing to the
influence of Atlantic airmasses, the land of the North is
here confined to the poleward side of the 58th parallel.
By contrast, east of Lake Baikal, the Arctic and Subarctic
plunge southward to between 150 and 500 kilometers of the
Chinese-Mongolian borders. Sharply increased continentality and rugged topography are responsible for that near
pinch-out of the habitable, temperate zone, so that a mere
10 percent of the enormous Soviet Far East is out of the
Northland.

The main direction of orientation in southern Siberia
is east-west. The regions of this temperate zone are
linked to each other and to the European USSR by east-west
railways. In Trans-Baikalia and the Far East, this narrow
belt is served by the single Trans-Siberian (the new Baikal-
Amur Mainline Railway [BAM] runs through virtually uninhab-
ited territory within the Northland almost in its entire
length). West of Lake Baikal there are two east-west
railways now and west of the Kuzbas three, in addition to
those connecting Siberia with Central Asia. By contrast,
the regions of the Siberian North are almost completely
isolated from each other and have virtually no direct link
to the European USSR. Their orientation is southward to
the Trans-Siberian, by the few existing north-south spur
lines, through the chiefly north-flowing rivers and, in the
Far East, by coastal shipping. The single-track Baikal-
Amur Railway will be the first east-west link in the
Siberian Arctic and Subarctic regions, making the emergence
of an east-west development zone possible. The Siberian
North, therefore, depends on the Trans-Ural south both
directly and indirectly for its development--for its
supplies, some of its labor force, and its export routes.
Only Tiumen' Oblast and the Norilsk-Igarka node near the

mouth of the Enisei are able to ship much of their resources directly to the European USSR (and abroad), the former because of relative proximity and the specialized transport modes represented by oil and gas pipelines, the latter because of lighter ice conditions and better developed navigation on the western half of the Northern Sea Route. However, even these two areas depend overwhelmingly on supplies shipped in from and through southern Siberia. The Asian North, therefore, may be regarded as a huge frontier zone that itself leans on and is linked functionally to the more established Trans-Ural hinterland.

West Siberia-North Kazakhstan

Among the Siberian regions, West Siberia is distinguished by its relative proximity to the economic core area west of the Urals. External orientation, the existence of diverse economic links to the metropolis (in certain periods also to the world at large), and persistent attempts to strengthen them can be traced right back to the late 1500s, with the first arrival of the Russians. The early links, however, fed by the fur trade, excluded the large volume of traffic flows which have typified the more recent periods. These large flows, generated by mining, agricultural, and, to some extent, lumbering activities, began much later (in the eighteenth and nineteenth centuries) and accelerated in the Soviet era, reaching phenomenal levels in the present decade. Robert North, who has traced the historical evolution of the province's economy in detail, finds that, with the exception of the late nineteenth and early twentieth centuries, when local initiatives became significant, most developmental impulses have originated from outside the area. Since the late 1920s, "the region has seen several of the Soviet government's most spectacular developmental schemes, from the Ural-Kuznets Combine to the Virgin Land Schemes and the current West Siberian oil and gas boom." The primary goal of regional development has been and remains "the growth of national economic and military strength. Regional viewpoints, and the viewpoints of sectors which contribute little economic and military strength are subordinated."[19]
Because of pressing national needs for and the relative transportability of its energy resources, West Siberia (with North Kazakhstan) became the primary energy colony of the USSR during the Brezhnev era. Today, it accounts for over 55 percent of all fuel production in the

country, all the increments and the bulk of Soviet hard
currency earnings.[20] The region is tied to the European
USSR by a dozen large-diameter gas, petroleum, and petroleum product pipelines, the most heavily used railway lines
in the world, and a unified power grid. Some three-fourths
of all its fuel output and nine-tenths of its oil and gas
are shipped out of the province, overwhelmingly westward,
to the European USSR (including the Urals) and abroad. In
heat content, this huge energy flow, all of it overland,
today well exceeds the fuel imports of the European
Community and approximates that of all Western Europe.[21]
Other bulk commodities, such as ores, wood, and grain,
further raise the share of primary materials in total
regional export. Adding up freight by all transport media
(converting natural gas by coal equivalent), outshipment
exceeds inshipment in tonnage by perhaps ten times.[22]

Notwithstanding the high cost of development,
especially in the West Siberian North, the massive input of
resources during the Brezhnev years was more than paid for
by that huge commodity export to the metropolis and abroad.
New transport technologies, especially the pipelines, have
increased the volume of westerly commodity flow many times
above preWar level, while the discovery of vast, new
resources with high value on the domestic and world markets
multiplied the region's contribution to national income.
When world prices were assigned even to a fraction (i.e.,
the export portion) of oil and gas output, West Siberia
appeared as a hefty net contributor to the nation's output
in the middle through late 1970s. It gave more to the rest
of the country than it received.[23] This is unlikely to be
true today. In recent years, the investment and manpower
needs of the West Siberian oil and gas complex have risen
far beyond the levels even of the late 1970s (Chapter 3).
Meanwhile the volume of oil production is sagging and world
oil prices have dropped precipitously.

Physically, the region consists of the huge West
Siberian plain occupying the central and northern parts of
the area, the Kazakh Upland, and the Altai Mountains on its
southern and southeastern flank. The concave, extremely
low-lying plain, larger than the Amazon Basin, is subject
to extensive flooding and marsh formation. "The stagnant
pools, huge slow moving rivers and high water tables . . .
render West Siberia one of the wettest regions on earth,
with four-fifths of the area or almost 2 million square
kilometers considered to be saturated or supersaturated."
Its torpid flood waters encourage the breedings of swarms
of insects which, in summer, constrain human activity as

much as the swamps.[24] This forbidding surface environment,
however, is complemented by untold riches of the subsur-
face. The West Siberian Basin represents possibly the
largest sedimentary accumulation in the world. Its proven
and potential hydrocarbon reserves, though much more gas
than oil, approach those in the great petroliferous
provinces around the Persian Gulf. The southern portion of
the lowland, however, forms the eastern wedge of that
continuous agricultural zone that ends at the Altai
Mountains, to reappear only in isolated basins in East
Siberia and the Far East. Within this belt, the Altai
steppe and foothills are distinguished by the most fertile
soils and most reliable precipitation. Elsewhere, poorer
soils and lower and more erratic rainfall impair farming,
which peters out on the Kazakh uplands for lack of
moisture. The density of population in the well-settled
southern zone of West Siberia averages 13 to 14 per square
kilometer, a relatively high figure due to the high urban
concentration in the Kuzbas and two cities (Novosibirsk and
Omsk) with populations of well over one million each. By
contrast, the Near North of West Siberia averages 1 to 1.5
persons per square kilometer, despite the enormous recent
efforts at petroleum exploration and extraction. The Far
North has less than 0.5 person per square kilometer.[25]

The Kazakh Uplands are ancient, worndown mountains,
seldom exceeding 3000 feet. Highly mineralized, they are
one of the most important sources of metals in the USSR.
The rugged high Altai, extending into the country from
China and Mongolia, has undergone several cycles of uplift
and folding, with older rocks brought near the surface. It
is thus also rich in polymetallic ores and precious metals,
and contains, in a syncline between two of its ranges, the
largest accessible black coal deposit of the USSR. Coal of
much poorer quality is also found extensively in and on the
flanks of the Kazakh Uplands. The hydrocarbon reserves of
the plain have been discovered only in the last thirty
years but the mineral riches of the south have been known,
and to some degree exploited, long before the Revolution.
This is especially true of the Altai, where the mining of
precious and base metals began before the mid-eighteenth
century, and by the mid-1800s "ranked second to the Urals
among mining and metallurgical regions of Russia."[26]
Although not rivalling the current oil and gas boom of the
plain, mining in the south has expanded spectacularly
throughout Soviet times, while the Virgin Land Program of
Krushchev, confined mostly to this region, probably represented the most spectacular advance of the agricultural

frontier anywhere in the world. Given more arid conditions for agriculture than in the forest steppe zone of West Siberia, plus lower levels of urban-industrial concentration, North Kazakhstan has population densities generally well under 10 persons per square kilometer, declining to one per square kilometer and even lower in the central desert.[27]

What gives economic unity to these sharply different and very unevenly settled physical divisions is their relationship to the European core. Relative proximity and accessibility, the movement of huge amounts of bulk commodities westward, most of it by specialized and quasi-specialized transport media (pipelines, coal trains, high tension wires). Indeed, Soviet planners and experts today seem to recognize that unity, stemming from that relative position and similar economic relationship, by searching for a coherent macroregional policy for the area, designated as the Midland Region.

The Far East

The burden of remoteness and space increases sharply east of the Enisei and becomes a determining factor for development. Until Lake Baikal is reached, however, the Pacific remains as distant as the Urals. Irkutsk is closer to Sverdlovsk than to Vladivostok and nearer to Cheliabinsk than Khabarovsk.[28] The Buriat ASSR and Chita Oblast (Transbaikalia in Soviet parlance) are a little closer to the Pacific. However, their connection with the Amur lands and the coast is restrained by the great northern bulge of Manchuria even more effectively than the links of the Maritime Provinces with the rest of Canada are obstructed by the wilderness of northern Maine. The new Baikal-Amur Railway will hardly alter this situation, given its location well north of the populated zone. Transbaikalia is part of the official economic region of East Siberia and most of its population centers are tied in the Central Siberian Power Grid. Its transport links are mainly with provinces west of Lake Baikal. Nearly half of all railway freight loading handled in the Buriat ASSR is destined for the rest of East Siberia, which accounts for well over half of all incoming freight.[29]

One cannot, therefore, speak of a Pacific or even East Asian orientation in the economic sphere west of that Manchurian bulge. In fact, freight movements between the Far East and Siberian provinces further west became much weaker during the 1970s than before (Tables 2.1). On the other hand, Chita, from whose vicinity the historic Manchurian Railway to Vladivostok began, is the headquarters of the Transbaikal Military District, which briefly may have been placed under the same command as the Far Eastern Military District and the Soviet group of forces in Mongolia.[30] As Chapter 4 will show, an East Asian and, beyond it, an extraregional orientation in the military sphere are indeed realities today for the USSR east of Lake Baikal. Economically, however, such an orientation remains only a potential, and one that is pushed increasingly further into the future.

Delimiting Pacific Siberia in the north is somewhat easier, though not without some problems. The southern portion of the Yakut ASSR (Autonomous Soviet Socialist Republic) is now served by the BAM, and the southern Yakut TPC (territorial-production complex) represents the first and most important developmental node made possible by the new railway. The center of this ASSR is connected to the Pacific (at Magadan) by an important gravel highway, but most of the freight to and from this zone moves on the Lena River and is transhipped to the East Siberian Railway.[31] However, the extension of the BAM to the Aldan River and, later on, to Yakutsk (a project whose construction has just begun but which will not be completed much before the end of the century) should tie most of Yakutia into the BAM service area and thus more closely to the Pacific in the future. One is justified, therefore, to include the Yakut ASSR with the Far East. It is indeed so considered by Soviet specialists and was officially transferred to that Major Economic Region in 1963.

Geographically this enormous territory, composing over one-fourth of the entire USSR, is even more in need of internal differentiation than West Siberia-North Kazakhstan. Some 90 percent of it lies in the Northland, the bulk of it in the Far North. The effectively settled, temperate portion, essentially the only part of the Far East free of permafrost and with accumulated temperatures suitable for mid-latitude crops, is basically confined to the Middle Amur and Ussuri valleys, to the Khanka Lake plain north of Vladivostok, and southern Sakhalin. It is in this zone, within a hundred miles of the Trans-Siberian, aside from Sakhalin, that close to 5 million of the region's 7.7 million population is found.[32] With widespread peatbogs, acidic soils, and a heavy precipitation maximum that causes frequent and disastrous flooding in late summer (i.e., at harvest time), this is a rather

TABLE 2.1 Origin and Destination of Freight Shipment to and from the Far East (in percent of all tonnage shipped to and from Far East by rail, sea and river)

Regions of Origin and Destination	1966		1970		1977	
	Origin of inshipment	Destination of outshipment	Origin of inshipment	Destination of outshipment	Origin of inshipment	Destination of outshipment
North–West	1.2	2.7	1.8	2.4	5.59	6.60
Central Regions[a]	6.2	11.0	5.0	10.6	20.32	13.79
Baltic–Belorussia	0.6	1.6	0.5	2.5	8.58	3.72
Ukraine–Moldavia	3.2	4.6	3.1	5.81	12.91	16.52
Caucasia[b]	2.4	1.9	1.8	2.9	8.80	8.63
Volgo–Urals	19.1	12.7	12.9	14.1	21.53	21.90
Kazakhstan	1.8	13.8	4.0	11.2	4.50	8.02
Central Asia	1.3	4.4	1.4	4.8	3.87	1.64
West Siberia	24.7	15.3	29.0	12.6	8.76	9.78
East Siberia	39.5	32.5	40.5	33.1	2.79	7.80
Unaccounted freight (residual)	---	(0.5)[c]	---	---	2.36	2.60
USSR	100.0	100.5	100.0	100.0	100.0	100.0

[a]Center, Central Chernozem, Volgo–Viatka
[b]North and Transcaucasus
[c]Minor discrepancy. Exceeds total.

Source: L.I. Kolesov, Mezhotraslevye problemy razvitiia transportnoi sistemy Sibiri i Dal'nego Vostoka (Novosibirsk: Nauka, 1982), pp. 106–107.

uninviting environment. Yet it is far better than in the
Northland that makes up most of the Far East. The Far
Eastern North is the coldest part of the globe outside
Antarctica, the cold aggravated along the slightly warmer
Arctic and Pacific coasts by the high frequency of gale-
force winds and a wind chill index measuring from -60ºC to
-140ºC minima.[33] Aside from the Middle Lena-Viliui Lowland
and plains facing the Arctic Sea, the whole area is distinguished by rugged topography. Continuous permafrost,
reaching south almost to the Amur, and high seismicity over
much of the area severely complicate any building activity
and raise construction costs far above all other regions of
the USSR.

The vast Northland of the Far East is still inadequately explored, but its known mineral resources alone are
huge. Yet most of these riches may remain forever
untouched or be exploited only on a small local scale. Few
such minerals command the per ton value or lack alternative
sources of supplies in less forbidding regions to justify
exploitation for the national and international markets.
The construction of the BAM some 160 to 400 kilometers
north of the Trans-Siberian has made a wide east-west zone
much more accessible for resource development than the rest
of the Far Eastern North. Here a broader range of metallic
ores may eventually be worked, while even now, the recently
opened South Yakutian Basin furnishes 1.6 percent of all
Soviet coal, with one-third of it contracted to Japan.[34]
However, given the exceptional harshness of the environment, this coal has turned out to be the most expensive in
the USSR, and Japan now would like to reduce its purchase.
Similar difficulties may face other resources in the BAM
zone as well. At any rate, no timetable for their
exploitation has yet been announced and the development of
several remains controversial (Chapter 4).[35]

North of the BAM zone, only precious metals, diamonds
and tin are mined today or are likely to be for the rest of
the century.[36] Enormous coal reserves will stay untouched,
except for local power generation. Similarly, the big
reserves of natural gas are finding no markets outside
central Yakutia, though one field near the northeastern
extremity of Irkutsk Oblast may eventually be able to
supply the Irkutsk area some 600 miles to the southwest.
(The export of Yakutian gas no longer appears feasible to
anyone.) Along the more accessible Pacific coast, petroleum long produced on northern Sakhalin is being augmented
by much bigger off-shore finds of hydrocarbons, though
mainly of gas. Exploration is underway on Kamchatka and

may begin off-shore in the promising Okhotsk Basin in the future.[37]

Central Siberia

In between these two macroregions lies a third, Central Siberia. Its position basically corresponds to the official major economic region of East Siberia. This latter designation, however, makes sense only if the Far East is regarded as outside the framework of Siberia altogether, which is untenable and maintained in neither Russian, Soviet, or foreign research. The land between the Kuznets Alatau (Ala Mountains) and Lake Baikal, along the upper courses of the Enisei and Lena Rivers and the whole length of the Angara, form the core of that region. Most of Trans-Baikalia, that awkward area between Lake Baikal and the northward bulge of Manchuria should also be added, though it is somewhat cut off from the Enisei-Angara center.[38] As in the case of the Far East, a vast Northland adjoins the area, while in the south it is flanked by a far smaller unresponsive territory occupied by the forbidding ranges of the Saian Mountains. The economically responsive area of Central Siberia, therefore, covers less than 7 percent of the Siberian hinterland between the Pacific and the Urals and only a quarter of the official region of East Siberia (Figure 2.1). Population densities here average 5 to 6 per square kilometer, while north of the Angara mean density drops to less than one and to less than 0.5 in the Far North.[39]

Central Siberia is far less isolated from the main economic centers of the USSR than is the Far East. Krasnoiarsk lies nearer to the Volga than to the Pacific even via the BAM; it is also much closer to Moscow than to Vladivostok. The freight ties of this region with the rest of the country are some 40 to 50 percent greater than is true for the Far East when measured by the value of shipment and still greater when measured in tonnage.[40] Still, remoteness from the national market and the main centers of economic power is a much more crushing burden for Central Siberia than for West Siberia-North Kazakhstan and this has been a major formative influence on its development.

The enormous interregional flows of natural gas, so important for West Siberia, is entirely missing here and those of oil are on a far smaller scale. Consequently, the aggregate tonnage of commodity movement between Central Siberia and the rest of the country amounts only to a fraction of that which links West Siberia with the economy of the state as a whole. As is the case with the Far East, however, freight links with the European USSR have become far stronger than with neighboring Siberian regions, despite the remoteness from the metropolis. Just as for the Far East, the relative importance of such links with other Trans-Ural regions has been sharply reduced during the 1970s. By tonnage, barely over a fifth of all interregional freight movement to and from Central Siberia originated and terminated east of the Urals and the Caspian Sea in 1977 (Table 2.2).

Central Siberia represents the largest storehouse of accessible coal, waterpower, and forest reserves in the USSR and is rich in metal ores as well. By one authoritative estimate, the Angara-Enisei area concentrates a third of the nation's economically exploitable hydroelectric and forest potentials, two-fifths of its coal reserves and large reserves of nonferrous and ferrous metals, magnesium, apatite, asbestos, salt, and the like.[41] Oil, gas, diamonds, and gold (with the exception of one nearly exhausted deposit), however, are not on that list. Future prospects for petroleum and gas (hydrocarbons) appear good only in the Arctic and, farther south, only at great depth in an area of extreme geological complexity, greatly reducing the effectiveness of exploration work.[42]

In contrast to precious and rare metals, or even tin and petroleum, the minerals available here have relatively low per ton value. They are also untransportable in raw, unrefined form and must be processed locally before shipment. The vast hydropower and low-grade coal reserves, in particular, cannot be delivered outside Central Siberia in large quantities. Their utilization depends on the development of massive energy users in the area and in immediately adjacent provinces, such as the Kuzbas.

The adjoining Northland remains basically a wilderness, which, on the whole, has experienced much slower economic growth than northwest Siberia or even the Far Eastern Arctic and Subarctic. It is apparently regarded as a "reserve area" in developmental plans.[43] The massive resources of the Tunguska coal field (the largest in the USSR) lie untouched and so do vast deposits of tar sands along the Olenek River astride the border of the Yakut ASSR. However, on the western edge of the Putorana Mountains near the mouth of the Enisei, geology and greater accessibility have combined to give rise to one of the largest polymetallic mining complexes in the world. Very rich nickel-copper deposits, with the coproducts cobalt and

TABLE 2.2 Origin and Destination of Freight Shipment to and from East Siberia (in percent of all tonnage shipped to and from East Siberia by rail, sea and river)

Regions of Origin and Destination	1966		1970		1977	
	Origin of inship-ment	Destina-tion of outship-ment	Origin of inship-ment	Destina-tion of outship-ment	Origin of inship-ment	Destina-tion of outship-ment
North-West	2.2	0.8	1.9	0.6	5.59	6.60
Central Regions[a]	6.2	2.1	8.1	2.6	20.28	13.80
Baltic-Belorussia	0.5	0.1	0.6	0.2	3.62	2.12
Ukraine-Moldavia	3.9	3.3	5.3	4.2	12.91	16.52
Caucasia[b]	1.8	4.2	3.3	4.6	10.71	8.44
Volgo-Urals	44.3	13.9	29.2	10.8	21.54	21.90
Kazakhstan	3.4	14.0	6.7	8.7	4.50	8.02
Central Asia	1.3	12.2	1.6	10.4	3.87	1.64
West Siberia	27.3	31.4	32.2	37.4	8.76	9.78
Far East	8.6	16.7	10.3	18.3	2.74	0.87
Unaccounted freight (residual)	0.5	1.3	0.8	2.2	5.5	10.3
USSR	100.0	100.0	100.0	100.0	100.0	100.0

[a]Center, Central Chernozem, Volgo-Viatka
[b]North and Transcaucasus

Source: L.I. Kolesov, Mezhotraslevye problemy razvitiia transportnoi sistemy Sibiri i Dal'nego Vostoka (Novosibirsk: Nauka, 1982), pp. 106-107.

platinum, and initially important coal reserves lie near
the Kara Sea and the western half of the Northern Sea
route, which is open through most of the year. That
complex at Norilsk has recently undergone a major expansion.[44] It exemplifies the Soviet desire and determination
for mineral self-sufficiency (indeed surplus), and demon-
strates Soviet ability to exploit northern reserves against
tremendous odds wherever bulk transportation for such
minerals is possible.

NOTES

1. Narodnoe khoziaistvo SSSR v 1985 godu, pp. 12–17,
538 and 546.
2. Atlas SSSR (Moscow: Glavnoe Upravlenie Geodezii i
Kartografii, 1985), p. 99.
3. Densities in Tadzhikistan's Gissar Valley actually
exceed 500 per square kilometer with the prospect of
reaching 1000 by the turn of the century. Andizhan Oblast
in Uzbekistan has a density of 336 per square kilometer,
greater than that of Moscow City and Moscow Oblast
combined. Molodoi kommunist, 1982, No. 9, pp. 67–72.
Translated in Current Digest of the Soviet Press, Vol. 34,
No. 45 (December 8), 1982, p. 12.
4. Leslie Dienes, "Pasturalism in Turkestan: Its
Decline and Its Persistence," Soviet Studies, Vol. 27,
No. 3 (July), 1975, pp. 343–365.
5. Arthur A. Meyerhoff, "Soviet Petroleum: History,
Technology, Geology, Reserves, Potential and Policy," in
Robert G. Jensen, Theodore Shabad and A.W. Wright, eds.,
Soviet Natural Resources in the World Economy (Chicago:
University of Chicago Press, 1983), p. 335.
6. Michael Kaser, "The Soviet Gold Mining Industry,"
in Jensen, et al., Soviet Natural Resources, pp. 580–581;
Theodore Shabad, "Geography of Uranium Resources," in
Leslie Dienes and Theodore Shabad, The Soviet Energy
System: Resource Use and Policy (Washington: Winston &
Sons, 1979), pp. 174–179 and Theodore Shabad, Basic Indus-
trial Resources of the USSR (New York: Columbia University
Press, 1969), pp. 309–346.
7. Tsentral'noe statisticheskoe upravlenie SSSR
(TsSU), Chislennost' i sostav naseleniia SSSR (Moscow:
Finansy i statistika, 1984), pp. 110–137.
8. Even among the Kazakh, the birthrate during the

1970-1978 period averaged 30.6 percent. Among the Uzbeks it stood at 40.8 percent and among the Tadzhiks as high as 41.8 percent. E.K. Vasil'eva, ed., Rozhdaemost': izvestnoe i neizvestnoe (Moscow: Financy i statistika, 1983), p. 22.

9. A.G. Granberg, "Sibir' v narodnokhoziaistvennom komplekse," Ekonomika i organizatsiia promyshlennogo proiz-vodstva (EKO), 1980, No. 4, pp. 102-103.

10. Victor L. Mote, "Environmental Constraints to the Economic Development of Siberia," in Jensen et al., Soviet Natural Resources, pp. 15-71, especially pp. 20-27 and 42-46.

11. Narodnoe khoziaistvo SSSR v 1975 godu, p. 20 and Narodnoe khoziaistvo RSFSR v 1975 godu, p. 162.

12. Narodnoe khoziaistvo Kazakhstana v 1984 godu, pp. 5 and 84-85.

13. S.V. Riashchenko, "Medico-Geographical Investigations in Siberia," Soviet-American seminar on the Social-Geographical Aspects of Environmental Change (USSR Academy of Sciences, Institute of Geography, Irkutsk, August, 1983), p. 7.

14. S.V. Slavin, Osvoenie Severa Sovetskogo Soiuza (Moscow: Nauka, 1982), pp. 12-14.

15. L.M. Kaplan and I.Iu. Murav'eva, Ekonomicheskie problemy upravleniia stroitel'stvom na Severa (Leningrad: Stroiizdat, 1983), p. 26.

16. N.S. Iag'ia, Zdorov'e naseleniia Severa (Lenin-grad: Meditsina, 1980), pp. 202-214.

17. Riashchenko, "Medico-Geographical Investigations," p. 9.

18. Narodnoe khoziaistvo SSSR v 1985 godu, pp. 12-17 and Slavin, Osvoenie Severa, p. 22.

19. Robert N. North, Transport in Western Siberia: Tsarist and Soviet Development (Vancouver: University of British Columbia Press, 1979). Citations from pp. 8, 10, and 236.

20. Theodore Shabad, "New Notes," Soviet Geography, Vol. 27, No. 4 (April), 1986, pp. 248, 252, 258, and 266.

21. In the early 1980s, over 490 million tons of oil equivalent of fuel was shipped from Siberia to the European regions and the Urals (N. Kazanskiy and N. Singur, "Sibir' i Dal'nii Vostok v narodnokhoziaistvennom komplekse strany," Planovoe khoziaistvo, 1984, No. 4, p. 99. Adding shipments from North Kazakhstan, this flow reached over 520 million tons of oil equivalent. The European Economic Community in 1982 imported a total of 419 million tons of oil equivalent of fuel, with 422 million tons projected for 1983. Commission of European Communities, The Energy

38

Situation in the Community. Situation 1982, Outlook 1983. Paris, 1983), pp. 7 and 31.

22. Rough estimate. In the early 1980s, railway freight from the Asiatic to the European parts of the country reached 245 million tons, while freight from the opposite direction amounted to only 126.5 million tons. Well over half of the eastward moving shipment must have originated and terminated in West Siberia-North Kazakhstan, where less than half of all freight movement is local freight and transit. A.A. Mitaishvili, ed., Ekonomicheskie problemy razvitiia transporta (Moscow: Transport, 1982), p. 20 and S.K. Danilov, Ekonomicheskaia geografiia transporta (Moscow: Transport, 1982) pp. 283-366. One should add some 200 million tons of oil and over 160 billion cubic meters of gas shipped through pipelines, the latter equivalent to over 200 million tons of coal to the westward moving freight (not counting transit), which must have thus reached 500 to 550 million tons. Shipment into West Siberia-North Kazakhstan from all directions amounted to no more than 60 to 70 million tons.

23. Leslie Dienes, "The Development of Siberian Regions: Economic Profiles, Income Flows and Strategies for Growth," Soviet Geography, Vol. 23, No. 4 (April), 1982, pp. 219-223.

24. Mote, "Environmental Constraints," p. 33.

25. A.G. Granberg, ed., Ekonomika Sibiri v razreze shirotnykh zon (Novosibirsk: Nauka, 1985), p. 30.

26. North, Transport in Western Siberia, pp. 23.

27. Atlas SSSR, pp. 130-131.

28. Computed from tables in Atlas zheleznykh dorog SSSR (Moscow: Glavnoe upravlenie geodezii i kartografii, 1982), pp. 137-58.

29. For the Buriat ASSR, inshipment from East Siberia west of Baikal exceeds inshipment from the Far East by almost 6 times. For outshipment, the ties with East Siberia are 50 to 60 percent greater. The Far East accounts for less than one-tenth of the Buriat ASSR's total freight movement. For Chita Oblast, freight links with the Far East are doubtless somewhat stronger. G.Sh. Radnoev, Narodnokhoziaistvennyi kompleks Buriatskoi ASSR (Novosibirsk: Nauka, 1979), p. 94.

30. Peter Kruzhin, "General Govorov Heads All Forces in the Far East," Radio Liberty Research Bulletin, RL78/82, 1982, February 17, pp. 1-3.

31. The gravel road from Magadan accounted for only 6.6 percent of inshipment and 0.7 percent of outshipment in 1970. E.B. Aizenberg and Iu.A. Sobolev, Kompleksnye

programmy razvitiia vostochnykh raionov SSSR (Moscow: Ekonomika, 1982), p. 68 and B.V. Belinskii, ed., Napravleniia intensifikatsii raboty transporta Iakutskoi ASSR (Iakutsk: AN SSSR, Iakutskii filial, 1975), pp. 12-13.

32. Slavin, Osvoenie Severa, pp. 22 and 173 and Narodnoe khoziaistvo SSSR v 1985 godu, pp. 12-14.

33. Mote, "Environmental Constraints," pp. 24-26.

34. Victor Mote, "A Visit to the Baikal-Amur Mainline and the New Amur-Yakutsk Rail Project," Soviet Geography, Vol. 26, No. 9 (November), 1985, pp. 704-710 and Ekonomicheskaia gazeta, 1986, No. 6 (February), p. 3.

35. Leslie Dienes, "Soviet Japanese Relations: Are They Beginning to Fade?" Soviet Geography, Vol. 26, No. 7 (September), 1985, pp. 516-518.

36. Theodore Shabad, "News Notes," Soviet Geography, Vol. 25, No. 9 (November), 1984, pp. 705-707 and Kaser, "The Soviet Gold Mining Industry," pp. 556-596, esp. 557-567.

37. Arthur A. Meyerhoff, "Hydrocarbon Resources in Arctic and Subarctic Regions," in A.F. Embry and H.R. Balkwill, eds., Arctic Geology and Geophysics. Memoir 8. 1982, December, pp. 496-506 and Ekonomicheskaia gazeta, 1985, No. 52 (December), p. 10.

38 A.G. Aganbegian, ed., Sibir' v edinom narodnokhoziaistvennom komplekse (Novosibirsk: Nauka, 1980), pp. 282-284 and M.K. Bandman, Territorial'no-proizvodstvennye kompleksy (Novosibirsk: Nauka, 1980), pp. 49 and 80-81.

39. Granberg, Ekonomika Sibiri, p. 31.

40. L.I. Kolesov, Mezhotraslevye problemy razvitiia transportnoi systemy Sibiri i Dal'nego Vostoka (Novosibirsk: Nauka, 1982), pp. 100-102.

41. Aganbegian, Sibir' v edinom . . . komplekse, p. 269.

42. Meyerhoff, "Hydrocarbon Resources," pp. 480-489.

43. G.A. Privalovskaia and T.G. Runova, Territorial'naia organizatsiia promyshlennosti i prirodnye resursy SSSR (Moscow: Nauka, 1980), pp. 178-151 and 214-215; Granberg, Ekonomika Sibiri, p. 167 and Figure 1.

44. Theodore Shabad, "News Notes," Soviet Geography, Vol. 24, No. 3 (March), 1983, pp. 256-259.

PART TWO

National Policy Issues and Soviet Asia

3

Energy Policy
and Siberian Development

The spatial distribution of economic activity is the cumulative expression of past preferences, embodied in a wide range of fixed capital and infrastructure. As such, this geographic pattern is subject to pronounced inertia. Huge efforts and long lead times are needed to modify it significantly. This observation applies to energy use also and especially so in the USSR, where locationally concentrated heavy industries dominate demand even more than in the West. In contrast to the spatial inertia of energy consumption, the geographic pattern of supply and flows is more prone to change. Individual fuel deposits, particularly of hydrocarbons, even of easily minable coal over several decades, are subject to depletion. They must be replaced and this leads to changes in comparative fuel costs. Such shifts in supply costs, combined with the relative substitutability of energy sources and technological improvements in utilization technology and transport, can and do result in more rapid changes in regional energy mixes and the pattern of energy flows.

The enduring commanding position of the European USSR in the Soviet economy (only briefly challenged during the abnormal years of World War II) remains the cardinal geographic fact of the country. Substantial diffusion of industry within this core area has occurred over time. Yet, over three-fourths of the demand for Soviet energy, as roughly for most other resources, continues to originate in these parts.[1] Similarly, export opportunities and obligations historically have always centered on Europe, and this dominance was only strengthened by the dependency of the East European CMEA on Soviet natural resources. Given this geographic inertia of energy demand, the first call for supplies has also been on the European USSR, which remained self-sufficient and a <u>net</u> fuel exporter until almost the mid-1960s. The pressure of escalating fuel demand, however, has seriously depleted reserves west of the Urals, and exploration efforts, which until the later 1970s continued to focus on the European USSR, have failed to improve the situation. By the latter part of the 1970s, total fuel production in the European USSR was in an absolute decline, a trend which the accelerated nuclear program could not even remotely counterbalance.[2] The most critical task of Soviet energy policy has become the massive westward shipment of fuel from the Asian hinterlands to replenish the energy deficit of the European USSR, which today exceeds that of the whole European Economic Community (EEC), and to provide the additional export flows, nearly all of which goes through western border points and ports. The energy policy choices made since the early 1970s to deal with this east-west issue have had momentous regional and structural consequences. Presently, they are affecting the economy more than any other single decision in the civilian sphere.

THE FORCED DEVELOPMENT OF TIUMEN' OIL AND GAS AND ITS EFFECTS

I have long argued that during the 1970s, Soviet leaders had no choice but to turn to the giant oil fields of Tiumen' Oblast and throw <u>that</u> resource into the huge energy breach. At that time, no other fuel source could guarantee the required massive increments and also bridge the spatial gap between demand and supply. A coal-centered energy strategy, or even one which would try significantly to moderate the decline in the share of solid fuels, therefore, was to be short-lived, while technological and transport constraints would delay the full-scale contribution of Siberian gas to the Soviet energy economy.[3] The oil fields of the Middle Ob', still remote but more accessible than West Siberian gas, were thus crash developed, leading to premature peaking and admitted damage to some reservoirs. In a mere ten years (1970-1980), the production <u>increment</u> in the West Siberian oil fields reached 282 million tons and in thirteen years (1970-1983) 338 million tons, an expansion unprecedented anywhere in the world. The region, whose output in the 1965-1966 period was negligible, had by the end of 1984 cumulatively produced over 3.1 billion tons of oil, as much as the Volga-Ural fields until the latter part of the 1970s during <u>three</u>

decades of exploitation.[4]

The choices made during the 1970s set the stage for the energy strategy in the 1980s and for its consequences. To a very large degree, they also set the <u>course</u> of that strategy, despite the wide surface swings of Soviet energy policy--from coal, to more oil, and finally to the current gas program, the biggest economic crusade since the 1930s. Thane Gustafson has documented these erratic changes and they are important in illuminating the decision-making process.[5]   Yet the failure of these ephemeral strategies during the middle and late 1970s has been preordained; they left virtually no impact before they were overwhelmed by the massive shift to Big Gas. The performance of the 1970s in petroleum could not be duplicated even in West Siberia: during that decade, one single supergiant, Samotlor, contributed a full half of all Siberian (and 56 percent of all Soviet) <u>increment</u>. However, no other supergiants have been found and, because of forced development, the deposits put on line before 1971 entered the declining phase by 1980, and those put on line before 1975 peaked by 1982.[6]

In 1985, West Siberian oil production, as a whole, declined absolutely by about 6 million tons after an unbroken, meteoric rise through the previous decade and a half.   In fact, this formerly successful province was responsible for one-third of the drop in Soviet petroleum output.[7]   While the rapid decline at Samotlor, the country's largest field, has been slowed, some other districts in the province continue to do poorly and with 376 million tons produced during 1986, West Siberian output is still 5.8 million tons behind plan.[8]   The reserve situation remains worrisome: in September 1985, Gorbachev revealed that the ratio of explored reserves to production here is no better than in the country as a whole.[9]   In addition, by January 1986 almost 31 percent of these explored reserves were in complex, hard-to-work reservoirs, as opposed to 22 percent in 1980. Such fields contributed 42 to 47 percent of all reserve addition in Tiumen' during 1982-1983.   Soviet experts admit that the exploration, prove-up, and exploitation of such deposits pose a very serious problem for the Soviet oil industry.[10]   Complex fields, particularly the hard-to-identify limestone reservoirs of the deeper Jurassic age, also present a tremendous challenge further upstream in the prospecting stage.

The massive shift to gas in the early 1980's and the increasingly costly efforts to keep Tiumen' oil output growing (at least to compensate for declines elsewhere in the country) have had a momentous impact on Soviet regional development and economic structure. While unquestionably rational, the shift to gas has been too sudden and undertaken on too immense a scale. It was embarked on without adequate preparation for the intersectoral, interregional, and foreign trade requirements and impacts of its unprecedented resource demand, and it was confounded by the world's volatile energy market. At the same time, the worsening conditions in the Tiumen' oil industry also made a sharp rise in capital allocation to petroleum necessary, especially by 1985 and after.[11] Within the West Siberian gas and oil province, the 50 billion rubles of investment during the 1965–1980 period have had to be matched by a similar amount in the single Five-Year Plan (FYP) of the 1981–1985 period, while a staggering 82 billion rubles is envisaged for the second half of the current decade.[12] This could not but produce distortions, huge amounts of waste, and a sharp rise in cost.

The all-out emphasis on oil and gas in the West Siberian Lowland has produced an industrial structure overwhelmingly tied to the extraction of these two fuels. As Table 3.1 shows, extraction of the two hydrocarbons contributed less than 23 percent of the industrial output of Tiumen' Oblast as late as 1970, but over 60 percent a decade later. Little change was expected by 1985, except in the gaining of gas on oil in relative importance. Virtually all other branches, save the forest and wood-processing industries, are closely tied to hydrocarbon extraction. However, the favorable trend in the economics of the Tiumen' oil and gas complex, observable until the mid-1970s, has long since come to an end. The decline in the production cost of natural gas in the 1976–1980 period was already more than counterbalanced by the rise in transport outlays and still more by the mounting costs in the oil industry, continuing in the 1980s at an ever-increasing rate.[13] For the rest of the century, this unfavorable trend will accelerate, as the sharply deteriorating economic condition in the Tiumen' oil industry coincides with the shift in the center of construction activity to the northern gas fields. According to a programming model developed by the Economic Institute of the Soviet Academy of Sciences' Siberian Branch, the amount of freight shipped into Tiumen' Oblast should double even during the 1980s, while the energy intensity of the oil and gas complex should increase fivefold by the beginning of the next century.[14]

As Table 3.2 shows, one-third or more of all Siberian

TABLE 3.1 Branch Distribution of Industrial Output in Tiumen' Oblast (in percent of gross value)

Industry Branches	1960	1970	1980	1985 (plan)
All industry	100.0	100.0	100.0	100.0
Oil		19.4	46.0	34.8
Natural gas		3.4	14.3	22.2
Electric power	1.2	1.8	3.5	4.5
Machine building— metal working	14.7	17.3	11.5	12.4
Chemicals and petrochemicals	2.3	2.1	0.5	4.3
Forest products, wood processing, pulp & paper	24.5	15.2	5.5	4.8
Building materials	2.3	3.7	2.8	3.3
Light industries	12.5	11.3	8.7	7.3
Food industries	41.9	22.6	7.2	6.4

Source: V.V. Voskresenskii and V.K. Abramov, "Intensifikatsiia i kompleksnost' v razvitii tiumenskogo neftegazovogo kompleksa," Ekonomika gazovoi promyshlennosti, 1982, No. 1, p. 22.

48

TABLE 3.2 Investment in Siberia and the Far East, 1971–1990 by FYP (billion rubles)

	1971–1975 Official	1976–1980 Estimates (USSR figure official)	1981–1985 Estimates for original Plan (USSR figure official)	1986–1990 Plan
Tiumen' and Tomsk Oblasts	14.6	35	50–55	82
Rest of West Siberia	20.9	26	26	
Krasnoiarsk Krai	10.5	14.5	13	
Buriat ASSR	1.6	2.3		
Rest of East Siberia	10.6	12–13	12–13	
Yakut ASSR	3.35	3.24		
Kamchatka Oblast	1.34	2.4		
Rest of Far East	17.75	22–23	30–35	
Total for Siberia and the Far East	80.6	121	130–135[a] 142[b]	
Total for USSR	562.8	717.7	843.2	994

[a]Original plan.
[b]Assumes that investment in Siberia and the Far East as a whole grew at the national rate.

Notes: Subregional breakdown of table largely dictated by data availability. Official statistics on regional investment stopped after 1975. Column 1 from Nar. Khoz. RSFSR, 1975 g., p. 329. For columns 3 and 4, the shares of investment in Siberia and Far East were estimated as follows. 1976–1980: The chairman of the RSFSR Gosplan stated that during 1976–79 the two regions received 1.5 times as much investment as during the 1971–74 period (Maslennikova, in

EKO, 1980, No. 12, p. 6.) 1981-1985: We have the statement that over 120 billion rubles of investment was earmarked for Siberia and the Far East, a figure which I take to be state investment, or else outlays in Siberia would grow no faster than for the entire USSR. The head of Gosplan RSFSR also declared that in 1983 capital outlays of more than 27 billion should be allocated to Siberia (Planovoe khoziaistvo, 1984, No. 4, p. 99 and Izvestiia, December 1, 1982). With a similar ratio between state investment and investment from all sources that was the case in the RSFSR during the Tenth Plan, on the one hand, or multiplying the Izvestiia figure by 4.8 to 5 times the total of 130 to 135 billion for Siberia and Far East emerges. In reality, investment during 1981-1985 ran significantly above the Plan in the USSR as a whole and these overruns are at least as likely to apply in Siberia as elsewhere. Figures for Tiumen' and Tomsk Oblasts from Ekonomika gazovoi promyshlennosti, 1982, No. 1, p. 21; Problemy Severa, Vyp. 21, 1983, p. 44; Leningradskaia Pravda, January 8, 1981, p. 1; Planovoe khoziaistvo, 1981, No. 9, p. 8; Sovetskaia Sibir', June 8, 1986, p. 2 and interview by author in Soviet Academy of Sciences, Siberian Branch, IEOPP, Novosibirsk, August, 1986. Figures for USSR from Nar. khoz. SSSR v 1985 g., p. 365 and Pravda, June 19, 1986, p. 3. Sources for other rows may be obtained from the author.

investment already flows to a single province, Tiumen' (and, combined with Tomsk Oblast, over 35 percent), the seventeen other provinces that compose Siberia and the Far East have to share the remaining two-thirds. Tiumen' Oblast, with less than 6 percent of Siberia's population in 1970, has also accounted for almost 23 percent of its population growth and some two-fifths of all net immigration into Siberia since that time.[15] A mechanical increase of 400,000 to 450,000 (i.e., net immigration) in Tiumen' Oblast during the past thirteen years, however, is the consequence of a total migration (arrivals plus departures) 7 to 7.5 times as large. Each year in Tiumen', 300,000 to 350,000 persons take part in the migration process, one-third of the province's population.[16]

Demand for labor is growing at an exponential rate. The required increments for the 1981-1985 period was claimed to equal the growth during the previous fifteen years and another 1.4 million increase is thought to be needed during the second half of this decade. The province was expected to supply less than two-fifths of that demand from its own population and even immigration has proved unable to satisfy it.[17] Therefore, in addition to the population registered in Tiumen', itself highly unstable, a very large cohort of temporary workers are taking part in the development of the oil and gas complex. Flown in mostly from the European USSR on a rotating basis for a period of up to three months, this temporary or expeditionary work force has swelled greatly in the last few years. Its number reached some 90,000 by 1984, some four-fifths as many as those rotating to isolated outposts from within Tiumen' Oblast.[18] Expeditionary brigades were responsible for a full 40 percent of all drilling already in 1984 and the share of outsiders were only slightly less in the preparation and construction of drilling sites.[19]

The issues of employment, population, and settlement policy in the West Siberian oil and gas region (and elsewhere east of the Urals) will be examined in greater detail in Chapter 6. Suffice it to say here that General Secretary Gorbachev revealed in September 1985 that at that time 1.5 million workers were engaged in the development of the West Siberian oil and gas industries, more than the entire population of Tiumen' Province twelve years earlier. Gorbachev announced that construction organizations from five additional republics will undertake projects in the region during the Twelfth FYP (1986-1990).[20] Henceforth also "the Tatar and Bashkir oil associations have each been allocated whole fields in the Nizhnevartovsk area, for which they will be entirely responsible."[21]

The pressure on labor in West Siberia will only inten- sify during the Twelfth FYP. Already in 1984, each maintenance brigade, composed mostly of women, under Glav- tiumenneftegaz (the Chief Administration for Oil and Gas Extraction in Tiumen') had to service 68 wells, compared to 29 wells per brigade in Azerbaidzhan. In the Surgut region it had to service 85.[22] More than 2,000 wells that were capable of producing oil in West Siberia were inoperative in 1984.[23] At the same time, the program to convert 4,000 wells from pumps to gas lift, which requires far less frequent servicing, was badly delayed. Eight months after its target date of mid-1984, the program of well conversion was no more than half accomplished and only in 1987 does it appear to be completed.[24] The new, 1986-1990 Plan calls for a 50 percent increase in the total meterage drilled in the region, with a similar rise in geophysical work and a doubling of drilling in prospecting and exploration, all of which demand more workers even with substantial improvement in productivity.[25] V. Kuramin, the deputy minister of Construction of Oil and Gas Industry Enterprises, claims that a 60 percent increase in the labor force will be needed by the end of the current decade, while the programming model by the Economic Institute of the Soviet Academy's Siberian branch, cited above, calls for a 2.5- fold growth in employment by the turn of the century.[26]

These pressures are heightened by recent wholesale dismissals, disciplinary actions, and transfer of personnel in the Tiumen' Oblast administration, which may spur efforts but are unlikely to be conducive to rational decision making and allocation of resources. At the Nizhnevartovsk Association almost the entire leadership has been fired, the Variaganneft administration has had six directors in four years, and throughout the West Siberian oil and gas region two-thirds of the executives of petro- leum and gas extraction have received various penalties. Even the newspaper Sovetskaia Rossiia wonders whether such measures are not counterproductive and questions if one should really expect production and construction organi- zations to operate normally with such disruptions.[27] Gorbachev's speech to Party and government officials of Tiumen' and Tomsk Oblasts at a major conference in September 1985, however, made clear that the heat on them will continue.[28]

Tremendous distortions and wastage are the inevitable side effects of such a "supercampaign." This is true both inside Tiumen' Oblast and outside it and in the interregional and sectoral portions of the Siberian, and even the whole Soviet, economy. Internally, such pell-mell growth leaves infrastructural and social development even further behind, and especially so per capita, despite the strenuous efforts to correct the lag. In the Tenth FYP (1976-1980), for example, the share of all "nonproductive" investment in the total capital outlays of Tiumen' Oblast as a whole composed a mere 19 percent, significantly smaller than in most developed areas of the USSR.[29] Social infrastructure and housing receive only a part of that, especially in the northern oil and gas areas, where only 5 billion rubles, less than a tenth of total investment have been so allocated for the Tenth and Eleventh FYP.[30] As a result, at the close of the 1970s only 6 square meters of housing space was available per capita in the oil and gas regions of Tiumen'; at Noiabr'sk and Novo-Urengoi 2.7 square meters and 2.3 square meters per capita were reported respectively in 1980.[31] (Table 3.3.) Given the huge growth of population since that time and the fact that by the end of 1983 Tiumengazprom (Tiumen' Gas Industry), for example, fell 25 percent behind housing construction goals set by the Eleventh FYP, a significant impovement is very unlikely.[32] Even in Surgut, with a population of close to 200,000 in the more developed Middle Ob' region, the construction of the huge electric station was accompanied by the fulfillment of the housing plan to only 70 percent during the past ten years. In 1985, power workers received eight times less housing space than was promised. Public health fares even worse than housing. Only 0.5 percent of the monies allocated for "nonproductive" construction has gone for public health, that is, one-eighth of the norm.[33]

For the rest of the century, a continued surge in population is foreseen while prospecting, field development, and pipeline construction will demand still greater volumes of capital. The share of social infrastructure and all supporting industries, therefore, is expected to decline even further--to 18 percent of total investment according to a programming solution developed by the Academy of Sciences.[34] This means that capital allocation in the social sphere will hardly be able to keep ahead of population increase, leading to stagnation, in some cases even decline, on a per capita basis. In the prevailing conditions of Tiumen' Province, the delays in the commissioning of facilities serving the population will likely to be even greater. Every sign points to the further hardening of "departmentalism" and a rampant sauve qui peut spirit among enterprises and trusts. They have seen their

TABLE 3.3 Housing and Educational Infrastructure in Tiumen' Oblast, 1979

Indices	Total for Oblast	Branches of the Economy			
		Oil Industry	Gas Industry	Geology	Construction
Housing space sq. meter/ person	10.6	7.8	5.5	7.3	5.3
Nurseries and kin- dergarten (% of demand)	70.0	43.0	50.8	39.0	40.8
Schools	84.5	73.0	51.1	36.0	----

Source: I.T. Baseliia and A.Yu. Reteium, "Razvitie gornodobyvaiushchei promyshlennosti, infrastruktura i rasselenie," in MNTsNITI & AN SSSR, Komitet po sistemnomu analizu, Dostizheniia i perspektivy, No. 11, Prirodnye resursy i okruzhaiushchaia sreda. 1984, p. 85.

hands strengthened by the sharp decline in the share of budgetary allocations in total investment and a corresponding rise in that coming from their own resources (the latter share rose to almost one-third in the West Siberian oil and gas complex in 1980, with the expansion of bank credits further reducing the proportion of budgetary disbursement).[35]

Gustafson described recent Soviet efforts to deal with this old problem in the Tiumen' oil and gas complex, which is so big and crucial that it demands new or improved instruments of coordination. The creation of a special thirty-six-member commission of Gosplan, located directly in Tiumen' city, is the most notable of these efforts (according to Gustafson, such a thing with headquarters right in the field of action has never been done before). However, the powers of this commission have been described by its chairman in strikingly weak language. It may actually have lost power since its establishment and it is evidently undermined not only by the major ministries, but by the Tiumen' "Party apparatus that does not welcome potential rivals."[36]

The interregional distortions of this oil-and-gas-focused energy policy, with its huge resource requirements centered mainly in one province, are also obvious. During the 1981–1985 Plan, for example, the entire growth in the volume of capital allocation to West and East Siberia (which was 2.5 times as fast as in the country as a whole) was channeled to the ministries of oil and gas industries; that in fact means Tiumen' and (to some extent) Tomsk Oblasts to an overwhelming degree.[37] As my estimates in Table 3.2 show, the mounting capital needs of Tiumen', combined with that of the BAM and the military build-up in the Far East, has led to stagnation or very slow growth of investment in most other regions of Siberia. Particularly remarkable is the sharp, 6.5 percent absolute decline of state investment from 1980 through 1983 in Krasnoiarsk Krai, the most important industrial province east of the Kuzbas, containing the Kansk-Achinsk and Saian TPCs (territorial production complexes), the Norilsk mining and smelting concentration and major military installations.[38] In addition, investment in such a crucial part of the European core area as the Ukraine (as no doubt elsewhere west of the Urals) also suffered an absolute decline from 1978 through 1982, though it recovered afterwards.[39]

The Trans-Ural frontier zone is critically dependent on machinery and technology supplies from the metropolis. In the early 1970s, for example, West Siberia had to ship

in 73 percent of all the machinery utilized (nearly all
from the European Soviet Union) and East Siberia 85
percent.[40]   Since that time, the two regions lost further
ground, their relative contribution to the country's engineering output declined and their dependence on supplies
from centers west of the Urals could only have increased
(Table 3.4).   A decade later, West and East Siberia
combined must bring in three-fourths of all machines
used.[41]

THE SOUTHERN ECUMENE: FROM THE URALS TO
BAIKALIA

    National energy policy choices have the greatest influ-
ence on economic structure and development in the southern
zone of West Siberia-North Kazakhstan and in Central
Siberia as well (see Chapter 1 for the regional framework).
These regions, however, are characterized by very different
energy endowments with respect to resource mobility, labor
requirements, and markets than Tiumen' and Tomsk Oblasts.
This southern wedge of the Siberian ecumene is very rich in
coal and, east of the Altai Mountains, in hydroelectric
potential as well. It also has big reserves of metallif-
erous ores and, again east of the Altai, timber resources.
Thanks to better climate and considerable agricultural
land, this wedge is more habitable than the regions farther
north.   In diminishing degree from west to east, this Ural-
Baikal zone has been tied to the country's economic core by
railways for several decades. It has become an integral
part of that vital economic triangle which David Hooson
called "the effective national territory" of the Soviet
Union.[42]
    The vast resources of this zone, however, are expen-
sive, difficult, or outright impossible to ship over very
long distances. In contrast to Tiumen' gas and oil, for
example, the coal reserves of North Kazakhstan and the
Kuzbas can play but a relatively modest role in the fuel
supply of the energy-short Urals and European USSR.   The
still larger coal and waterpower riches of Central Siberia
cannot play a direct role at all without radically new
technologies.   Therefore energy policy choices in this zone
involve broad national industrial location decisions and
regional development issues to a far greater extent than in
the oil and gas regions of West Siberia.   These issues
determine prospects for Central Siberia and appear prominent in the provinces from the Urals to the Kuzbas as well.

TABLE 3.4 Siberia's[a] Share of Soviet Industrial Output and Changes in Its Industrial Structure, 1975–1980 (by gross value of output, in percentages)

Industrial Branches	Siberia's[a] Share of National Output		Industrial Structure of Siberia[a]			
	1975	1980	1970	1975	1980	1985 (estimated)
All industries	9.0	9.2	100	100	100	100
Electric power	15.3	15.0	5.4	5.2	5.2	5.0
Fuel industries	21.1	26.7	12.6	14.4	17.0	18.6
Ferrous metallurgy			5.0	n.d.	3.8	3.4
Chemicals and Petrochemicals	9.4	9.2	6.6	7.2	7.3	8.2
Machine building–metal working	7.7	7.4	19.8	21.3	23.4	23.5
Forest products, pulp and paper	16.0	16.0	9.3	8.2	6.9	6.3
Building materials	9.0	9.5	4.4	4.0	3.7	3.5
Light industries	5.4	5.9	10.8	10.5	10.6	9.7
Food industries	6.3	6.0	17.4	14.7	11.9	11.6
Other branches			8.7	n.d.	10.1	10.6

[a]West and East Siberia; excludes Far East.
Source: T.B. Baranova, "Osnovnye pokazateli razvitiia promyshlennosti Sibiri v Desiatoi Piatiletke," Izvestiia SO AN SSSR, Seriia obshchestvennykh nauk, 1982, No. 11, pp. 72–73 and A.G. Granberg, "Vzaimosviaz' strukturnoi i prostranstvennoi politiki ekonomicheskogo razvitiia Sibiri," Izvestiia SO AN SSSR, Seriia ekonomiki i prikladnoi sotsiologii, 1986, No. 1, p. 25.

(Oil production from the Mangyshlak-Gur'ev fields on the Caspian shores, representing less than 4 percent of the Soviet total, may be ignored here. Though in Kazakhstan, the extreme westerly location of these deposits link them closely to the Volga-Ural and Caucasian petroleum provinces both geologically and economically. See Figure 2.)

Ever since the days of the Ural-Kuznetsk Combine and the opening of the Karaganda Basin, this western half of the Ural-Baikal wedge has been furnishing coal to the Soviet heartland. Until the end of the 1960s, however, from 40 to 50 percent of that total (which reached less than 66 million tons in 1970) was coking coal tranported to the blast furnaces of the Urals.[43] Aside from coking coal, the European USSR was still essentially self-sufficient in fuels, its modest shipments of steam coal and crude oil (from Siberia, Kazakhstan, and Poland) and larger quantities of gas (piped in from Central Asia, Siberia, and Iran) were more than counterbalanced by their net exports.[44] The very rapid growth of fuel deficit in the European provinces--to some 350 million tons of oil equivalent by 1983 and more today--has multiplied demand for all fuels that could be transported out of the Asiatic USSR.[45] Coal shipment during the 1970s rose by almost 90 percent, from less than 66 million tons in 1970, to around 120 million in 1980, with perhaps a slight increase since.[46] Yet the growth of that coal shipment (virtually all from the three coal fields of the Kuzbas, Karaganda, and Ekibastuz)--just as its absolute quantity--pales in comparison with the almost 23-fold rise in the transport of oil and gas from Tiumen' Oblast westward, the quantity of which exceeded 500 million tons of oil equivalent in 1983.[47] During the 1970s, North Kazakhstan and the Kuzbas also fell well behind Central Asia as fuel suppliers to the European USSR. In heat content, their share in the total outshipment of fuel from the Asian USSR dropped from about 38 percent in 1970 to a mere 4 to 5 percent by the third or fourth year of the present decade.[48]

The comparatively modest growth in the contribution of the Ural-Kuznetsk zone to the fuel supply of the metropolis is related to the poor performance of the Soviet coal industry and the lack of railway capacity east of the Urals. Since 1960, investment in coal consistently rose slower than investment in the total economy or in the energy complex as a whole. Within the energy industries, a relentless shift of outlays towards the oil and gas sector (including pipelines) is especially observable since the end of the 1960s, with the share of that sector in fuel and

58

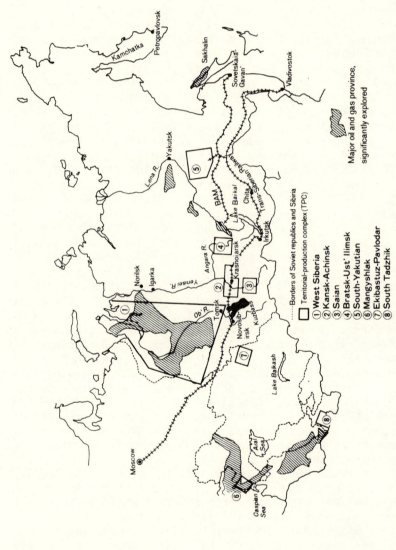

FIGURE 2 Aspects of Resource Development and Territorial Production Complexes in the Asian USSR.

energy investment growing from 56 percent during the first half of the 1970s to about three-quarters of the total in the first half of the 1980s.[49] Inevitably, the coal industry got starved and, by the Tenth FYP (1976-1980), depletion ratios, i.e., the share of new capacity needed to compensate decline in worked-out mines, exceeded 80 percent.[50]

Soviet coal basins east of the Urals generally enjoy much more favorable geological conditions than those elsewhere. In the more settled regions along existing railways, therefore, they represent a solid potential for large expansion in output and are the only regions of the country where noticeable increase did, in fact, take place. During the 1970s, production in Siberia and Kazakhstan grew by 46 percent, representing an annual rate of almost 3.9 percent, but from 1980 through 1985 only a 1.4 percent increase was observable. (Except for the largest fields, the disappearance of the data hampers analysis for the most recent years.[51]) It is important to note, however, that--given the poor quality of most eastern coals apart from those from the Kuzbas--the 127 million tons of increment in output during the 1970s was equivalent in heat content to only 53 million tons of oil, and to still less in the way of effective energy, i.e., with the efficiency of heat capture taken into account. Since 1970, the Ekibastuz Basin of North Kazakhstan contributed almost two-fifths of all growth in physical output east of the Urals.[52] The famed Kuzbas increased production much more slowly and has been essentially stagnating since 1978; mining in the Kansk-Achinsk Basin doubled through the Ninth, Tenth, and Eleventh FYPs, but that expansion still amounted to less than 22 million tons of increment, equivalent to only 7 million tons of oil in heat content.[53]

Of all coals of the Asian USSR, only those from Ekibastuz, the Kuzbas, and Karaganda can withstand regular transport to the Urals (and in the last two cases beyond), but opportunities for expansion at Karaganda today are very limited. Relative proximity and accessibility to power stations in the Urals, plus to those of North Kazakhstan and Omsk Oblast explain the rapid development of Ekibastuz as much as low mining costs. The recent stagnation of the Kuznetsk Basin, therefore, is all the more surprising, given the much higher quality of its coals, their greater transportability, and favorable production costs. Since 1978, output in the Kuzbas actually declined slightly, and the target of the Eleventh FYP, projecting a modest 1.7 percent annual increase during the first half of the 1980s, has been missed by a wide margin.[54] Not a single new coal mine has come on line in the Kuzbas for two decades, and the reconstruction of old collieries takes sixteen to seventeen years on the average.[55]

The intense rivalry for scarce investment within the coal industry pits the Kuzbas most directly against the Donbas, its long-term rival. Despite much more difficult geological conditions, due partly to more than a century of intensive exploitation, location and institutional factors both favor the Donets Basin. Besides a more developed infrastructure and huge markets west of the Volga, the institutional arrangements of the coal industry under a union-republic rather than all-union ministerial structure (which is the case for the other energy branches) permit Ukrainian regional interests a strong play. Having long experienced a net outflow of resources for regions east of the Caspian Sea and the Urals, Ukrainian pressure groups seem to have been much more successful in protecting investment in their coal industry.[56] Despite poor performance since the late 1970s, about one-third of all allocation to coal is today channeled into the Donbas, with apparent reduction in outlays, at least relatively, in the Kuznetsk Basin.[57] Continued vigorous lobbying by the Ukrainian Coal Ministry will guarantee very stiff resistance to a substantial shift of resources away from that principal Ukrainian field in favor of its Siberian rival.[58]

Aside from insufficient investment to exploit their full potential, the Kuznetsk and Ekibastuz Basins are also hampered in making a larger contribution to the energy supply of the European USSR by inadequate transport capacity. The rail lines leading to the Urals from the east are the most overburdened in the country, and the share of coal in total freight on these lines is much higher than the average for the country. In 1980, for example, coal composed 29 percent of all off-loading from railways in the Urals (almost exclusively from Kuznetsk and Kazakh mines), while in the country as a whole only 20 percent.[59] Through the Ninth FYP (1971-1975), 60 to 65 percent of all the coal carried in the Asian USSR was hauled on two main lines leading from the Kuzbas, Ekibastuz, and Karaganda coal fields to the Urals; if the chief distribution lines in the Urals are included, these railroads transported three-fourths of all coal outside the European USSR.[60] As of the early 1980s, this high share apparently has not dropped appreciably, since new loadings from East Siberian fields and the South Yakutian Basin onto other railroads were largely counterbalanced by further shipments from Ekibastuz to the Urals. The growing burden Ekibastuz coal has placed on the railways is aggravated by the steady worsening of its already low quality (a deterioration shared by nearly all coal fields in the USSR).61 From 1970 through 1983, the mean heat content of this coal declined from 4,030 kilocalories per kilogram to 3,814 kilocalories, and average ash content rose to almost 44 percent (from 41.3). However, two-fifths of all Ekibastuz coal mined by 1981 already had an upward deviation of up to 53 percent ash, the shipment of which is now officially permitted to power stations equipped to handle it, and transport with up to 60 percent ash has been recorded.62

In its present state, the railway system handling coal to the Urals has reached maximum carrying capacity. "By 1980, up to 3,000 carloads of coal [were] leaving Ekibastuz every day" for some seventeen power stations in Kazakhstan, the southwest portion of West Siberia, and as far as the western slopes of the Urals.63 Shipments from the Kuzbas also increased substantially until 1978, but not afterwards because of stagnation in production. Yet, in some parts of this basin, particularly the Mezhdurechensk-Myshi region which concentrates one-fourth of its coal output, a severe disproportion in railway loading and carrying capacity and mine performance continues to constrain severely the outshipment of that fuel.64 A CIA research report stated in 1980 that, with improvement and upgrading, including some new construction and double tracking on key links of limited length, the existing rail system could handle another 40 to 50 million tons.65 To what extent these improvements have actually been made is unclear. At least in Ekibastuz, further increments in output are planned to be consumed in nearby and mine-mouth power stations, with the electricity itself transmitted largely out of the region.

This "coal by wire" approach, however, is experiencing significant delays. Production at the Ekibastuz 1 station is somewhat behind schedule and the high-voltage transmission system is still limited to 500 kilovolt lines. Work on the far larger 1,150 kilovolt AC system to the Urals and the Kuzbas (which will provide much stronger interconnection between the Siberian and European Unified Grid via Ekibastuz than presently available) is in progress, but the long-heralded 1,500 kilovolt DC line to Tambov, west of the Volga, is in abeyance.66 The USSR State Construction Trust (Gosstroi), in fact, wants to abandon the latter DC project. Even those who continue to fight for it admit that this line will not be able to carry much, if any, power westward because electricity demand east of the Urals will outgrow the capacity of power stations in those regions to supply it by about 1990. Instead, those championing the project argue for its construction as a key link in the Unified Electricity Grid. And, ironically, they argue for that line as a transmitter of electricity eastward, as the burgeoning, poorly adjustable nuclear capacity west of the Urals will lead to the production of substantial surplus power at night.[67] In the wake of the Chernobyl accident and the expected slowdown in the Soviet nuclear program, this argument appears much less persuasive today. Chernobyl may revive high-level support for long-distance DC transmission and may provide the necessary push to get the Ekibastuz-Tambov line finally underway.

Finally, Soviet scholars and planners are well aware of the great potential of coal slurry pipelines, a technology which in part has already proved itself economically and environmentally in the United States. (Besides the 440-kilometer-long Black Mesa line, successfully operating for fifteen years, 90 percent of the right-of-way for the new 1,380-mile, 25-million-ton-capacity ETSI project has been acquired despite bitter opposition from the railroads. The water supply has been secured and a favorable environment impact statement received from the Department of Interior.[68]) Since the early 1970s, calls for the development of long-distance slurry transport have been appearing in the Soviet press and in more specialized journals. Yet "all available evidence suggests that the USSR is not very far along in creating slurry pipeline technology" because Soviet industry has not yet produced the proper pumping equipment.[69]

Currently, the feasibility of a 33-million-ton-capacity slurry line is under evaluation by Gosplan. One of its boards (Kollegiia Gosplana) recently directed the Institute of Complex Transport Problems and the Institute of Complex Fuel-Energy Problems to prepare a technical-economic report on the optimum version of coal transport to the European USSR. Yet, as of late 1985, this board has received only sharply contradictory, incompatible proposals. Even the construction of the 250-kilometer Belovo (Kuzbas)-Novosibirsk slurry pipeline of 3-million-ton yearly capacity, which was decided some years ago, is proceeding very slowly.[70] Yet intensive study of the performance of this line will have to precede any attempt to undertake the far larger slurry project to the Urals. Campbell's assessment made in the late 1970s continues to apply: "The strongest impression one has . . . is how little R and D work has been done and how vague and irreso- lute policy seems to be in setting any kind of directions and goals for moving ahead with some kind of demonstration work on slurry pipelines, given the urgency of finding a solution to the problem of transporting Eastern coal."[71]

Energy Policy and Industrial Structure

Given the difficulties of further increasing coal shipments to the European USSR even from this comparatively accessible part of the Asian Soviet Union, a much greater local use of the region's fuel resources assumes great significance. The expansion of energy-intensive industries east of the Urals is an indirect way of reducing the burden of fuel transport from east to west or at least severely curtailing its growth. The Ural-Altai region was long ago described as "a new Russian Mid-East--a rather more raw counterpart of the American Mid-West," with its crucial grain- and meat-farming economy combined with an equally crucial metal-smelting, fabricating, heavy engineering industrial one.[72] Environmental conditions, of course, are much more like those of the Canadian prairies than of Illinois or Iowa, while nonferrous metals in this Soviet "Mid-East" have always played a much larger role vis-a-vis ferrous metals than in its U.S. counterpart.

Be that as it may, the dominance of mining, metal smelting, casting and fabricating denotes an energy inten- sive industrial structure, even if energy per se in these activities rarely proves to be the controlling locational factor. The advocates of a more rapid "eastern" develop- ment strategy have always used the growing fuel (and water) deficit west of the Urals and the increasing agricultural value of land there as the chief economic argument for shifting much more heavy industries to the Ural-Baikal zone. Though no longer advocating full-scale, multifaceted development, they have continued to press for the expansion of a broad range of such industries: fuel, electrometal- lurgical, electrochemical, ferrous and nonferrous branches, heavy machinery, wood processing, basic chemicals, and virtually the whole line of petrochemical synthesis. All except wood processing and some other heavy water users would appear suitable for southwest Siberia and North Kazakhstan, though locational economics for some may favor Siberia east of the Altai to this Ural-Altai zone.

Southern Siberia-North Kazakhstan does have a large

share of heavy resource and energy-using industries and
substantial heavy machine-building branches as well. Yet
much of that is the legacy of World War II, and, despite
some modernization, those industries are technologically
obsolete. Others were built during Khrushchev's Seven-Year
Plan (1958-1965), when the organization and management of
industry via the economic councils (sovnarkhozy) probably
contributed to some dispersion of manufacturing both
towards underdeveloped labor surplus regions of the
European Soviet Union and the selective resource rich areas
of the Asian USSR.[73] However, most of that eastward shift
had petered out by the Brezhnev era, if not before. From
the mid-1960s to 1980, West and East Siberia actually lost
ground relative to the rest of the country in machinery and
chemicals and barely held their share in ferrous metallurgy. Since 1975, at least, their combined contribution
to national output remained the same in the forest and pulp
and paper industries as well (Table 3.4).[74]

The sharp decline in industrial expansion particularly
affected the southern provinces of West Siberia. By the
Ninth FYP (1971-1975) the rate of industrial growth here
declined almost to approximate the national mean, but
during the Tenth FYP (1976-1980), it dropped noticeably
below it. Only Novosibirsk Oblast continued to show
sufficient vigor, while the Kuzbas-Altai area became an
especially obvious loser. In the Kuzbas (Kemerovo Oblast),
total industrial production consistently increased slower
than the national mean even since 1960 and in Altai Krai at
least since 1970, but perhaps earlier.[75] For that citadel
of heavy industry, the poor performance of the 1960s was
mainly associated with the importance of slowly growing
industries and the dearth of dynamic branches. In the
traditional heavy industries, which have become the
region's mainstay, growth rates in the Kuzbas still kept up
or ahead of the national average for the given branch
during the 1960s. The coal industry in the Kuznetsk Basin
also did much better than elsewhere during that decade. In
addition, the injection of some light industry into the
region to provide greater employment opportunities for
women has proved highly successful. In the 1970s, however,
the disadvantageous industry mix effect and Soviet failure
to introduce more modern manufacturing into the province,
has become increasingly compounded by below average
performance of the Kuzbas within these slowly growing
branches themselves (Table 3.5). In other words, the
province was losing out to other regions even in some of
these industries, especially iron, steel, and chemicals.

TABLE 3.5 Growth of Industrial Output and Labor Productivity in the Kuzbas Compared to the USSR as a Whole, 1960-1980 (by industrial branches and in percentages)

Industrial Branches	Growth of Industrial Output				Growth of Labor Productivity			
	1960 – 1970 (1960 = 100)		1970 – 1980 (1970 = 100)		1960 – 1970 (1960 = 100)		1970 – 1980 (1970 = 100)	
	Kuzbas	USSR	Kuzbas	USSR	Kuzbas	USSR	Kuzbas	USSR
All industries	195	227	149	178	160	166	137	156
Fuel industries	140	181	126	154	133	193	127	157
Ferrous metallurgy	196	194	131	141	158	157	125	138
Non-ferrous metal-lurgy	213	n.d.	100.5	n.d.	201	n.d.	120	n.d.
Chemicals	346	349	209	218	210	200	169	175
Machine building	277	324	192	268	168	205	165	214
Electric power	191	274	164	180	126	176	170	151
Forest and forest products	151	168	120	139	169	157	124	142
Building materials	285	229	87	156	154	187	131	139
Light industries	296	171	230	148	170	137	191	142
Food industries	194	189	127	140	146	149	127	131

Sources: Taken or computed from E.P. Dubrovskaia ed., Gorizonty Kuzbasa. Ekonomicheskii ocherk (Kemerovo, 1982), pp. 14–15; Narodnoe khoziaistvo SSSR v 1970 g., pp. 136 and 161 and Narodnoe khoziaistvo SSSR v 1980 g., pp. 127 and 136.

The rise in labor productivity, too, lagging only slightly behind that for Soviet industry during the 1960s, fell far below the Soviet average (itself very sluggish) in the following decade and did so in all but two major branches (Table 3.5).

Whether because of economic reasons or its republic status, Kazakhstan has continued to make both absolute and large relative gains not only in the fuel and electric power industries, but also other heavy resource-oriented branches that demand huge quantities of energy. Being a union republic gives this area more political clout in regional competition for development than enjoyed by mere oblasts of Siberia, with the probable exception of Tiumen'. While the share of all Kazakh industries in Soviet industrial fixed capital rose quite impressively from 3.6 percent in 1961 to 5 percent by 1974, that of chemicals grew by almost 50 percent (though to a still modest 3.6 percent share of the Soviet total), that of construction materials increased from 5.4 to 7 percent, that of ferrous metallurgy doubled from 3.5 to 7 percent. Data for nonferrous metallurgy, Kazakhstan's leading specialty, whose contribution to the industry mix is about 2.5 times that in the USSR as a whole), is unfortunately lumped in a catchall category, "all other branches" in Soviet statistics where, however, it should dominate. It appears, therefore, that by the value of fixed capital, the share of Kazakhstan in Soviet nonferrous metallurgy rose from around one-tenth in 1961 to about one-eighth in 1974.[76]

The fuel-energy, metallurgy, chemical, and some heavy machine building industries will doubtless dominate the capital stock in Kazakhstan. Even by value of output, these resource-oriented branches accounted for over half of this republic's industry in 1979 and are expected to contribute three-fifths or more by 1990 (Table 3.6). The energy intensity of the Kazakh economy, therefore, should continue to exceed that in the European USSR and should conform to the planners' desire to encourage heavy energy-consuming activities east of the Urals and restrict them west of it. Yet, in aggregate terms, the shift of big fuel- and power-using industries to Kazakhstan has been too modest to make much of a dent on the huge mounting energy deficit in the European parts. It is also worth noting that the projections concerning the 1990 industrial structure in Kazakhstan, shown in Table 3.6, differ sharply, indicating considerable uncertainty about the development of principal branches.

Given the failure to accelerate the expansion of

TABLE 3.6 Structure of Industrial Output in Kazakhstan for 1979 and Projections for 1990 (in percent of total)

Industrial Branches	Structure in 1979	Projections for 1990	
		By NIEIPiNa	By Authors of Study
Electric power	4.0	5.6	5.2
Fuel industries	10.52	8.0	13.0
Non-ferrous metallurgy	10.7	6.6	7.2
Ferrous metallurgy	5.84	7.6	6.0
Chemical industries	4.34	14.4	6.3
Machine building—metal working	17.12	22.0	21.3
Light industries	16.92	13.1	16.2
Food industries	20.61	11.8	16.8
Others	10.58	10.9	8.0

Source: T.A. Ashimbaev, ed., Fondoemkost' produktsii v promyshlennosti Kazakhstana (Alma-Ata: Nauka, 1981), pp. 169-170.

energy-intensive activities in the Kuzbas-Altai area of West Siberia and the uncertainties in the Kazakh projections, I draw the following conclusion. The direct impact of national energy policy decisions on regional development of these Ural-Altai "midlands" has been strong, but not nearly as overwhelming as in the Tiumen'-Tomsk oil and gas provinces. Supply inelasticities, transport, and quality constraints on coal will prevent the fuel resources of the region from playing a greatly enhanced role on the national scene and serving as the primary vehicle of economic growth, as is the case in Tiumen' Oblast. The indirect impact, expressed in the shift of heavy energy-using industries to that zone in order to effect a modification in the spatial structure of national energy demand, has been even more modest, especially since the early 1970s. What shift has taken place was largely confined to select areas of central and northeast Kazakhstan and was induced more by locational considerations in nonferrous and ferrous metallurgy than by the abundance of fuel resources per se. The Kuzbas and neighboring Altai Krai, in particular, have lost ground both in energy-intensive activities and by broad measures of economic development.

In addition, very slow retirement of fixed assets characterized most industries of this Soviet "midland," especially its heavy energy-using ones, with generally declining rates through the 1970s. For example, in Kazakh industry as a whole, 2.3 percent of the assets were retired in 1971, but that share never exceeded 1.6 percent for the remaining years. However, in ferrous metallurgy retirement rates were well under one percent in every year of the decade and in nonferrous metallurgy and chemicals they surpassed 2 percent in only two years. By 1979, a third of industrial fixed capital in that republic was amortized and still in use (even though amortization rates are very low in the USSR), but in nonferrous metallurgy over 43 percent and in the fuel industries almost two-fifths.[77] Part of the energy intensive economy of the Ural-Altai "midlands," therefore, is simply due to the obsolescence of equipment constructed two to three decades ago or even earlier. The relief it provides for the European USSR, while real, must be qualified to reflect this adverse factor.

Central Siberia

Central Siberia resembles but surpasses the Ural-Altai "midlands" in energy riches, and this fact is the guiding character of the region's development and its role in the national economy. Large, accessible reserves of metals and other minerals show further similarity to the Ural-Altai "midlands," but with first-class forest stands adding to the resource potential. More than anywhere else in the USSR, national energy policy decisions with respect to the development of Central Siberia must involve major modifications in the geographic, technological, and sectoral pattern of energy use and in the location pattern of Soviet industry in general.

The huge coal and hydroelectric resources of this region cannot make a direct contribution to the economic core of the European USSR at all and are very unlikely to do so in this century. So far, they have defied attempts to ship or transmit them over great distances. In the case of the highly varigated, troublesome coals of Kansk-Achinsk, even large-scale local consumption encounters serious technical difficulties. Though close to the surface, no other basin of the country has such a complex cover of overburden,[78] the coals are extremely diverse and prone to caking, spontaneous combustion, and explosion.[79] Existing power stations burning this fuel have suffered reduced efficiency and availability, and their use in much larger 800-megawatt units (boiler and turbine blocks) is still not fully solved.[80] In addition, the environmental consequences of the massive burning of this fuel in huge power stations in unprocessed form is today judged unacceptable. Earlier plans for eight, then six, giant stations (in one source even twelve) of 6,400 kilowatts have now been abandoned. The latest sources claim feasibility for only two to three or, in case of a most sanguine advocate of Siberian energy development, three to four.[81]

In the latest scholarly publications, Kansk-Achinsk coal still appears as one of only five national fuel bases able to provide for future growth and compensate for declines elsewhere. (The others are West Siberian and Central Asian oil and gas with Ekibastuz and Kuznetsk coal.) However, it is now envisaged to furnish only 9 to 11 percent of the increment in total fuel supply and 4 to 6 percent of gross output even in the next 15 to 20 years.[82] Equally important, no massive movement of energy from the Kansk-Achinsk Basin (either in the form of fuel or electricity) out of Siberia is now contemplated. Instead, Kansk-Achinsk lignite is to be used entirely in Siberia—initially to raise the share of thermal versus hydroelectric capacity in the Central Siberian Grid (see below), then to free more Kuznetsk coal for Western regions, and finally to create a large synfuel and coal chemical complex in the area, which, with the thorough processing of the lignite and the recovery of much waste products, would be environmentally more acceptable than the massive burning of raw coal.[83]

None of these ideas are new, and I had already discussed them in 1977.[84] However, statements that little, if any, coal and probably even electricity from east of the Kuzbas will make it to and across the Urals, and that the development of the Kansk-Achinsk complex is feasible only in the long term are now unequivocally voiced and seem to be more or less accepted by the whole energy establishment. There is also a consensus that the further development of the Kuzbas and the Kansk-Achinsk Basin represents one integral problem that must be approached as one. And the former, not the latter, has the main task of supplying consumers further west. Whether a large-scale synfuel and coal chemical industry based on Kansk-Achinsk coal, acknowledged to be very costly, will ever materialize, however, is far less certain. Two pilot plants (with 175-ton and 100-ton per hour capacity) to process that lignite via two competing routes are under construction, one at least for six to seven years.[85] Clearly, a final decision has not yet been made, but renewed anxiety about the prospect of petroleum may have given a fillip to the project.

In the more immediate future, accelerated growth in coal production in Central Siberia does appear to be called for. The preponderance of hydrostations in the region has led to an instability and vulnerability of the power supply in dry years, while the insufficiency of peaking and semipeaking capacity (a perennial problem in the Soviet Union) has further reduced the utilization factor. In the early 1980s, hydrostations represented 52 percent of all capacity of the Unified Siberian Grid that extends westward to Omsk, which means that east of the Kuzbas this share must have exceeded two-thirds.[86] Hydrostations here have often been forced to operate at greatly reduce availablity-- a mere 36 percent of the time (3,118 hours) in Krasnoiarsk Krai during 1980--and whole settlements, many factories, and collective farms have suffered from power cutoffs over the past years.[87] At the same time, the rate of utiliza- tion of Siberian thermal plants have become excessive, far beyond the limit warranted by economics and safety consider- ations. In 1975, for example, a year of very low water flow, thermal stations of the Unified Siberian Grid operated at 6,600 hours of availability (i.e., more than 75 percent of the time), with some plants running for 7,200 to 7,500 hours.[88] These rates were unquestionably the highest in the world, preventing proper maintenance and repair and incurring damage in the long run. These strains and shortages of electricity supply, surely an ironic situation for Central Siberia, may further retard the already slow shift of energy-intensive industries eastward, in the opinion of two of the foremost Soviet authorities.[89] While the plans call for the rapid expansion of wood processing, pulp and paper, petrochemicals, and nonferrous metallurgy in the region, and the Eleventh Five-Year Plan (1981–1985) reportedly earmarks a 3.5-fold growth of investment in the Kansk-Achinsk Basin,[90] KATEK (Kansk-Achinsk Fuel-Energy Complex) is well behind schedule.[91]

At the same time, Siberian officials have also expressed some dissatisfaction about the excessively coal-oriented fuel strategy (ugol'nyi perekos) in the area, which aggravates living conditions and results in excessive labor expenditures in an already difficult environment plagued by manpower shortages and high turnover.[92] While close to 60 percent of the urban heat supply in East and West Siberia (though only half in the Far East) is furnished centrally from coal-fired cogenerating plants and large boilers, the remainder and practically all rural heat is still derived from the direct burning of unsorted solid fuels (much of it still gathered by the population) on the premises.[93] In the mid-1970s, this represented over a quarter of all gross energy use in Siberia, and the servicing of thousands of small boilers alone was said to employ over 100,000 persons, not counting those engaged in the transport of coal and ash.[94] Scholars pressing for the more rapid development of Central Siberia (as of the Far East) argue for the expansion of cogeneration even into much smaller settlements than in the European USSR. They would also like to raise the flow of Tiumen' natural gas to the Tomsk-Kuzbas-Novosibirsk area (though they appear to recognize that it is increasingly less probable)[95] and eventually secure gas from Yakutia both for Irkutsk Oblast and the Far East.[96]

The much greater use of Central Siberia's energy potential for the processing of the region's rich natural resources has been seriously hindered by the underdevelopment of Siberian machine building and a profile that matches very poorly the needs of the area. In 1980, the whole of East and West Siberia combined contributed a mere 7.4 percent of the country's machine-building and metalworking output (a slightly smaller share than five years

earlier) and only a quarter of that output originated east
of the Kuzbas.[97] Obsolescence is a serious problem and
apparently is not improving. In Irkutsk Oblast, for
example, the share of investment channeled into the
reequipment and retooling of enterprises is only half as
high as in the country as a whole and is much lower still
in the Buriat ASSR, where a mere 7 percent of capital is
planned to be earmarked for that purpose during the Twelfth
FYP.[98] The level of automation in Siberian factories is
likewise well below that west of the Urals, leading to
generally less efficient utilization of labor. A recent
source claims that the use of manpower is 2 to 2.5 times
higher than in the "better" enterprises of the country.[99]
Even today, some three-fourths of Siberia's machinery
production is shipped to other parts of the USSR, while
Siberia continues to rely on distant enterprises in the
Urals and European regions for its equipment. Similarly,
design institutes and organizations working for Siberian
projects are located thousands of kilometers away and "are
unaware of the conditions in which they are being
built."[100] As Boris Rumer has put it:

> As long as Siberia maintains such a [small] share
> of machine building production and ships in 80
> percent of its equipment requirements, largely
> from the European part of the country, it is
> unrealistic to count on dynamic development of its
> economy and the opening up of its vast unsettled
> and inaccessible areas. And this relates not only
> to economic but to social development: the location
> of machine building there helps to retain the labor
> force, to prevent its migration to other regions.
> Developing only extractive industry will not solve
> these problems.[101]

A more dependable developmental strategy for Siberia,
and especially Central Siberia, even a strategy that
stresses its resource potential, would require the creation
of a more balanced economic structure. This had been obviously recognized in the few years even before Gorbachev
took the helm. In 1978, the production association, Kras-
tiazhmash (Krasnoiarsk Heavy Machinery Association), was
organized to unite both existing and to-be-reconstructed
enterprises with a new giant plant for the production of
heavy mining and energy equipment for the Siberian resource
industries. Yet after six years, the completion of its
first new block was delayed until 1988, and no one dares

even to guess when the whole plant may be operational. For 1985, the association was woefully short of labor and 4,507 tons short of metal, and the excavator it did produce cost four times more than planned.[102]

Under Gorbachev, the expansion of Siberian machine building may become a more articulated policy. At a recent conference in Novosibirsk, Valentin Koptig, vice-president of the USSR Academy of Sciences and chairman of its Siberian Division unequivocally stated:

> Siberia can no longer obtain its advantage . . . through the extractive branches. Today's Siberian strategy envisages a shift in the center of gravity towards the processing branches and mainly towards the comprehensive processing of fuel and raw materials. . . . One of the first tasks [also] is the redirection of specialization in machine building. It is no secret that all the basic branches of Siberia's economy would be sharply accelerated if Siberian machine building were to address itself directly to their needs."[103]

Politbureau member Vitalii Vorotnikov (thought to be attuned to Gorbachev's views) was also a key speaker at that conference. While emphasizing the fuel and power complex of Siberia, he clearly stated that the goal must be the harmonious development of the region, and constant concern must be shown to all spheres of the economy and not just to the branches that determine its specialization.[104] This could indicate high-level political support for the more complex development of the southern zone of Siberia than was the case during the Brezhnev era and the years of his two short-lived successors.

Whether such a reorientation will be possible in practice, however, is much less certain. It is, in fact, in the more buoyant first dozen or more of the Brezhnev years when such a significant structural transformation could have been more easily accomplished. During that period, with large postwar cohorts entering the labor force and with rapidly growing oil and gas production from more accessible deposits, then with huge windfalls from soaring fuel and gold prices, the economy possessed considerable reserves and enjoyed maneuvering room. Today these reserves no longer exist. Major economic policy decisions will likely demand not merely a relative shift of resources among sectors and regions, i.e., a shift in the rate of growth of new investment, but also more and more and an absolute shift. Resource allocation is not yet a zero sum game, but it is approaching that state as the expansion of the labor force and of capital formation slows to a snail's pace and their productivity continues to decline.

It is significant that Soviet scholars themselves mistrust official statistics which claim a roughly 3.5-fold rise in the production of machinery and equipment from 1970 through 1984, in value terms, and an unbroken increase even since the late 1970s. Output growth in value terms does not correspond to improvements in the productivity of Soviet machines. At the same time, when measured by its aggregate energy, transport, and loading capacity (i.e., its ability to do work), the bulk of the Soviet machinery sector which lends itself to such physical measurement registered very slow expansion, experiencing an absolute decline since 1980. Soviet machine building today is unable to satisfy the growing demand for capital goods and one-third of all equipment installed must be imported.[105] Under Gorbachev's leadership, the Twelfth FYP (1986-1990) calls for a huge 80 percent rise in investment in the machinery sector.[106] This would greatly aid pro-Siberian planners in their push to broaden the region's industrial structure. Where Gorbachev hopes to find the capital for modernizing the machinery industry is unclear. Such huge new demands on investment resources cannot come at the expense of the energy sector, whose center of gravity has shifted to the harsh regions east of the Urals and, especially, the Siberian North. Indeed, while planned growth rates of investment in the energy industries are lower than in the machinery sector, the ruble increase in allocation will be almost as large, and total capital requirements will be far larger even without the enormous investment in pipelines.[107]

In the past, as Rumer has written,

> Every argument about high expedience always fell into the background when faced with the immediate need for the rapid satisfaction of acute require-ments for some sort of raw material, a metal, or fuel, whether it was Kolyma gold during the war years or Tiumen' oil and gas in our day. Such a narrowly directed tactic, which in essence boils down to pumping out unique resources with a barbarian attitude towards the ecological problems of the region . . .

has determined much of the character of Siberian develop-

ment.[108]   Even during the economically less constrained
Eighth and Ninth Five-Year Plans (1966-1975), this attitude
was the prevailing one. The creation of a more balanced
economic structure in the southern zone of Siberia, with
some elements of autarchy, is indeed a desirable direction
for population stability and economic health, if the
process is allowed to take place in a relatively autonomous
fashion.   Such a development strategy would need to emphasize the satisfaction of   local demand, through local
linkages and enterprises.   Apart from the fact that the
harnessing of local enterprise would require considerable
decentralization of   management,   perhaps   through much
greater territorial autonomy (I discount radical economic
reforms), the creation of reasonably balanced economic
profiles in outlying regions is a very slow process.
Accelerated, forced development on the basis of autarchic
principles, on the other hand, is always very costly and
fraught with its own dangers.
    The Gorbachev leadership, with all its pressing prob-
lems and mounting fuel and material needs, may lack the
time for the slow process of autonomous evolution of more
balanced regional structures in Siberia, even if it is
prepared to loosen significantly the reins of central
control.   Yet it also lacks the resources (financial,
human, technological) to force and accelerate the more
comprehensive development even of the better located
provinces east of the Urals. The recent stress on reconstruction and retooling in investment allocation bodes ill
for finding resources for such a strategy, especially since
"the share of replacement in machine building in Asian
regions must be higher [possibly twice as high] than in
European regions" because the stock of equipment is much
more worn out. "Thus, much larger investments [would be]
required per unit of net increase in machine-building
capacity" east of the Urals.[109]   Failure to broaden
Siberia's economic structure and to develop its regions
along more diversified, comprehensive lines in more
propitious times may have already foreclosed that option in
this century for the new leadership.
    Siberian scholars I talked to also appear quite
pessimistic about the short-term prospects of that vast
region, a contrast to the enthusiastic, confident tone that
marked their writings ten to fifteen years ago. They are
obviously aware of the likely consequences of the apparent
shift in economic policy under Gorbachev even as they
sincerely support his drive towards improved economic efficiency and performance.   Yet, as Theodore Shabad has

written:

>If irreplaceable regional development programs, such as the oil and gas efforts in West Siberia, are taken out of the equation, the very essence of the Gorbachev economic policy, with its stress on improving the <u>existing</u> economic potential, implies a shift in orientation, however subtle and small, from vast, undeveloped open spaces of the east to the great centers of economic activity in the west.[110]

The 1985 Party Program (published on October 26) for the country's long-range development calls for the doubling of national income by year 2000, implying an average rate of growth of about 4.7 per year, but supplies only a few notions of how is that to be accomplished. Keith Bush has shown that in order to sustain such a desired annual increase for the rest of the century, it would be necessary to raise "total factor productivity to levels ranging from +2.4 to +2.8 percent per annum, i.e., a rate never achieved by the Soviet economy in peacetime," and up from the −0.5 to −0.8 yearly average rate prevailing since 1971.[111] Such a radical improvement in productivity is completely improbable. Yet without it, hopes of restructuring Siberia's economy towards a more broadly based pattern of self-sustained growth must remain unrealized.

Certain specialists continue to hope that, through the more intensive processing of fuels and raw materials and the rapid development of construction and transport, the Siberian economy can still grow above the national average. Yet it is significant that the director of the Central Economic Research Institute at the Russian Republic Gosplan declared recently that such an above average increase for Siberia is simply unfeasible in the near future. The thesis concerning the more rapid development of the region should be filled with new meaning: the success of that development should be judged by the role Siberia plays in accelerating the growth of the whole national economy.[112] In other words, a regional emphasis at the present time can be justified only insofar as it helps the expansion of the national system.

Such open assertion of metropolitan priorities may not be a conscious admission of Siberia's peripheral, dependent status. Yet, in truth, Siberia has been a net recipient of large capital, labor, and technological inflow through the past decades. Unless one assigns some intrinsic mystical value to minerals, forests, fish, and widelife, apart from the ecological role of the last three, they become resources only through human effort. And a mostly empty resource frontier remains a net recipient of such effort until a stage of self-sustained growth is reached. It is clear from this chapter that Siberia has not yet reached that stage. Given the 33 million people today in East and West Siberia and Northern Kazakhstan, a more autonomous, balanced development, geared more to local demand and markets is theoretically possible but extremely unlikely. Even if greater autonomy were granted, the economic structure of the region has become too distorted by metropolitan needs for such a course.

Ironically, the Center today is also paying the price for such an unbalanced development, since the burden of that policy, an inordinate resource dependence on increasingly remote and harsh areas, is detrimental to intensification in the metropolis itself. One can argue, of course, that the economy of the Canadian North is even more narrow. However, the Northlands of that country are exploited on a far more modest scale and are still largely in a pristine state. While they may be subsidized, their impact on the economy as a whole is slight. The Siberian economy today is sizable enough to affect the whole of the USSR and affect it critically through the supply of fuels and some minerals. Unfortunately, one-sided metropolitan priorities also left it too distorted, with harmful consequences for its own prospects and even for the country as a whole.

NOTES

1. L.A. Melent'ev and A.A. Makarov, eds., Energeticheskii kompleks SSSR (Moscow: Ekonomika, 1983), p. 193.
2. Ia.A. Mazover, ed., Problemy razvitiia i razmeshcheniia toplivnykh baz SSSR (Moscow: Nauka, 1982), pp. 13-14.
3. The author has pointed this out as early as 1975 and 1977. Leslie Dienes, "Energy Self-sufficiency in the Soviet Union," Current History. Vol. 69, No. 407 (July-August), 1975, pp. 10-14 and 47-51 and Leslie Dienes, "The USSR: An Energy Crunch Ahead," Problems of Communism, Vol. 26, No. 5 (September-October), 1977, pp. 41-60.
4. Theodore Shabad, "News Notes," Soviet Geography, Vol. 25, No. 4 (April), 1984, p. 266; Leslie Dienes and

78

Theodore Shabad, The Soviet Energy System: Resource Use and Policy (Washington, D.C.: Winston and Sons, 1979), pp. 46-47 and Izvestiia, December 7, 1984, p. 2.

5. Thane Gustafson, The Soviet Gas Campaign. Politics and Policy in Soviet Decisionmaking (Santa Monica: Rand, June, 1983), Chapter 3.

6. S.N. Starovoitov, ed., Problemy razvitiia Zapadno-Sibirskogo Neftegazovogo Kompleksa (Novosibirsk: Nauka, 1983), pp. 80-81.

7. Theodore Shabad, "News Notes," Soviet Geography, Vol 27, No. 4 (April), 1986, p. 251 and V.I. Vorotnikov, "Razvitie proizvoditel'nykh sil Sibiri i zadachi uskoreniia nauchno-tekhnicheskogo progressa," Ekonomika i organizatsiia promyshlennogo proizvodstva (EKO) 1986, No. 1 (January), p. 47.

8. Ekonomicheskaia gazeta, 1986, No. 18 (April), pp. 1 and 3; and Sotsialisticheskaia industriia, May 27, 1986, p. 2.

9. Pravda, September 7, 1985, p. 1. See also statements by Politbureau member Vorotnikov and specialist Maksimov about the inadequacy of reserves. Vorotnikov, "Razvitie," p. 54 and G.M. Mkrtchian and N.I. Pliaskin, eds., Aktual'nye problemy osvoeniia toplivno-energeticheskikh resursov Sibiri (Novosibirsk: IEOPP, 1985), p. 6. The first source also reveals that the opinion of specialists is divided about the probability of further large discoveries in West Siberia.

10. Starovoitov, ed., Problemy razvitiia, p. 79; F.K. Salmanov and F.Z. Khafizov, "Itogi deiatel'nosti Glavtiumen'-geologii," Geologiia nefti i gaza, 1984, No. 3 (March), p. 5 and G.A. Gabrieliants, V.I. Poroskun and Iu.V. Sorohin, Metodika poiskov i razvedki zalezhei nefti i gaza (Moscow: Nedra, 1985), pp. 6-7.

11. In 1986, investment in the oil industry rose 16.2 percent over that of the previous year. During the first nine months of 1986, government capital outlays in the industry increased 19 percent compared to the first nine months of 1986. Narodnoe khoziaistvo SSSR v 1985 g., p. 368; Narodnoe khoziaistvo SSSR v 1984 g., p. 15 and Ekonomicheskaia gazeta, No. 44 (October), 1986, p. 15.

12. Leslie Dienes, "The Energy System and Economic Imbalances in the USSR," Soviet Economy, Vol. 1, No. 4 (October-December), 1985, p. 364; Sovetskaia Sibir', June 8, 1986, p. 2. The somewhat ambiguous language of that newspaper article (from the daily of the Novosibirsk Obkom) was clarified by an interview in IEOPP of the Siberian branch of the Soviet Academy of Sciences. The 82

billion is unequivocally planned for the West Siberian oil and gas region alone.

13. L.A. Charuizkaia, "Analiz vliianiia razlichnykh faktorov na sebestoimost' dobychi gaza," Ekonomika gazovoi promyshlennosti, 1981, No. 11, pp. 10-11.

14. N.I. Pliaskina, O.V. Savinykh, V.I. Skorobogatova and V.N. Kharitonova, "Issledovanie perspektiv razvitiia Zapadno-Sibirskogo Neftegazovogo Kompleksa s ispol'zovaniem setevoi modeli," AN SSSR, SO, Seriia ekonomiki i prikladnoi sotsiologii, Izvestiia 1985, No. 1, p. 25.

15. Natural increase in Siberia during recent years has been only slightly above the average for the Russian Republic and is probably not much higher in Tiumen' Oblast. Therefore, the difference between the actual population and that projected on the basis of a natural increase representative of the RSFSR should roughly equal net immigration (Narodnoe khoziaistvo SSSR v 1985 godu, pp. 12-14.

16. A.D. Khaitun, Ekspeditsionno-vakhtovoe stroitel'-stvo v Zapadnoi Sibiri (Leningrad: Stroiizdat, 1982), pp. 8-9.

17. Starovoitov, Problemy razvitiia, pp. 212-213 and Vorotnikov, "Razvitie," p. 56.

18. A. Ananev and A. Silin, "Obespechenie predpriiatii i stroek Zapadno-Sibirskogo Neftegazovogo Kompleksa rabochei siloi," Planovoe khoziaistvo, 1984, No. 1, p. 96 and Sovetskaia Rossiia, December 9, 1983, p. 3.

19. Pravda, April 3, 1984, p. 2 and Neftianik, 1983, No. 9 (September), pp. 9-12. The share of outside teams in the construction of drilling sites was 35 percent in 1981, according to the latter source and increased 54.5 percent in that single year.

20. Pravda, September 7, 1985, p. 1.

21. Thane Gustafson, "The Origins of the Soviet Oil Crisis, 1970-1985," Soviet Economy, Vol. 1, No. 2 (April-June), 1985, p. 128.

22. Izvestiia, December 7, 1984, p. 2 and Pravda, April 3, 1984, p. 2.

23. Pravda, November 21, 1984, p. 2 and Izvestiia, May 28, 1985, p. 2.

24. Matthew J. Sagers and Theodore Shabad in PlanEcon Report, Vol. 2, Nos. 29-30 (July 24), 1986, pp. 8-11 and Sotsialisticheskaia industriia, March 2, 1985.

25. Izvestiia, May 13, 1986, p. 2; May 27, 1986, p. 2; Ekonomicheskaia gazeta, 1985, No. 21 (May), p. 6; Pravda, January 14, 1986, p. 2; and Sovetskaia Sibir', June 8, 1986, p. 2.

26. Platt's Oilgram News, Vol. 63, January 15, 1985,

80

p. 2 and Pliaskina et al., "Issledovanie perspektiv," p.25.
27. Izvestiia, December 7, 1984, p. 2 and Sovetskaia Rossiia, April 20, 1985, p. 2.
28. Pravda, September 7, 1985, pp. 1-2.
29. S.D. Agaeva and B.D. Orlov, "Nekotorye cherty investitsionnogo protsessa v Zapadno-Sibirskom Neftegazovom Komplekse," AN SSSR, SO, Seriia obshchestvennykh nauk, Izvestiia, 1982, No. 11, p. 88.
30. Ekonomicheskaia gazeta, 1984, No. 36 (September), p. 9.
31. S.N. Zhelezko, Sotsial'no-demograficheskie problemy v zone BAMa (Moscow: Statistika, 1980), p. 40 and E.I. Pilipenko, "Formirovanie kadrov gazovoi promyshlennosti Zapadnoi Sibiri," in V.V. Alekseev, S.S. Bukin, A.A. Dolgoliuk and I.M. Savitskii, eds., Sotsiali'nye aspekty industrial'nogo razvitiia Sibiri (Novosibirsk: Nauka, 1983), pp. 76 and 78.
32. Ekonomicheskaia gazeta, 1984, No. 36 (September), p. 9.
33. Sotsialisticheskaia industriia, May 28, 1986, p. 2 and Sovetskaia Rossiia, December 9, 1983, p. 3.
34. Pliaskina et al., "Issledovanie perspektiv," pp. 25-26.
35. G.V. Poliak and V.N. Annenkov, "Finansovye aspekty formirovaniia territorial'no-proizvodstvennykh kompleksov," AN SSSR, SO, Seriia obshchestvennykh nauk, Izvestiia, 1983, May, p. 26.
36. Gustafson, The Soviet Gas Campaign, pp. 23-26.
37. A.G. Granberg, "Vzaimosviaz' strukturnoi i prostranstvennoi politiki ekonomicheskogo razvitiia Sibiri," AN SSSR, SO , Seriia ekonomiki i prikladnoi sotsiologii, Izvestiia 1986, No. 1, p. 26.
38. Narodnoe khoziaistvo Krasnoiarskogo Kraia (Krasnoiarsk, 1985), p. 97.
39. Narodnoe khoziaistvo SSSR v 1979 godu, p. 373; Narodnoe khoziaistvo SSSR v 1983 godu, p. 365.
40. A.G. Aganbegian, ed., Sibir' v edinom narodnokhoziaistvennom komplekse (Novosibirsk: Nauka, 1980), p. 183.
41. Granberg, "Vzaimosviaz'," p. 26.
42. David Hooson, "The Outlook for Regional Development in the Soviet Union," Slavic Review, Vol. 31, No. 3 (September), 1972, p. 537.
43. Coal shipped in from the Asian USSR from A.M. Nekrasov and M.G. Pervukhin, eds., Energetika SSSR v 1976-1980 godakh (Moscow: Energiia, 1977), p. 148. Coking coal flow in 1980 was approximately 31 million tons. Matthew J. Sagers, "Coal Movements in the USSR," Soviet Geography,

Vol. 25, No. 10 (December), 1984, p. 727. That flow could
not have increased much since 1970, since pig iron output
in the Urals grew by only a fifth during the decade, while
technological improvement and the growing volume of natural
gas available must have reduced specific coke consumption
per ton of pig iron. Theodore Shabad, "News Notes," Soviet
Geography, Vol. 18, No. 4 (April), 1977, p. 279 and Vol.
21, No. 4 (April), 1980, p. 255.

44. Nekrasov and Pervukhin, eds., Energetika SSSR,
p. 148; Vneshniaia torgovlia SSSR za 1971 god (Moscow:
Mezhdunarodnye otnosheniia, 1972), pp. 27 and 41.
45. In 1980, over 75 percent of all fossil fuels were
still consumed in the European USSR (including the Urals).
Assuming a 73 percent share in 1985, the European USSR used
1,300 tons of standard fuel (SF) or almost 910 million tons
of oil equivalent that year. Melent'ev and Makarov, eds.,
Energeticheskii kompleks SSSR, p. 193 and PlanEcon Report,
Vol. 2, Nos. 29-30 (July 24, 1986), p. 5. Siberia produced
over 1,000 million tons of SF equivalent, while output in
Kazakhstan and Central Asia can be estimated from physical
output as 260 million tons of SF. A.G. Aganbegian,
"Glavnoe zveno-intensifikatsiia," Nauka i zhizn', 1984,
No. 10, p. 7 and Theodore Shabad, "News Notes," Soviet
Geography, Vol. 26, No. 4 (April), 1985, pp. 288-301.
46. Sagers, "Coal Movements," p. 727.
47. Nekrasov and Pervukhin, eds., Energetika SSSR,
p. 148 and Aganbegian, "Glavnoe zveno-intensifikatsiia,"
p. 7. Aganbegian claims that outshipment from Siberia
reached over 800 million tons of SF in 1983.
48. Shipment from Central Asia and Kazakhstan should
add some 130 million tons of SF. Estimated from production
figures and approximate known exports to RSFSR. Theodore
Shabad, "News Notes," Soviet Geography, Vol. 27 No. 4
(April), 1986, pp. 250-71.
49. Leslie Dienes, "The Energy System and Economic
Imbalances in the USSR," Soviet Economy, Vol. 1, No. 4
(October-December), 1985, p. 349.
50. Ed A. Hewett, Energy, Economics and Foreign Policy
in the Soviet Union (Washington: The Brookings Institution,
1984), p. 85.
51. Theodore Shabad, "News Notes," Soviet Geography,
Vol. 21, No. 4 (April), 1980, p. 248 and Vol. 27, No. 4
(April), 1986, p. 266.
52. Sources in footnote 51 and V.E. Popov and P.V.
Shemetov, eds., KATEK i razvitie otraslei khoziaistva
Sibiri (Novosibirsk: Nauka, 1984), p. 8 for Siberia. For
Kazakhstan, increment in heat equivalent computed sepa-

82

rately from the calorific content of Ekibastuz and Karaganda coals.

53. Theodore Shabad, "News Notes," Soviet Geography,
Vol. 21, No. 4 (April), 1980, p. 248 and Vol. 27, No. 4
(April), 1986, p. 266.
54. Theodore Shabad, "News Notes," Soviet Geography,
Vol. 26, No. 4 (April), 1985, p. 301 and Vol. 27, No. 4
(April), 1986, p. 266.
55. Pravda, October 6, 1983, p. 2; Sovetskaia Rossiia,
January 21, 1984, p. 2 and V.E. Popov, K.M. Zviagintseva
and A.P. Kuz'min, "Dolia Kuzbassa," EKO, 1984, No. 4, p. 5.
56. Ihor Gordyew and I.S. Koropeckyj, "Ukraine,"
chapter 8 in I.S. Koropeckyj and Gertrude E. Schroeder,
eds., Economics of Soviet Regions (New York: Praeger,
1981), pp. 295-299 and James W. Gillula, "The Economic
Interdependence of Soviet Republics," in U.S. Congress,
Joint Economic Committee, Soviet Economy in a Time of
Change, Vol. 1 (Washington, D.C., U.S. Government Printing
Office, 1979), pp. 630-636. See also Chapters 9-11 in I.S.
Koropeckyj, ed., The Ukraine within the USSR. An Economic
Balance Sheet (New York: Praeger, 1977).
57. Ekonomicheskaia gazeta, 1985, No. 31 (July), p. 10
and Theodore Shabad, "News Notes," Soviet Geography,
Vol. 26, No. 4 (April), 1985, p. 302.
58. Izvestiia, December 4, 1984, p. 2 and G.I. Iovenko
and V.I. Rudenko, "Voprosy obespecheniia uglem energetiki
Uk. SSR," in Razvitie proizvoditel'nykh sil UkSSR i
kompleksnoe ispol'zovanie prirodnykh resursov (Kiev, 1982),
pp. 44-52. Abstracted in Referativnyi zhurnal. Geografiia,
1983, No. 10, E123 and Theodore Shabad, "News Notes,"
Soviet Geography, Vol. 27. No. 4 (April), 1986, p. 267.
59. M.A. Sergeev and A.P. Cherviakov, Problemy povysheniia effektivnosti transporta krupnogo ekonomicheskogo
raiona (Moscow: Nauka, 1982), p. 29.
60. P.K. Dubinskii, Analiz raboty zheleznodorozhnogo
transporta ugol'noi promyshlennosti v deviatoi piatiletke
(Moscow: Ministerstvo Ugol'noi Promyshlennosti SSSR,
TsNIEIugol', 1977), p. 48 and I.V. Nikol'skii, V.I. Toniaev
and V.G. Krasheninnikov, Geografiia vodnogo transporta SSSR
(Moscow: Transport, 1975), pp. 53-58.
61. Theodore Shabad, "News Notes," Soviet Geography,
Vol. 25, No. 4 (April), 1984, pp. 277-278 and K.F. Roddatis
and K.V. Shakhsuvarov, "O poteriakh v narodnom khoziaistve
iz-za ponizhennogo kachestva uglei dlia teplovykh elektro-
stantsii," Elektricheskie stantsii, 1985, No. 1, pp. 6-10.
62. Roddatis and Shakhsuvarov, "O poteriakh," p. 8.
63. Theodore Shabad, "News Notes," Soviet Geography,

83

Vol. 25, No. 4 (April), 1984, p. 282.
64. Pravda, October 23, 1985, p. 2.
65. U.S. CIA, National Foreign Assessment Center, USSR: Coal Industry. Problems and Prospects (Washington, D.C.: 1980), pp. 12-13.
66. Theodore Shabad, "News Notes," Soviet Geography, Vol. 25, No. 4 (April), 1984, pp. 282 and 290-291 and Vol. 26, No. 4 (April), 1985, pp. 302-303 and 306.
67. Pravda, February 1986, p. 2.
68. Edward J. Wasp, "Slurry Pipelines," Scientific American, Vol 249, No. 5 (November), 1983, pp. 48-55.
69. Robert W. Campbell, Soviet Energy Technologies (Bloomington: Indiana University Press, 1980), p. 173.
70. Pravda, October 21, 1985, p. 2 and S.P. Arsen'ev et al., Ekonomicheskie problemy transporta SSSR (Moscow: Transport, 1985), p. 150.
71. Campbell, Soviet Energy Technologies, p. 175.
72. David J.M. Hooson, The Soviet Union: Peoples and Regions (Belmont, CA: Wadsworth Publishing Co., 1966), pp. 192-212. Citation on page 192.
73. Allan Rodgers, "The Locational Dynamics of Soviet Industry," Annals of the Association of American Geographers, Vol. 64, No. 2 (June), 1974, pp. 235-236.
74. A.G. Aganbegian et al., eds., Razvitie narodnogo khoziaistva Sibiri (Novosibirsk: Nauka, 1978), p. 215; T.V. Baranova, "Osnovnye pokazateli razvitiia promyshlennosti Sibiri v Desiatoi Piatiletke," AN SSSR, SO, Seriia obshchestvennykh nauk, Izvestiia, 1982, No. 4, pp. 42-73; L. Gramoteeva, Effektivnost' territorial'noi organizatsii proizvodstva (Moscow: Mysl', 1979), pp. 139-140 and A.G. Granberg, "Strukturnye sdvigi i intensifikatsiia promyshlennosti Sibiri," EKO, 1985, No. 6, pp. 10-11 and 13.
75. A.G. Granberg, ed., Ekonomika Sibiri v razreze shirotnykh zon (Novosibirsk: Nauka, 1985), pp. 53, 123, 136, 143 and 157.
76. James W. Gillula, The Regional Distribution of Fixed Capital in the USSR. Foreign Economic Report No. 17 (Washington, D.C.: U.S. Bureau of the Census, 1981), p. 31.
77. T.A. Ashimbaev, ed., Fondoemkost' produktsii v promyshlennosti Kazakhstana (Alma-Ata: Nauka, 1981), pp. 109-110 and 112. For both machine building and metallurgy, the volume of worn-out assets retired was ten to eleven times less than the volume of fixed investment brought into production and in the electric power industry more than twenty-two times less. Investment, therefore, mostly creates new employment and does not replace obsolete technology. In five of Kazakhstan's nineteen oblasts the

84

share of capital spent on reconstruction and technological retooling ranges from a mere 7 to 14 percent. V.P. Krasovskii and G.M. Merkin, eds., Rezervy povysheniia effektivnosti regional'nykh kapital'nykh vlozhenii (Moscow: AN SSSR, Institut ekonomiki, 1985), pp. 97-98 and AN Kazakhskoi SSR, SOPS, Problemy razvitiia proizvoditel'nykh sil Kazakhstana (Alma-Ata, 1983, unpublished), p. 61.

78. Trud, August 10, 1983, p. 2. This came as a surprise to me. To my knowledge, no such statement about this basin has yet been made in the open literature where the incomparably low extraction cost of this coal has always been stressed.

79. Iu.L. Marshak, et al., "Osnovnye voprosy szhiganiia uglei Kansko-Achinskogo basseina," Elektricheskie stantsii, 1981, No. 1, pp. 18-24 and Popov and Shemetov, eds., KATEK i razvitie, pp. 53-61.

80. Sotsialisticheskaia industriia, November 19, 1977, p. 2 and sources in footnote 79.

81. Popov, et al., "Dolia Kuzbassa," p. 6 and Trud, August 10, 1983, p. 2.

82. Mazover, ed., Problemy razvitiia, p. 38.

83. Popov and Shemetov, eds., KATEK i razvitie, pp. 16-22 and 61-85; Popov, et al., "Dolia Kuzbassa," p. 11; Sotsialisticheskaia industriia, January 13, 1983, p. 2 and February 13, 1983, p. 2.

84. Dienes, "The USSR: An Energy Crunch Ahead," pp. 51-60.

85. Ekonomicheskaia gazeta, 1986, No. 36 (September), p. 3; Sotsialisticheskaia industriia, January 13, 1983, p. 2 and Popov and Shemetov, eds. KATEK i razvitie, p. 78. An earlier report on one of these plants being under construction in 1979 was made in P.S. Neporozhnii and Z.F. Chukhanov, "Comparative Analysis of Traditional and Complex Processing Methods for Deriving Liquid Fuels from Coal" (paper presented at U.S.-Soviet seminar under energy agreement, 1979).

86. L.L. Peterson and A.Sh. Reznikovskii, "Rol' GES i GRES v OEE SSSR," Elektricheskie stantsii, 1983, No. 8, pp. 33-37.

87. Elektricheskie stantsii, 1983, No. 5, p. 7 and Pravda, January 28, 1979 and March 22, 1979.

88. V.V. Alekseev, ed., Ocherki ekonomiki Sibiri (Novosibirsk: Nauka, 1980), p. 169.

89. Melent'ev and Makarov, eds., Energeticheskii kompleks SSSR, p. 170.

90. Pravda, February 16, 1982, p. 2 and March 22, 1979.

91. Ekonomicheskaia gazeta, 1983, No. 35 (August), p. 6 and 1986, No. 1 (January), p. 8. The start of the first block of the Berezovo GRES has been delayed for the third time and is now three years behind schedule. So are other power projects in East Siberia.

92. Aganbegian, ed., Razvitie, pp. 173–179.

93. V.P. Korytnikov et al., "Osnovnye napravleniia razvitiia teplosnabzheniia i teplofikatsii v gorodakh Sibiri i Dal'nego Vostoka," Teploenergetika, 1979, No. 2, p. 11 and G.P. Dobrovol'skii, "Nauchnye issledovaniia po tselevoi programme "Toplivno-energeticheskii kompleks Sibiri," AN SSSR, Vestnik, 1982, No. 5, p. 43.

94. Aganbegian, ed., Razvitie, p. 175 and Korytnikov et al., "Osnovnye napravleniia," p. 11.

95. L.S. Khrilev et al., "Opredelenie effektivnosti i masshtabov primeneniia teplofikatsii," Teploenergetika, 1983, No. 8, pp. 2–6 and Korytnikov et al., "Osnovnye napravleniia." Even major industries are not getting the needed gas. The construction of two ammonia plants in Kemerovo Oblast and a huge methanol unit in Tomsk are nearing completion without the doubling of the Nizhnevartovsk-Kuzbas pipeline, which has not even been approved yet, they will not have the needed raw material. Izvestiia, January 5, 1984, p. 2. Also Popov and Shemetov, eds., KATEK i razvitie, p. 120.

96. A.G. Aganbegian, A.A. Kin and V.P. Mozhin, eds., BAM. Stroitel'stvo. Khoziaistvennoe osvoenie (Moscow: Ekonomika, 1984), p. 71.

97. Baranova, "Osnovnye pokazateli," pp. 72–73 and Gramoteeva, Effektivnost', p. 142.

98. Izvestiia, January 3, 1986, p. 2 and P.M. Ivanovich et al., eds., Analiz razvitiia territorial'nykh sistem (Novosibirsk: AN SSSR, SO, IEOPP, 1986), pp. 119–120.

99. Sotsialisticheskaia industriia, September 12, 1985.

100. Sotsialisticheskaia industriia, July 20, 1985, p. 3 and Pravda, July 30, 1985, p. 2.

101. Boris Z. Rumer, Investment and Reindustrialization in the Soviet Economy (Boulder, Co.: Westview Press, 1984), p. 106.

102. Tatiana Boldyreva and Valerii Lavrov, "Liliputskie shagi Gulivera," EKO, 1985, No. 12, pp. 46–69.

103. Sotsialisticheskaia industriia, July 20, 1985, p. 3.

104. Pravda, July 19, 1985, p. 2.

105. V.K. Fal'tsman, "Mashinostroenie: puti peremen,"

86

EKO, 1985, No. 12, pp. 3-5.
106. N.I. Ryzhkov, Ob osnovnykh napravleniiakh ekonomicheskogo i sotsial'nogo razvitiia SSSR na 1986-1990 god i
na period do 2000 goda (Moscow: Politizdat, 1986), p. 30.
107. In comparison to the 1981-1985 Five-Year Plan,
the 1986-1990 FYP calls for a 35 percent investment growth
in the fuel-energy complex (apparently without investment
in pipelines) and a 47 percent growth in capital allocation
for the production and transportation of fuels. Capital
allocation to the economy as a whole is to rise by less
than 12 percent. According to the Plan, investment in the
machine building and metal-fabricating industries is to
grow from 73 billion rubles in 1981-1985 to about 131
billion in 1986-1990. Without pipelines, investment in the
fuel and energy industries (including petroleum refining
and associated petrochemical branches) is slated to rise
from 131 billion to 177 to 180 billion rubles. N.I.
Ryzhkov in Pravda, June 19, 1986, pp. 2-3 and in Ob
osnovnykh napravleniiakh, p. 31 and Narodnoe khoziaistvo
SSSR v 1985 godu, p. 368 and footnote 106.
108. Rumer, Investment and Reindustrialization, pp.
134-135.
109. Ibid., pp. 109-110.
110. Theodore Shabad, "The Gorbachev Economic Policy:
Is the USSR Turning Away from Siberian Development?" Paper
presented at the Conference on Siberia, University of
London, April 1986.
111. Keith Bush, "USSR--The Growth Targets of the 1961
and 1985 Party Programs" (Munich: Radio Liberty Research,
October 28, 1985, unpublished).
112. V.E. Seliverstov, "Razvitie Sibiri v narodnokhoziaistvennom komplekse SSSR," AN SSSR, SO, Seriia ekonomiki
i prikladnoi sotsiologii, Izvestiia 1986, No. 1, p. 50.

4

Economic and Strategic Position of the Soviet Far East

The vast region of the Soviet Far East abuts on the Pacific Basin, where in recent years the most vigorous growth in world trade has taken place and where some of the most dynamic economies are found. At the same time, remoteness from the country's economic core, harsh physical environment, and lack of infrastructure present greater barriers to effective economic integration with the metropolis than for the two other Siberian regions farther west. By contrast, problems with socio-political integration, as manifest among the Moslem population of the Central Asian periphery, do not arise. Equally important, nowhere in the USSR do issues of development intertwine with strategic concerns over so extensive a territory than east of Lake Baikal. These concerns indeed go back to the mid-nineteenth century, when the Amur lands were first annexed.[1]

National policy towards the development of the Far East has been strongly influenced by these factors of geographic position and strategic concerns. On the one hand, the intensifying involvement of the USSR in the world economy during the 1970s appeared to mark out this huge area for a particularly important position in Soviet exports. Big projects geared to foreign trade were to be the main thrust and the chief engine of economic growth. On the other hand, the traditional regional concerns in the strategic sphere have become overshadowed by an extraregional, more or less global, orientation. As this chapter will show, the outward foreign trade orientation of Siberia's eastern half remains essentially a potential, and a potential that is increasingly remote. By contrast, the Pacific provinces today play a pivotal role in Soviet strategy well beyond the East Asian theater. This has strongly influenced the economic position and links of the area with the rest of the USSR and has intensified the one-sided dependency of this region on the distant metropolis.

If, as Chapter 2 has shown, relative proximity permits West Siberia-North Kazakhstan to play the pivotal role in energy and raw material supply to the European core (and thus the economy as a whole), more than paying for the cost of development in the process, remoteness in the extreme denies such a role to regions east of the Enisei and even more to those east of Lake Baikal. Remoteness from the metropolis, however, is not compensated for by proximity and easy access to the Pacific Basin for most of Transbaikalia and the Far East (supra, Chapter 2). Nor does much more than a third of the population of Siberia east of Baikal live within 100 kilometers of the coast, in contrast to the U.S. Pacific states where over 85 percent of the population resides in that zone.[2] This situation also distinguishes the Soviet Far East from other maritime regions of the USSR, such as the Northwest, Baltic, and Black Sea areas. Only in the immediate coastal provinces and in the zone along the BAM, can one speak of accessibility to the Pacific even in the purely geographic, let alone economic, sense.

What does this remoteness from the metropolis, and in large part also from the Pacific, mean for the eastern half of Siberia in economic terms--in the role these eastern provinces play in the Soviet economic system, including foreign economic relations? And what does it mean in strategic terms for the Soviet Union as a global superpower and a major Pacific and East Asian power? In East and Southeast Asia, the USSR faces one-third of the world's population (1.5 billion people) and some of its most dynamic and fastest-growing economies with a burgeoning share in world trade. Across the ocean, the relative importance of the Far West in the U.S. economy and trade has also sharply increased in recent decades, with most of its foreign economic ties being with countries of the Pacific Basin.

Confronted with this Pacific vigor, the easternmost provinces of the USSR suffer not only from the general stagnation of the Soviet economy, but in recent years seem to be losing ground relatively among Soviet regions themselves despite the huge construction work of the BAM, touted as the railway project of the century. Nor have these provinces benefited from the expansion of trade in the Pacific Basin. Not counting Mongolia and Vietnam, which are members of the CMEA, East and Southeast Asia plus

Oceania account for a miniscule 5 percent of Soviet trade turnover, a share smaller than in 1970.[3] Perhaps even more serious, not much over a fifth of all Soviet export shipment to countries of the Pacific Basin originate in the Soviet Far East.[4] Parallel with this weak and subordinate relationship within the Soviet spatial economic system, however, the Pacific provinces have long been accorded special attention in the strategic-military sphere. This attention by Soviet leaders has become particularly pronounced over the last two decades.

WEAK INTEGRATION AND PARASITIC RELATIONSHIP

The Far East and even Transbaikalia are much less integrated into the mainstream of the Soviet economy than regions farther west. Both by tonnage and value, the movement of goods to and from the Far East amounts to a small fraction of that for West Siberia-North Kazakhstan and is much less even than that for East Siberia west of Lake Baikal. In addition, in stark contrast to the rest of the Trans-Ural hinterland, shipment into the Far East exceeds outshipment 2.5 times by volume and 1.8 times by value.[5] This is conclusive proof that, despite the region's natural riches, remoteness and the harsh environment have so far prevented the generation of major export flows to pay for the high cost of development and the expense of naval and military installations so prevalent through its territory. Siberia east of the Enisei River, and still more east of Lake Baikal, is heavily subsidized. Recently published estimates by a Soviet economist have enabled me to calculate that in 1975 all twelve provinces east of that river were recipients of large unreturned inflows of national income. This subsidy exceeded 700 million rubles in six of the twelve provinces, and for the area east of Lake Baikal it approximated one-third of national income utilized in the region. As a percentage of the Soviet NMP (net material product), the subsidy amounted to some 2 percent or 7.5 to 8 billion rubles.[6]

Specific examples of this "parasitic" relationship between the Far East and the rest of the USSR abound. Demand for some 95 percent of all products of ferrous metallurgy, 80 percent for those of the chemical industry, 71 percent of those of light industry, and over half of those of machine building must be shipped in from elsewhere.[7] Of rolled metal alone, 2.1 million tons are railed in each year at a cost of 32 to 35 million rubles, and even the reconstruction of the old Komsomolsk steel mill and the building of a new plant will not satisfy more than 50 to 60 percent of demand. The products of the ten machinery branches that operate in the Far East match up very poorly with regional needs and are sent mostly to other parts of the country.[8] At the same time, overseas exports to defray the cost of developmental efforts so far have proved disappointing. Not much over a fifth of all Soviet shipment to countries of East and Southeast Asia and the Pacific Basin, itself a mere 3.75 percent of all Soviet exports, originate from the Far East Economic Region.[9] Fish and forest products compose 70 to 80 percent of this with little prospect for significant expansion for either category. The very modest exports of machinery products are directed overwhelmingly to the European socialist states, with only 5 to 7 percent marketed in countries around the Pacific Basin.[10]

The economic indicators for the development of the Far East are deteriorating sharply, far more rapidly than for the USSR as a whole. According to the calculations of Soviet scholars, the growth of factor inputs during the 1960–1980 period accounted for almost four-fifths of the increment in the net output of the region's industry; growth in factor productivity contributed less than 21 percent. The corresponding ratio for Soviet industry as a whole was 53 and 47 percent (Table 4.1). The increase in labor productivity has been significantly slower than in the Russian Republic as a whole, according to official data up to 1975 and partial evidence since. Capital productivity in the Far East during the 1970s declined with notable rapidity and at an increasing rate (Table 4.2). For agriculture and construction, the contribution of factor productivity to output growth was computed only for the 1976–1980 period. It appeared even lower than for industry, being actually negative for construction, with factor inputs rising somewhat faster than the net value of production in this branch.[11] In the Far East, the time lag before production factors yield any return is longer than elsewhere and in 1984 the value of unfinished construction reached 97 percent of capital investment by the state. Still more serious, capital and labor are used with lower coefficients of intensity.[12]

The extreme instability of the labor force is well known through ample anecdotal evidence. In Chapter 6, I show that the average hours spent on the job by an industrial worker in the Far East and Siberia in the mid-1970s amounted to a mere 1,300 hours, only 70 percent of

TABLE 4.1 The Share of Extensive and Intensive Factors in
the Growth of Industrial Output in the Soviet Far East
from 1960 to 1980 (in percent)

| Regions and country | Percent of total increment in final (net) industrial product attributable to | |
	Growth of factor input	Improvement in factor productivity
Far East	79.2	20.8
Southern zone	72.3	27.7
Northern zone	69.7	30.3
USSR	53.2	46.8

Note: The author assumes a modified Cobb-Douglas production function. Final product in the industry of the Far
East and its zones was estimated as Gross Output –
Material Costs + Turnover Tax, available by industrial
branches for the Russian Republic, and corrected according
to the branch structure characteristics of the Far East.

Source: P.A. Minakir, Ekonomicheskoe razvitie regiona:
programnyi podkhod. Moscow: Nauka, 1983, pp. 185-191.
Reprinted from L. Dienes, "Economic and Strategic Position
of the Soviet Far East," Soviet Economy, Vol. 1, No. 2
(April-June), 1985, p. 155.

the time his counterpart in Alaska spent working. As a
result of the low efficiency in employing labor, industry
as a whole and the majority of its major branches required,
in 1977, significantly more manpower per unit value of
output in the Far East and Siberia than in the European
regions of the Russian Republic. Despite a statistically
higher than average level of capitalization (due entirely
to the higher zonal pricing of structures), the labor force
in the Far East is less mechanized than in developed
regions west of the Urals. Automation is even less
advanced and manual labor more common. In construction,
greater isolation and dispersion over a vast territory is
further aggravated by departmental and ministerial autarchy
and lack of coordination. This results in too many small

TABLE 4.2 Dynamics of Industrial Growth in the Far East by Time Period (in percent)

Factors	1960–1965	1966–1970	1971–1975	1976–1980
Percent of total increment attributable to growth in factor productivity	35.2	32.5	2.6	-50.5[a]
Labor productivity	36.2	36.0	33.9	27.9
Productivity of capital	- 1.0	- 3.5	-36.5	-78.4
Percent of total increment attributable to growth of factor inputs	64.8	67.5	97.4	150.5[a]
Growth in employment	35.8	23.2	25.6	18.7
Growth in value of fixed assets	29.0	44.3	71.8	131.8

[a]Combined inputs of capital and labor growing some 50 percent faster than industrial output.

Source: P.A. Minakir, Ekonomicheskoe razvitie regiona: programnyi podkhod. Moscow: Nauka, 1983, p. 192. Reprinted from L. Dienes, "Economic and Strategic Position of the Soviet Far East," Soviet Economy, Vol. 1, No. 2 (April–June), 1985, p. 155.

and inefficient construction organizations, much duplication, and ineffective use of labor, especially through the vast Northland.[13]

Subregional Differences

For analytical purposes, the enormous territory of the Far East is in need of careful geographic differentiation. As shown in Chapter 2, some 90 percent of it lies in the Northland, the bulk of it in the Far North, which experiences the coldest winters on the globe outside Antarctica.[14] Along the slightly warmer Arctic and Pacific coasts, the high frequency of gale-force winds make conditions almost as harsh. Aside from the Middle Lena-Viliui Lowland and plains facing the Arctic Sea, the whole area is distinguished by rugged topography. Continuous permafrost, reaching south almost to the Amur, and high seismicity over much of the area severely complicate any building activity and raise construction costs to above all other regions of the USSR. Not surprisingly, only 5 to 6 percent of the area is developed (osvoennaia territoriia) and this whole huge region contains only some 3.3 million inhabitants.[15]

The effectively settled, temperate portion of the Far East, a mere 10 percent of its territory, is basically confined to the Middle Amur-Ussuri Valleys, to the Khanka Lake plain north of Vladivostok, and to southern Sakhalin. Essentially, this is the only part of the region free of permafrost and with temperature regimes suitable for mid-latitude crops, though widespread peatbogs, acidic soils, and heavy precipitation that causes frequent and disastrous flooding in late summer (i.e., at harvest time) severely limit its potential. Nearly the entire coastline is frozen in winter, even here, and is troubled by raw, thick fog through the summer and autumn months. This uninviting environment, the best the Soviet Far East offers for human habitation, is home for a little over 4 million people. In the two Transbaikal provinces of East Siberia (i.e., the Buriat ASSR and Chita Oblast), over 700,000 persons out of a total of 2,362,000 also reside in the southern zone.[16] Within a radius of 3,000 kilometers around Khabarovsk, barely reaching Lake Baikal on the west, this minuscule Soviet population of about 5 million faces one hundred times as many people in North China, Korea, and Japan.

Besides this north-south dichotomy, the continental maritime division within the Far East appears almost as sharp. As mentioned, less than half of the population of the Far East and little more than a third that of the Far East and Transbaikalia combined live within 100 kilometers of the Pacific Ocean. The coastal provinces situated within the Trans-Siberian and BAM supply zones are linked by the two railways with the rest of the Soviet Union. In the northern interior, as noted in Chapter 2, the vast Yakut ASSR with half the area of the Far East has the bulk of its freight linkages with regions west of Lake Baikal via the Lena River, but is destined to be served much more by the BAM in the future.[17] However, three oblasts on the Pacific littoral--Sakhalin, Kamchatka, and Magadan--with a combined population of 1.6 million people, have links with the rest of the country essentially only by sea. The first two oblasts lack and will continue to lack land communication altogether; the one gravel road from Magadan to Yakutsk is rather tenuous overland connection.[18] The near-complete dominance of maritime links justify treating these three provinces as separate in some respect. On the other hand, in its economic structure and linkages with other Soviet provinces, Magadan Oblast appears quite distinct from Kamchatka and Sakhalin and instead closely resembles the Yakut ASSR.

Given the above, recent Soviet research tends to divide the Far East in the following way: (1) the Southern Zone (Amur Oblast, Khabarovsk Krai, Maritime Krai), population 4,965,000 as of January 1, 1986; (2) the Northeast (Yakut ASSR and Magadan Oblast), population 1,551,000; and (3) a Maritime Zone (Sakhalin and Kamchatka Oblast), population 1,135,000.[19]

As expected from the underdeveloped and imbalanced economy of the Far East, extraregional linkages with the rest of the country are more important than economic links among the provinces of the region.[20] Given the enormous expanse of the Far East, this of course multiplies the transport burden, especially since 73 percent of all interregional outshipment from the Far East was destined for the European USSR (including the Urals) and 80 percent of all inshipment originated from that part of the country in 1977. In fact, since 1970, the relative importance of the Far East's freight links with East and West Siberia has been drastically reduced while those with several areas west of the Urals increased substantially (Table 2.1). In part, this is due to the construction efforts on the BAM, in part also to the huge military build-up (see below). However, an excessively resource-dominated economic strategy, leading to an ever-decreasing degree of complementarity with other Siberian regions also appears to be a factor. At any rate, a sharply growing dependency relationship with the distant metropolis at the expense of economic ties with nearby areas appears reasonably clear.

All the provinces of the Far East depend on other regions of the USSR for a significant portion of total input in their net regional product. In two provinces this share approaches 30 percent, for two it is around 22 percent, and for the remaining three about 18 percent (Table 4.3). Surprisingly, Magadan Oblast appears the most self-sufficient with almost 72 percent of the total value of inputs originating from within the province's boundaries. Clearly, its extremely narrow industrial profile (four-fifths of its labor force employed in mining, with an additional 7 percent in fishing), and perhaps the contribution of penal labor reduces the share of input from the outside to a surprisingly low level.[21] The maritime oblasts, Sakhalin and Kamchatka, seem least self-sufficient: respectively less than half and less than three-fifths of the value of total inputs in their net regional products originate within their boundaries. The two, however, rely on other Far Eastern provinces for inputs almost as heavily as on regions outside the Far East and similarly distribute their output both inside and outside the Far East. By contrast, the economic links of the Northeast (Magadan Oblast and Yakut ASSR) with the rest of the Far East are weak and extremely one-sided. The Northeast receives only a small fraction of its inputs not produced within that zone from elsewhere in the Far East. It also ships virtually all of its products (overwhelmingly consisting of gold, diamond, tin, and fur) to the western regions of the USSR and, indirectly, for export.[22]

Strategic Considerations and the Military Build-up

Strategic considerations have always loomed large in Soviet regional issues. The USSR today is the only military power with land frontiers in three of the great geopolitical and cultural world regions, Europe, East Asia, and the Middle East. Such a position forces the Soviet state to defend itself on all these fronts but also allows it to project its power into all three geopolitical theaters from within its own territory. In this geopolitical context, the regional significance of the Far East (and also Soviet Central Asia) is greatly enhanced by the

TABLE 4.3 Territorial Structure of Total Inputs in the Production of Final (Net) Output. Far East (percent of total input)

| | Regions of demand | | | | | | |
Regions of supply	Amur Oblast	Khabarovsk Krai	Maritime Krai	Kamchatka Oblast	Sakhalin Oblast	Magadan Oblast	Yakut ASSR
Amur Oblast	69.9	2.7	0.8	3.2	9.1	1.5	2.4
Khabarovsk Krai	8.9	70.5	7.2	8.8	8.9	1.2	2.4
Maritime Krai	2.9	7.1	68.4	4.9	3.6	2.1	2.5
Kamchatka Oblast	0.0	0.0	0.0	59.4	1.3	0.0	0.0
Sakhalin Oblast	1.1	2.4	1.5	2.0	48.2	3.4	0.1
Magadan Oblast	0.0	0.2	0.0	0.0	0.0	71.8	0.5
Yakut ASSR	0.0	0.0	0.0	0.0	0.0	1.8	68.9
From outside Far East	17.2	17.1	22.1	21.5	28.9	18.2	28.2

Source: N.N. Mikheeva, "Analiz mezhotraslevykh i mezhregional'nykh vzaimodeistvii na osnove informatsii otchetnykh mezhotraslevykh balansov Dal'nego Vostoka," Izvestiia, AN SSSR, SO ser. obshch. nauk, 1983, No. 6, p. 78. Reprinted from L. Dienes, "Economic and Strategic Position of the Soviet Far East," Soviet Economy, Vol. 1, No. 2 (April–June), 1985, p. 161.

tremendous growth of the economic capacity of East Asia and the new pivotal role of the Gulf States in the oil supplies of a number of key industrial and industrializing nations. By the same token, U.S. concern with the Soviet naval and military build-up in the Far East is heightened by the fact that the Asian Pacific region represents the single largest economic area of U.S. interest--30 percent of U.S. foreign trade in 1982 ($136 billion). In addition, $106 billion worth of oil transited the Indian and Pacific Ocean that year (a recession year for many countries) en route to world markets.[23]

Together with the specter of a rival China, the relative shift in the importance of the three geopolitical regions does provide a partial explanation for the massive increase of Soviet military power in the Far East. Certainly the impressive growth of the Pacific fleet, which also has responsibility for the Indian Ocean, has provided the USSR with much greater ability to outflank the surrounding states on their sea sides. In my view, however, the focus of Soviet strategy in the Far East is found beyond the East Asian theater in the global environment and particularly in superpower relations. It is this extraregional dimension which has been the most important factor in shaping the strategic profile of the Pacific provinces in recent years.

The general contours of the Soviet naval build-up on the Pacific is well known. Still, it is worth noting that the 770 vessels assigned to the Pacific Fleet compose some 40 to 45 percent of Soviet blue-water and coastal forces.[24] This is more than double the share that the Pacific commercial fleet represents in all Soviet civilian tonnage,[25] although--given the near total lack of roads along most of the Pacific littoral--coastal shipping for the Far East is of exceptional importance. Since November 1985, three new principal surface combatants (one nuclear-powered guided-missile cruiser and two guided-missile destroyers) were transferred to the Pacific Fleet. Two of the USSR's four aircraft carriers for combatants with verticle take-off capabilities are also based there today. Almost a third of all Soviet submarines and 36 to 40 percent of all ballistic missile submarines are likewise assigned to the Pacific. Three-fourths of these are stationed at ice-free Petropavlovsk-Kamchatka, also homeport for almost 30 percent of all surface combatants operating from Pacific harbors.[26] With its supply satellites, such as Oktiabrskii on the Okhotsk Sea, this huge base may be over half the size of Murmansk-Severomorsk

on the Kola Peninsula, the biggest in the USSR.[27] Petropavlovsk is the largest city in the Siberian North and,
with 248,000 persons in January 1986, accounts for almost
three-fifths of the entire population of Kamchatka.[28]
According to my research, Kamchatka Oblast, with the second
smallest in population in all of Siberia, situated in the
most remote corner of the land, not only has the highest
share of "consumption" in gross regional income among all
Siberian provinces, but also has one of the highest per
capita levels of "consumption" (actually the slightly
larger category "real income") in the country.[29] Only the
huge naval base and the corresponding size of military
demand can explain that prominence. Altogether, the number
of Soviet naval personnel deployed in the Pacific, estimated at 134,000, is claimed to outnumber that of any other
region.[30]

Since the mid-1960s, the Soviets have also put about a
quarter of all their ground forces and some 26 percent of
their air force into Asia, chiefly along the Pacific coast
and the Chinese border.[31] The two military districts
located east of the Enisei account for over half of all
Soviet mechanized infantry divisions and four of the six
armored divisions stationed in Asia, including Mongolia and
Afganistan.[32] These Far Eastern ground forces possess
modern equipment, very strong air defense capability, and
some 11 million tons of war materiel, a fifth of it stocked
along the new BAM railway.[33] Finally, there were by 1984
144 SS-20s, with a total of 432 warheads, based in the
region. There are more today. "The estimates on the
number of SS-20s deployed in the whole Asian-Pacific
[region] range from a high 206 to a low 160."[34] As a
result of all this military build-up, in the border and
coastal provinces east of Lake Baikal (which includes all
oblasts, krais, and ASSRs, except Yakutia) one-fourth of
all adult males up to age sixty are in uniform today.[35]
Whether the reported 1987 changes in the Far Eastern
command (from a general to a lieutenant general for land-
based forces and from an admiral to a vice-admiral for the
Pacific navy) presages any downgrading of this vast arsenal
of military power in the future remains to be seen.[36]

Considering this military build-up overall, one is
impressed by the importance that the global-strategic
dimension has assumed during the last decade. From the
acquisition of the Amur-Ussuri lands until the early 1970s,
it was ambition and perceived military needs in the East
Asian theater which shaped the contours of Far Eastern
armed forces and installations. The Sino-Soviet break and

the outburst of rampant violence in China during its Cultural Revolution helped to prolong the primacy of this East Asian dimension, resulting in the massive Soviet ground forces along the Chinese border. To what degree the decision to construct the Baikal-Amur Mainline was a response to these regional concerns is a moot question. At present, however, the chief military significance of the railway (soon to be operational) may lie in the impressive logistic improvement it will provide for Soviet forces along the Pacific coast, whose mission reaches far beyond the regional theater.

The military build-up of the last decade seems to be driven by this wider reach and primarily by superpower realtions. Today, it is this global strategy that shapes the contours of military forces in the Far East, with their consequent geographic and economic impact. Central to Soviet Far Eastern military strength today is the SSBN, the nuclear submarine armed with ballistic missiles having a range of over 7,000 kilometers. With such range that includes most of the United States, domestic waters behind historic chokepoints can become sanctuaries rather than traps; the Sea of Okhotsk has in fact been used as a submarine-launched ballistic missile (SLBM) launching test range with sixteen such missiles fired from it since 1981.[37] To a degree, this extraregional strategy is also served by the land-based SS-20s, and long-range bombers, capable of reaching all of Asia and parts of the U.S. from the Far Eastern provinces.

Elements which form the vital core of a military strategy, however, have to be shielded and defended. The strong supporting role that Soviet surface ships and aircraft must play to ensure the success and survival of the submarine by denying the enemy approach to home waters appears frequently in Soviet naval writings, according to a U.S. expert.[38] Certainly, parallel with the sharp growth of the Soviet submarine force on the Pacific, the past years have seen an equally impressive rise in capabilities to protect the SSBNs and their bases and to guard the approaches to the Northwest Pacific and the Okhotsk Sea. Soviet determination to protect the approaches to the Okhotsk and Japan Seas, even at the price of permanently alienating Japan, is proved by the militarization of the Southern Kuriles, which the Japanese claim. These islands have been garrisoned with more than 14,000 men, and in 1986 reportedly received SSC-1 rockets, with a 450-kilometer range and capable of carrying nuclear weapons.[39] Iron-ically, this remarkable growth in Soviet power aimed at

Japan also seems to be driven more by extraregional considerations than by purely regional ones. So long as the strategic concerns of the USSR were confined to East Asia and the Northwest Pacific, the Soviet military threat to Japan remained far more restrained.

THREE MODELS OF DEVELOPMENT FOR THE SOVIET
FAR EAST

Given the isolation and remoteness of the Far East from the metropolis, there are three possible models of economic growth for the region. One represents a more or less autonomous and balanced line of development. It would concentrate on satisfying local demand with small-scale consumer industries that depend on local enterprise and the advantage of place. Foreign trade also would be autonomously conducted, its scope and reach again determined overwhelmingly by the need of the provincial market and the exchange value of local products. This is, in fact, the model the region was allowed to pursue before the Revolution and even during the 1920's.[40] Local initiatives were dominant, trade with neighboring states and regions-- especially Manchuria--virogous, but induced and shaped by regional forces. Russian political influence in Manchuria until the period 1904-1905, while beneficial, was not a sine qua non for such an evolution, since regional trade and cooperation continued after the Russo-Japanese War. Such a line of development today would require a radical modification, if not abandonment of central planning, which seems nowhere in the offing. And it would require an open regional economy and untrammeled local trade with Japan and China, where similar economic changes would be necessary. Irrespective of the merit of the model or its chances of success today, it is unlikely to be resuscitated in this century.

In theory, Soviet-Japanese coastal trade could put some minor features of this model into practice. From 1960 on, the Soviets have engaged in regional trade (between Leningrad and Finland, then between Baku and Turkey and Iran), and the establishment of Dalintorg (Far Eastern Foreign Trade Bureau) at Nakhodka in 1965 represented the third attempt.[41] Yet coastal trade has never fulfilled its promise. In 1981, it still made up less than 3 percent of total Soviet-Japanese trade, only to decline dramatically to 1.6 percent in 1983, and absolutely from a little over 90 million to between 45 and 50 million rubles. Dalintorg is still permitted to trade in only seventy or so items, mostly in a barter arrangement, which severely limits flexibility.[42] The lack of desirable Soviet products and their poor quality control, their high price compared to alternative sources, and the lack of a guarantee by Dalintorg (or its lack of authority to guarantee) to reciprocate with goods requested by the Japanese all limit expansion. A still more serious restriction is the definition of allowable commodities: (1) items "which are produced for the domestic market in planned quantities . . .[and, therefore] can be exported only if production is above planned targets; (2) surplus by-products or waste products, i.e., wood chips; and (3) minor local goods (valuable minerals, fur, etc., are thus excluded) which do not have a domestic market."[43] An autumn 1984, interview with the Chamber of Commerce of Nigata, a city and prefecture more strongly involved with Soviet coastal trade than most others, revealed a desire to increase participation in "big trade" (i.e., that via the Soviet Ministry of Foreign Trade in Moscow) rather than coastal trade.

There are also problems of complementarity in coastal trade on the Japanese side. Some circles in Japan have hoped that such trade with the USSR, and Soviet Far Eastern development in general, could spur economic growth in Hokkaido and northwest Honshu. The economic profiles of these prefectures, however, are the most biased towards primary products in all of Japan and show the least complementarity with that of the Soviet Far East. Soviet imports are mostly from the highly industrialized Tokyo-Osaka region of eastern Honshu.[44] The five- to sevenfold lag of export to the USSR versus imports from that country in Hokkaido's trade has not changed in over fifteen years (in 1983, the northern island accounted for 4.9 percent of Japanese imports from the USSR but contributed a mere 0.8 percent of Japanese exports to the same.[45] A Soviet participant in a July 12, 1984, symposium at Sapporo flatly denied the prospect of any increase in agricultural and similar primary imports from Hokkaido to the Far East.

The second model relies heavily on foreign trade to drive regional economic growth, but such trade is geared to the priorities of the metropolis and is initiated and directed by it. Given abundant natural resources but remoteness from the economic core, these resources would be exported almost exclusively abroad—in this case mostly to the Pacific Basin. The revenues would accrue to the center and would be disposed of in accordance with its overall sectoral and regional policy. The catch in this model is that natural resources for the world market face a competitive environment. Not only are there alternative supplies and frontiers for development, but technology may permit the reworking of abandoned deposits and the stabilization or decline of demand through conservation and substitution. To enhance the competitive position of a resource frontier, the metropolis may grant concessions and permit equity ownership for foreign firms. Failing that, it will have to direct vast amounts of capital and labor to build the transport and social infrastructure to make these resources physically accessible for export. The harsher the frontier area and more remote from the economic core, the longer and costlier the process, and physical accessibility still may not translate into competitive cost on the world market.

Since the start of the Five-Year Plan, concessions and equity participation have been ruled out in the USSR, and the serious push during the Brezhnev era to develop the Far East through foreign trade has had to rely on a huge domestic effort to provide accessibility. The construction of the BAM, beside its real or perceived strategic value, is the most recent and important manifestation of this effort. The enormous cost of Siberian development and the priority demand of the economy for Tiumen' gas and oil (which now receives over one-third of Siberian investment and some 8 percent of all state investment in the USSR [see Chapter 3]), however, have stymied the ambitious plans for resource development along the BAM, pushing them much further into the future. By Soviet admission, several of the Siberian and Far Eastern mineral deposits have also turned out to be much more complex geologically than originally anticipated because of inadequate prospecting.[46]

To aggravate the problem of development, the USSR has failed to foresee the long-term energy and material conservation measures put into effect throughout the industrial world following the two oil shocks. Nor did it anticipate the deep structural changes experienced by these economies, which reduced demand for most raw materials. By 1980, for example, Japan was spending 7.7 percent of all investment in plants and equipment on energy-saving investment, with another 1.7 percent on fuel conversion.[47] The shift away from heavy industries in the advanced countries is exemplified by a 25 percent (122-million-ton) drop in steel production between 1974 and 1983 throughout the OECD, one-sixth of that absolute decline taking place in Japan.[48] (The OECD or Organization for Economic Cooperation and Development includes all developed market economies in the world, except Finland.)

As a result of these momentous changes, Japanese interest (as that of other nations) in the importation of Soviet Far Eastern resources has declined sharply. Indeed, as lengthy interviews with officials of two major trading companies confirmed, the Japanese are trying to renegotiate their contract for South Yakutian coking coal, reducing the yearly purchases by over one-fifth. Japanese traders express almost uniform dissatisfaction with the quality and mix of Soviet commodities, their inability to specify the firms and factories from which (on the basis of past experience) they wish to import, and the high price of Soviet products. And they remain particularly unmoved by Soviet urging to advance loans for resource projects in the interior. Japan and the USSR remain at an impass even about the development of Sakhalin oil and gas, a project which would provide 3 million tons of LNG (liquefied natural gas) and 1.25 million tons of oil to Japan per year, beginning in early 1990. Although a general agreement was concluded recently after long years of wrangling, wide differences between the two sides may still frustrate the deal. The recent appreciation of the yen further complicates the project, which in the spring of 1987 remains in abeyance. Whatever its fate, Japanese businessmen today describe such form of trade as basically outdated. Other huge ventures in this century are extremely unlikely.[49]

Given these conditions and constraints, a third model for Pacific Siberia appears the most likely. Namely, the metropolis will continue to regard this remotest of its hinterlands, particularly the coastal provinces, as of crucial strategic value. Economically, too, it will view it as a potential asset, not to be isolated from the strategic factor. Even with very limited exploitation, the vast virgin resources of the region should guarantee self-sufficiency for the USSR in nearly every strategic mineral for the foreseeable future. The heavy subsidization of the Far East, therefore, will persist and, for the rest of this century at least, the area will remain an economic liability. Most of the subsidy, however, will go to existing production centers and to shore up the Soviet military position. New production centers in this century will be very few; the expansion of existing ones will proceed only slowly. Over the coming decade, perhaps longer, Soviet economic policy in the Far East will remain basically a holding action as efforts focus on more accessible regions farther west. The rationale for this proposition is briefly sketched below.

THE ECONOMIC SLOWDOWN AND FAR EASTERN DEVELOPMENT

Current difficulties in the Soviet economy are having a significant impact on Siberian and Far Eastern development, affecting both the sectoral and regional contours. Sectorally, the essence of this impact will be the further narrowing of the area's industrial specialization, an even more limited focus on fuel extraction plus the mining and smelting of a few precious and strategic metals, and an even greater relative neglect of social infrastructure and services. Even in gold production, so crucial for Soviet hard currency earnings, more easily accessible areas have almost overtaken Siberia. Regionally, the importance of Tiumen' Oblast, with its oil and gas resources, has sharply increased and is expected to grow further. Without oil and gas, industrial growth in Siberia has actually lagged behind the Soviet mean since the mid-1970s.[50] In the Far East, it has even trailed that in the rest of Siberia and fell behind the Soviet average throughout the 1970s.[51] The slowdown in the infrastructure and service sector has been even greater. In five provinces, four of them in the Far East, the net output of this sector suffered an absolute decline, though regions with major naval facilities have escaped such an absolute decrease (Table 4.4). The negligible absolute drop for Sakhalin is well within estimated error.

More recently, Gorbachev's stress on intensification and the retooling of existing enterprises signals a retreat from costly attempts to speed the development of the Far East. The forces that hinder growth and diversification west of Lake Baikal (Chapter 3) are magnified east of the Lake. Siberia proper also competes with the Far East for investment and labor and offers many of the same resources closer to the European USSR. Gorbachev's opposition to long-range massive projects, which divert funds away from modern electronic, machinery, and computer industries, is bound to affect the prospects of the Far East well into the future.

The BAM Program

Soviet plans called for the completion of the Baikal-Amur Railway (BAM) by the November 7, 1984, anniversary of the Revolution, a year ahead of schedule. While the laying of the tracks to achieve such a feat was apparently accomplished, only one of the eight major tunnels along the route and a mere third of the track itself were fully operational at the end of 1985. Complex geological conditions, combined with slipshod work, has led to "intolerable delay in the work connected with the opening of train traffic", in the words of a special investigative commission headed by Politbureau member Aliev.[52] In 1983 alone, the inspection service found about 1,400 instances of defective work along the railway.[53] Although 40 percent of the, mostly infrastructural, investment associated with the construction of the BAM still remained to be accomplished at the end of 1985,[54] the total cost of the project has already reached some 20 billion rubles at that time.[55] While a huge sum, this is no more than 22 to 24 percent of that which the USSR invested in the West Siberian oil and gas complex during the decade of 1976-1985, while BAM was under construction (Table 3.4). Tiumen', however, has provided a big payoff, which cannot be said for BAM. Without significant development along its route, the latter will not repay its investment in economic terms.

The larger BAM "program" for the development of that huge virgin territory, however, is at a virtual standstill. In only one new TPC (territorial production complex), South Yakutia, is work moving ahead today. Even here, only coal mining and electric power development is a reality, and the plan for coking coal production ran somewhat behind schedule.[56] As Theodore Shabad has reported, the preliminary draft of the Twelfth FYP envisaged the start of construction on a new underground mine in that coal basin with the Coal Ministry asking for one billion rubles of outlays for a mine with a 2.5 million-ton yearly capacity. However, "the project was dropped from the final version of the plan, apparently reflecting a reluctance to undertake major new projects" in such a remote area.[57] Plans are also under way to develop the Seligdar apatite deposit in southern Yakutia because the huge Far Eastern region entirely lacks fertilizer production, its soils are in great need of phosphorus, and its farms apply only up to 30 percent of the optimal dose, having to ship all of it from the Urals and beyond.[58]

None of the other proposals for new TPCs presented since 1975 have been approved by the authorities. The Aldan iron ore complex, also intended as part of South Yakutian TPC, was only slated for "research and planning" during the Eleventh FYP. Iron ore extraction is very doubtful before the end of the Twelfth FYP; the proposed new steel mill, if it is ever approved (and not even its

TABLE 4.4 Growth of Net Product in Industry, Construction, and Infrastructure in Siberian Regions

Regions and Provinces of Siberia	1970–1975 1970 = 100			1975–1980 (estimate) 1975 = 100		
	Industry	Construction	Infrastructure[a]	Industry	Construction	Infrastructure[a]
West Siberia	156	156	262	143	117	131
Altai Krai	146	145	244	141	101	141
Kemerovo Oblast	136	103	237	127	137	123
Novosibirsk Oblast	159	133	278	140	94	140
Omsk Oblast	158	150	256	134	102	134
Tomsk Oblast	139	119	188	138	118	120
Tiumen' Oblast	245	247	372	195	129	128
East Siberia	154	127	257	141	130	125
Krasnoiarsk Krai	155	121	259	143	147	123
Irkutsk Oblast	154	139	266	138	155	120
Chita Oblast	149	110	243	145	112	161
Buriat ASSR	152	135	221	141	113	137
Tuva ASSR	149	136	140	182	147	57

Far East	143	134	243	128	123	109
Maritime Krai	146	123	247	135	114	117
Khabarovsk Krai	151	128	272	138	129	122
Amur Oblast	131	212	228	131	113	91
Kamchatka Oblast	148	119	244	114	107	120
Magadan Oblast	120	124	231	112	127	89
Sakhalin Oblast	142	114	216	113	106	97
Yakut ASSR	154	136	234	124	148	84

aIncludes services directly related to material production, i.e., all transport, communication, material supplies and storage, water supply, foreign trade, retail trade, communal services, and commodity related household services.

Source: Computed from value of total net product and percentage in given branches for 1970, 1975, and 1980 in V.P. Mozhin, ed., Ekonomicheskoe razvitie Sibiri i Dal'nego Vostoka. Moscow: Mysl', 1980, 76-77. Reprinted from L. Dienes, "Economic and Strategic Position of the Soveit Far East," Soviet Economy, Vol. 1, No. 2 (April-June), 1985, p. 168.

location has been decided yet), will not come on stream
before the end of the century. The most serious difficulties, however, have probably arisen with the gigantic
Udokan deposit, best known for its vast copper reserves
which, however, are in association with half a dozen other
metals. The complicated diversity of the ores, it is now
believed, may make exploitation more difficult than
previously thought and correspondingly more costly.
According to the Economic Gazette, the USSR Ministry of
Nonferrous Metallurgy is proceeding very slowly with scientific research and projecting-surveying work concerning the
nature and location of the ore-concentrating combine
envisaged. Nor is there any agreement about the type and
location of the settlement to be established. Further
feasibility studies are called for to find a technical
solution to these problems before development gets under
way. The Kholodnaia lead deposits at the more accessible
northern end of Lake Baikal and the Molodezhnoe asbestos
deposit (the opening of which, however, will require an
additional rail spur) may have a better chance of being
started during the 1986-1990 FYP, but here, too, ore
concentration and infrastructural development are infea-
sible until well after 1990.[59]

It is significant that a recent volume claims uncertainty about the size of expected capital investment in the
BAM zone even among major project-making organizations of
Gosplan.[60] Three variants for development have been
proposed, two with greatly extended time horizons and
drastic curtailment of projects during this century. The
third variant, in particular, limits the BAM program to the
South Yakutian coal field, a number of forest conversion
mills at the western and eastern ends of the line, and a
later timetable for the opening of the Udokan and Molo-
dezhnyi deposits (see above). This scenario drops plans
for the new Far Eastern metallurgical base and for a number
of other smaller mineral projects, but more thorough
geological and other scientific studies of the territory
are envisaged.[61] The Twelfth FYP, however, still lists
preparatory work for that long-proposed integrated mill,
though no decision has been announced despite reportedly
twenty-five years of debate.[62] It may also be important
that, apart from the South Yakutian TPC, no other proposed
complexes along the BAM are listed in the most recent
edition of Atlas SSSR, and even the presence of very few
mineral resources are noted.[63] Under Gorbachev's steward-
ship, new resource projects in Siberia's remote eastern
half will have far fewer champions in the top adminis-

tration.   One rarely reads about the larger BAM program
today in the Soviet press. The work force on the railway
"has been sharply cut back, from 130,000 at the peak of
construction to 30,000 at the present time."[64]

The BAM program, in fact, seems to be focusing
primarily on the transport and transit aspects of the
railway, which provides an alternative route, shorter by
400 kilometers, to the Pacific coast than the old Trans-
Siberian.   In a concerted endeavor, Far Eastern ports are
being modernized and expanded. The capacity of the new
port Vostochnyi (opposite Nakhodka on Wrangel Bay, where
the greatest construction effort is concentrated) has
already reached 8 million tons, with a new container
terminal and five new piers included in the current FYP.
Its ultimate capacity is envisaged as 40 million tons,
which would make it perhaps the largest port in the entire
USSR, according to a Western expert. Although transship-
ment over the Trans-Siberian "landbridge" has slumped in
the early 1980s, the chief causes may have been transi-
tional and associated with the depressed status of world
trade during the deep recession and the temporary
difficulties in Iran, which also uses the route. With the
full completion of the BAM, "the Trans-Siberian route could
carry as much as 88 million tons of [container] cargo
during the rest of the 1980s," a 35 percent increase in
such tonnage (both domestic and international) that flowed
across that route in 1980.[65]   Other ports are also
undergoing less spectacular modernization or expansion.[66]

Not all of these port developments are related to
export or foreign transit. Given the geographic configuration and rugged topography of the Far East, marine
transport plays an exceptionally crucial role in the
economy of the coastal provinces. Ocean shipping represents 14 percent of all freight loading in the region as a
whole but provides the exclusive means of transport between
Sakhalin, Kamchatka, and the "mainland" and the primary
means between Magadan Oblast and the latter. These three
oblasts today account for 22 percent of the population of
the Far East[67] and over a quarter of its NMP (net material
product).[68]   The significance of Far Eastern ports, both
for domestic and international shipping, is underscored by
the fact that the approximately 20 percent of Soviet
civilian tonnage represented by the Pacific commercial
fleet exceeds the relative contribution of the USSR's whole
eastern half (East Siberia and the Far East) to Soviet NMP
by three times.[69]

In addition to the new east-west link provided by the

BAM, once it becomes fully operational, preparatory work on extending the north-south spur of the Little BAM towards Yakutsk has reportedly started. The first half of this line to Tomot (on the Aldan River) is planned for 1990; the second half to Yakutsk for the mid-1990s.[70] This new line, named AYAM (Amur-Yakutsk Mainline), will not, however, help in the development of the BAM zone. Indeed, by the premature transfer of construction brigades and equipment from that east-west line to the new north-south railway, it will contribute to the already drastic scaling down and postponement of projects along the BAM and may even delay the full completion of that railway itself. In addition, building organizations from the Kuzbas and the Kansk-Achinsk fuel-energy complex west of Lake Baikal are reportedly raiding construction brigades both on BAM and AYAM. These raiders offer the same pay and much better living conditions in their more established, climatically less extreme areas.[71]

The effect of the new AYAM railway, when and if it is completed a decade or more hence, will be felt in central Yakutia, chiefly by reducing sharply the cost of supplies into the region. While shipment out of Yakutia is projected to grow between 1985 and 2000 by 80 percent, shipment into that ASSR is expected to increase by almost two and a half times (from 6.4 million to 15.3 million tons). Well before that time, AYAM's southern section (the Little BAM which is in operation today) will have to be extensively upgraded, as it was badly in need of preventive maintenance and upgrading at the end of 1985 after seven years of operation.[72] AYAM will not alter appreciably the economic structure of the Yakut ASSR or the Northeast of Siberia in general. That economic structure is expected to remain extremely narrow, based overwhelmingly on the extraction and smelting of precious and strategic metals and tin. Excepting the extreme southwest corner of Yakutia, not even petroleum production is envisaged from the basins of the Northeast (Yakut ASSR and Magadan Oblast) in this century. A recent work designates most of this territory as "reserve areas" for the more distant future.[73]

The Military Significance of BAM

Allen Whiting, in his work on East Asian Siberia, states that "BAM would appear to have more military value in a precombat situation than in actual war," i.e., to provide "a major logistic supplement to the Trans-Siberian for strengthening Soviet forces throughout the area . . . and enhance Moscow's ability to prepare for war in East Asia. Once war begins, however, BAM's liabilities may outweigh its assets." Whiting acknowledges that "much will depend on the specific circumstances" but, in general, stresses the vulnerability of the BAM and questions its reliability under conditions of modern warfare.[74]

While I certainly agree with that author concerning the greater precombat significance of the railway, it seems to me that the stated and implied assailability of the line in time of war is perhaps overplayed. Although many chokeponts (i.e., bridges and tunnels) do make BAM vulnerable to air attack, it is also heavily defended from enemy aircraft. From Irkutsk eastward along the Trans-Siberian, nine or ten major Soviet air force bases interpose between the Chinese-Mongolian frontier and the new railway, not to mention those in Mongolia. A similar number of Soviet air bases (along the Lower Amur-Ussuri axis plus Sakhalin) shield BAM from attack coming from the Pacific and, along the Ussuri River, also from Manchuria. These two axes of bases command a total number of aircraft in the neighborhood of 750.[75]

Successful air attacks on the BAM, therefore, are highly improbable. Significant damage to those chokepoints would have to be inflicted by missile attacks for which such pinpoint accuracy is, as yet, less likely, especially when coming from submarines. Three bridges, over 400 meters long, and two tunnels, over 6 and 14 kilometers long, can more probably be hit by missiles, but tunnels would more easily survive a nonnuclear hit and, in a pinch, could be circumvented by temporary bypasses, as they will be in the first few years of the railway's operation.[76] The majority of these chokepoints (and both of the above tunnels) are also located on the western section of the line, least exposed to enemy attack. West of Manchuria, the old Trans-Siberian--rather less vulnerable here than along the Middle Amur and the Ussuri Valley--also can provide an alternate route to the eastern BAM through Tynda. At any rate, BAM does represent a significant logistic improvement in Soviet Far Eastern, and especially coastal, military capabilities. Assuming the two tunnels are successfully finished, a Chinese source expects the railway's annual capacity of 35 million tons to double in the future. Even without that expansion, the new line increases transit capacity between Central Siberia and the coast by 40 to 45 percent.[77] The fact that a fifth of all war materiel of the Far Eastern Military District is reportedly stocked along the line provides some indication of its strategic importance as perceived by the Soviet leadership.[78]

PROSPECTS FOR THE FAR EAST

The economic profiles and prospects of regions are a result of interaction between external and internal impulses. External forces, whether coming from the world at large or from the centers of power within the same state, tend to dominate in case of raw, pioneer areas with small population. In the centrally managed USSR, regional development is tightly intertwined with major national policy choices and priorities. The economic-strategic value placed on the different regions by the commanding metropolis and the role they play in the objectives of national policy are the crucial determinant in their development.

The role of the Far East in the Soviet regional system is conditioned by its extreme remoteness from the controlling power center, by its singularly harsh physical environment, and by its exceptional strategic importance. The region is weakly integrated into the mainstream of the Soviet economy. At the same time, its strongest economic ties are not with neighboring parts of the country or the world, but with the distant metropolis in a strongly dependent, parasitic relationship. Such dependence is further enhanced by the military importance of the Far East, especially of its coast, to the Soviet regime. The recent Herculean efforts by the Soviet government to open up its vast natural riches and accelerate regional growth via resource exports are proving largely unsuccessful despite the construction of the BAM. In a period of severe capital and labor constraints, national economic priorities are shifting to West Siberia, which is far more accessible to the country's economic core. Concurrently, reduced world demand for energy and raw materials, combined with the high costs and often poor quality, of Soviet natural resources, make them increasingly less attractive to countries of the Pacific Basin, especially Japan.

At present, there are no signs that the Soviet regime is willing to move towards a more autonomous strategy of development for the Far East, with much greater local initiative, budgetary freedom, and local trade with neighboring states. Nor is there yet much of an indication of major political concessions to Japan and/or China to induce

significant international cooperation to develop the area.
The vast military build-up and the strategic role assigned
for the Far East both in the East Asian and, more recently,
the global theater make major concessions very unlikely in
the foreseeable future. According to a well known Japanese
expert, "the Kremlin leaders have lately begun to perceive
Japan not as a function or an extension of its far more
important competition with the United States, but, rather,
as a important, independent source of political and
economic power in the world, particularly in the Asian-
Pacific region." Yet "the core of the Kremlin's current
Japan policy appears to lie in its stated intention of
improving relations with Tokyo on its own terms.[79]

The Soviet leadership will continue to subsidize the
Far East in a huge way, viewing it as a great strategic
value and, because of its natural riches, a <u>potential</u>
economic asset as well. Its short-term, even medium-term,
economic development, however, will be very slow and its
nature extremely unbalanced. New production centers, even
of resource extraction, will be very few. The important
position of rivaling other nations on the vast Pacific, a
position that Russia had hoped to gain since the mid-
nineteenth century[80] so far has become a reality mainly in
the military sense. In its seven Far Eastern provinces,
the USSR presently generates an economic output roughly
equal to that of Taiwan and an export contribution only 6
percent of that East Asian island.[81] This comparison is
not expected to become more favorable for the Soviet Far
East during the forthcoming decades.

NOTES

1. James R. Gibson, "The Sale of Russian America to
the United States," <u>Acta Slavica Iaponica</u>, Tomus 1, 1983,
p. 31.
2. A.I. Treyvish, "Rol' ekonomiko-geograficheskogo
polozheniia Dal'nego Vostoka," in AN SSSR, Dal'nevostochnyy
Tsentr and Tikhookeanskiy Institut Geografii, <u>Territori-
al'no-khoziaistvennye struktury Dal'nego Vostoka</u> (Vladivostok, 1982), p. 112.
3. <u>Vneshniaia torgovlia SSSR v 1985 godu</u> (Moscow:
Finansy i statistika, 1986), pp. 10-14.
4. N.L. Shlyk, "Eksportnaia spetsializatsiia Dal'nego
Vostoka: osnovnye napravleniia razvitiia," AN SSSR, SO,

114

Seriia obshchestvennykh nauk, Izvestiia, 1981, No. 6, p. 35.

6. My computations are based on economic estimates supplied in V.P. Mozhin, Ekonomicheskoe razvitie Sibiri i Dal'nego Vostoka (Moscow: Mysl', 1980), pp. 67–77. For further detail, see Leslie Dienes, "The Development of Siberian Regions: Economic Profiles, Income Flows and Strategies for Growth," Soviet Geography, Vol. 23, No. 4 (April), 1982, pp. 212–219, esp. Table 2.

7. P.M. Klin, T.I. Zabolotnikova, T.S. Pronina, L.F. Maslenko, and L.A. Stoliarova, "Mezhotraslevye sviazi i proportsii v narodnom khoziaistve Dal'nego Vostoka," in Retrospektivnyi analiz ekonomiki Dal'nego Vostoka (Vladivostok, 1982), pp. 13–32. Quoted in Referativnyi zhurnal. Geografiia, 1982, No. 11, E209.

8. Ekonomicheskaia gazeta, 1984, No. 30 (July), p. 9 and V. Chichkanov, "Problemy i perspektivy razvitiia proizvoditel'nykh sil Dal'nego Vostoka," Kommunist, 1985, No. 16 (November), pp. 98–99.

9. The 3.75 percent share is without Mongolia, Vietnam, Nicaragua, and North America. If exports to the United States, Canada, and Nicaragua are added, that share rises to 4.5 percent in 1985 Vneshniaia torgovlia SSSR v 1985 godu, pp. 10–14 and Shlyk, "Eksportnaia spetsializatsiia," pp. 8–12 and 35.

10. Shlyk, "Eksportnaia spetsializatsiia," p. 37.

11. P.A. Minakir, T.M. Mashteler, and O.M. Prokapalo, "Predplanovoie issledovaniie faktorov regional'nogo ekonomicheskogo rosta," AN SSSR, SO, Seriia obshchestvennykh nauk, Izvestiia, 1982, No. 1, pp. 40–46.

12. P.A. Minakir, Ekonomicheskoe razvitie regiona: programmnyi podkhod (Moscow: Nauka, 1983), pp. 194–95 and Chichkanov, "Problemy i perspektivy," p. 95.

13. L.M. Kaplan and I.Iu. Murav'eva, Ekonomicheskie problemy upravleniia stroitel'nym proizvodstvom na Severe (Leningrad: Stroizdat, 1983), pp. 31–39.

14. S.V. Slavin, Osvoeniie Severa Sovetskogo Soiuza (Moscow: Nauka, 1982), pp. 173–74.

15. Kaplan and Murav'eva, Ekonomicheskie problemy upravleniia, p. 26; Slavin, Osvoeniie Severa, p. 173; and B.F. Shapalin, "Territorial'naia organizatsiia khoziaistva Severa," Problemy Severa, 1983, No. 21, pp. 20–31.

16. As of January 1986, the population of all of the Far East reached 7,651,000, which would leave close to 5 million for the southern zone of the Far East proper. Shapalin, "Territorial'naia organizatsiia khoziaistva Severa," p. 28; Narodnoe khoziaistvo SSSR v 1985 godu,

pp. 12-14.

17. E.A. Zin', Ekonomika i organizatsiia raboty rechnogo transporta Sibiri i Dal'nego Vostoka (Moscow: Transport, 1979), p. 11; and E.B. Aizenberg, and Iu.A. Sobolev, Kompleksnye programmy razvitiia vostochnykh raionov SSSR (Moscow: Ekonomika, 1982), p. 68.

18. Atlas SSSR (Moscow: Glavnoie upravleniie geodezii i kartografii, 1985), p. 168.

19. N.N. Mikheeva, "Uchet produktov nedopolniaiu-shchego vvoza v analize mezhregional'nykh i mezhotraslevykh sviazei," AN SSSR, SO, Seriia obshchestvennykh nauk, Izvestiia, 1982, No. 6, pp. 52-58 and Narodnoe khoziaistvo SSSR v 1985 g., pp. 12-14.

20. N.N. Mikheeva, "Analiz mezhotraslevykh i mezhregional'nykh vzaimodeistvii na osnove informatsii otchetnykh mezhotraslevykh balansov Dal'nego Vostoka," AN SSSR, SO, Seriia obshchestvennykh nauk, Izvestiia, 1983, No. 6, p. 79.

21. Slavin, Osvoenie Severa, p. 190.

22. Mikheeva. "Uchet produktov," p. 53.

23. Robert L.J. Long, Adm., "The Military Balance in the Pacific," Defense, 1983, August, p. 13.

24. Long, "The Military Balance," p. 13 and Jane's Defence Weekly, 1984, April 14, p. 560.

25. V.I. Ivanov and K.V. Malakhovskii, eds., Tikho-okeanskii regionalizm: kontseptsii i real'nost' (Moscow, Nauka, 1983), p. 243.

26. Jane's Defence Weekly, 1984, April 14, p. 560; Terence Prittie, "Strategic Balance in the Pacific," Soviet Analyst, Vol. 11, No. 2 (January 27), 1982, pp. 3-5; and Soviet Military Power (Washington, D.C.: U.S. Government Printing Office, 1987), pp. 8-9, 17-18 and 68-69.

27. Based on the approximate number of submarines and surface ships in the two location and the size of the two cities' respective populations.

28. Narodnoe khoziaistvo SSSR v 1985 godu, pp. 13 and 22.

29. Leslie Dienes, "The Development of Siberia: Regional Priorities and Economic Strategy," in G.J. Demko and R.J. Fuchs, eds., Geographical Studies on the Soviet Union. Essays in Honor of Chauncy D. Harris (Chicago: The University of Chicago, Department of Geography, Research Paper No. 211, 1984), pp. 200-206.

30. Joseph M. Ha, "Soviet Policy in the Asian Pacific Region: Primary and Secondary Relationships," Acta Slavica Iaponica, Tomus V, 1987, p. 94

31. Herbert J. Ellison, ed., The Sino-Soviet

Conflict: A Global Perspective (Seattle: University of
Washington Press, 1982), pp. 200-206 and The Christian
Science Monitor, Feb. 17. 1983, p. 9.

32. Peter Kruzhin, "More Evidence that General
Govorov Heads All Forces in the Far East," Radio Liberty
Research Bulletin, RL78/82, 1982, February 17, and D.R.
Jones, Soviet Armed Forces Review Annual, Vol. 5 (Gulf
Breeze, FL: Academic International Press, 1981), p. 195.

33. Long, "The Military Balance," p. 83 and Jane's
Defence Weekly, 1984, April 14, pp. 560-62.

34. Yomiuri Shimbun, July 21, 1984 and courtesy of
Professor Hiroshi Kimura, Slavic Research Center, Hokkaido
University and Ha, "Soviet Policy in the Asian-Pacific
Region," p. 106.

35. The border and coastal oblasts and krais contain
87 percent of the population of the Far East, where in 1980
an estimated 2,043,000 of the males were in the 20 to 60
age group and 2,366,000 in the 15 to 60 age group. Eighty-
seven percent of this would amount to less than 1.8 million
and 2.06 million respectively. The male population between
18 and 60, therefore, would approximate 1.9 million. With
roughly similar age structure, Chita Oblast and the Buriat
ASSR add another 700,000 to total 2.5 million in that age
group. Godfrey S. Baldwin, Population Projections by Age
and Sex: for the Republics and Major Economic Regions of
the USSR, 1970 to 2000 (Washington, D.C.: U.S. Government
Printing Office for the U.S. Bureau of the Census, 1979),
p. 102; Narodnoe khoziaistvo SSSR v 1985 godu, pp. 12-14.
The forty-seven or so divisions in Transbaikalia and the
Far East, though not all of them combat ready, represent
about half a million ground and air force personnel. In
1984, approximately 467,000 uniformed personnel served in
the Soviet navy Soviet Military Power, 1984 (Washington,
D.C.: U.S. Government Printing Office, 1985), p. 61. Some
190,000 of these, therefore, must be attached to the
Pacific fleet, giving a total military personnel of close
to 700,000 and more with border and special forces The
Japan Times, June 13, 1984, p. 1; Long, "The Military
Balance," pp. 10-17.

36. While the outgoing commanders were candidate
members of the Communist Party's Central Committee, the new
commanders are not. Nor is the current commander-in-chief
of all the Soviet Far Eastern forces, General Ivan
Voloshin, a member of the Central Committee. General
Stanislav Postnikov, commander of the Transbaikal Military
District, however, is a member. Foreign Report, Economist
Newspapers Ltd., April 2, 1987.

37. Jane's Defence Weekly, 1984, April 14, p. 560.

38. John J. Herzog, "Perspectives on Soviet Naval Development: A Navy to Match National Purposes," in Paul J. Murphy, ed., Naval Power in Soviet Policy, Vol. 2 (Washington, D.C.: U.S. Government Printing Office, 1978), pp. 51-53. The author gives three recent citations. He claims that Soviet naval analysts have concluded that "the Germans lost the submarine campaign in World War I and II because they failed to support submarine operations with surface and air forces."

39. Ha, "Soviet Policy in the Asian-Pacific Region," p. 96 and Novoe Russkoe Slovo (New York), February 7, 1986, p. 2. The latter source quotes the Japanese newspaper, Sankei Shimbun.

40. Minakir speaks of the "autonomization" of the Far East's economy during the 1920's. The Far Eastern budget was autonomous, affording considerable independence to regional planning and administrative organs in financing and trade. In 1928, international exports reached 7 percent of the region's gross output. Minakir, Ekonomicheskoe razvitie regiona, pp. 57-58.

41. Richard L. Edmonds, "Siberian Resource Development and the Japanese Economy," in Robert G. Jensen, Theodore Shabad and Arthur W. Wright, eds., Soviet Natural Resources in the World Economy (Chicago: The University of Chicago Press, 1983), p. 225.

42. V.K. Maksimov, "Rol' pribrezhnoi torgovli v sovetsko-iaponskikh torgovo-ekonomicheskikh sviaziakh." Paper presented at a Soviet-Japanese symposium, Slavic Research Center, Hokkaido University, Sapporo, Japan, July 12, 1984.

43. Elisa B. Miller, "Soviet Participation in the Emerging Pacific Basin Economy: The Role of 'Border Trade,'" Asian Survey, 1981, No. 5 (May), p. 567.

44. Edmonds, "Siberian Resource Development," p. 225.

45. Fumio Yamanaka (Northern Region Center Economic Specialist). Presentation at the Soviet-Japanese symposium. Slavic Research Center, Hokkaido University, Sapporo, Japan, July 12, 1984 and Hokkaido Profile, 1983 (Sapporo: Hokkaido Government, Department of General Affairs, November 1983), pp. 34-35.

46. A.G. Aganbegian, A.G. Klin, and V.P. Mozhin, eds., BAM. Stroitel'stvo. Khoziaistvennoe osvoenie (Moscow: Ekonomika, 1984), pp. 12 and 71.

47. Foreign Press Center/Japan, Japan's Energy Situation, 1981 (Tokyo: August, 1981), p. 10.

48. MEMO (Mirovaia ekonomika i mezhdunarodnye otno-

118

sheniia), Ekonomicheskoe polozhenie kapitalisticheskikh i
razvivaiushchikhsia stran. Obzor za 1983 god i nachalo
1984 god (Moscow: Pravda, 1984), p. 39.
    49. For more detail see Leslie Dienes, "Soviet-
Japanese Economic Relations: Are They Beginning to Fade?"
Soviet Geography, Vol. 26, No. 7 (September), 1985,
pp. 509-525 and Gordon B. Smith, "Recent Trends in Japanese-
Soviet Trade," Acta Slavica Iaponica, Tomus V, 1987, pp.
111-123.
    50. A.G. Granberg, "Vzaimosviaz' strukturnoi i pro-
stranstvennoi politiki ekonomicheskogo razvitiia Sibiri,"
AN SSSR, SO, Seriia ekonomiki i prikladnoi sotsiologii,
Izvestiia, 1986, No. 2, p. 25.
    51. Minakir, Ekonomicheskoe razvitie regiona, p. 83.
During the Eleventh FYP (1981-1985), the reduction in the
growth rate of capital investment allocated to the Far East
was more severe than that for the country as a whole. V.P.
Chichkanov and P.A. Minakir, eds., Analiz i prognozirovanie
ekonomiki regiona (Moscow: Nedra, 1984), p. 84.
    52. In 1983 alone, the inspection service has found
about 1,400 instances of defective work on BAM. Sovetskaia
Rossiia, June 3, 1984 and Victor Mote, "The Amur-Yakut
Mainline: A Soviet Concept of Reality," The Professional
Geographer, Vol. 39, No. 1 (February), 1987, p. 14.
    53. Gudok, March 6, 1984, p. 1.
    54. Ekonomicheskaia gazeta, 1985, No. 50 (December),
p. 5.
    55. In his September 7, 1985 Tiumen' speech, Gorba-
chev revealed that the cost of the railway project equalled
two years of investment in Tiumen' Oblast, which--as shown
in Chapter 3--amounted to about 20 billion current rubles.
Pravda, September 7, 1985, pp. 1-2.
    56. Victor Mote, "A Visit to the Baikal-Amur Mainline
and the New Amur-Yakutsk Rail Project," Soviet Geography,
Vol. 26, No. 9 (November), 1985, pp. 703-704.
    57. Theodore Shabad, "News Notes," Soviet Geography,
Vol. 25, No. 4 (April), 1984, p. 271.
    58. Theodore Shabad, "News Notes," Soviet Geography,
Vol. 27, No. 1 (January), 1986, p. 13, Ekonomicheskaia
gazeta, 1985, No. 50 (December), p. 5 and Atlas SSSR, pp.
140-141.
    59. Ekonomicheskaia gazeta, 1986, No. 3 (January), p.
7; Victor Mote, "Principal Natural Resource Development
Projects in East-Asian USSR, 1982-1990." Soviet Transport
Project Task C. Case Study of the BAM and East Siberia.
Transport Capacity Problem. Wharton Econometric
Forecasting Associates, December 1982; and Aizenberg and

Sobolev, Kompleksnye programmy, passim.
    60. Aizenberg and Sobolev, Kompleksnye programmy, p. 126.
    61. Ibid., pp. 124-27.
    62. Ekonomicheskaia gazeta, 1985, No. 50 (December), p. 5; and Theodore Shabad, "Geographic Aspects of the New Soviet Five Year Plan, 1986-1990," Soviet Geography, Vol. 27, No. 1 (January), 1986, p. 13.
    63. Atlas SSSR, esp. p. 132.
    64. Theodore Shabad, "The Gorbachev Economic Policy: Is the USSR Turning Away from Siberian Development?" Paper presented for the Second World Conference on Siberia. London, April 1986.
    65. Victor Mote, "Containerization and the Trans-Siberian Land Bridge," Geographical Review, Vol. 74, No. 3 (July), 1984, pp. 307, 310, and 314.
    66. B.V. Korovin, "Dal'nii Vostok v sisteme vneshne-ekonomicheskikh sviazei SSSR i Iaponii." Paper presented at a Soviet-Japanese symposium, Slavic Research Center, Hokkaido University, Sapporo, Japan, July 12, 1984.
    67. Narodnoe khoziaistvo SSSR v 1985 godu, pp. 12-14.
    68. NMP shares computed by me from data supplied in Mozhin, Ekonomicheskoe razvitie Sibiri, pp. 76-77.
    69. Ivanov and Malakhovskii, eds., Tikhookeanskii regionalizm, p. 243 and Mozhin, Ekonomicheskoe razvitie Sibiri, p. 78.
    70. Mote, "A Visit to the Baikal-Amur Mainline," p. 703.
    71. Ekonomicheskaia gazeta, 1985, No. 50 (December), 1985, p. 5 and Izvestiia, December 26, 1986, p. 2.
    72. Mote, "The Amur-Yamal Mainline," pp. 17 and 20.
    73. B.V. Robinson, Ekonomicheskaia otsenka neftianykh resursov novykh raionov (Novosibirsk: Nauka, 1985), pp. 98-106 and G.A. Privalovskaia, "The Concept of the Spatial Organization of Resource Use in Soviet Industry," Soviet Geography, Vol. 25, No. 5 (May), 1984, pp. 319-327.
    74. Allen S. Whiting, Siberian Development and East Asia (Stanford: Stanford University Press, 1981), pp. 101-104.
    75. Jane's Defence Weekly, April 14, 1984, pp. 560-62.
    76. Sovetskaia Rossiia, Sept. 19, 1984, pp. 1-2.
    77. Shan Cheng, "Second Siberian Provides Vital Link," Beijing Review, Vol. 28, No. 12 (March 25), 1985, p. 12.
    78. Jane's Defence Weekly, 1984, April 14, pp. 560-62.

79. Hiroshi Kimura, "Basic Determinants of Soviet-Japanese Relations: Background, Framework, Perception, and Issues," Acta Slavica Iaponica, Tomus V, 1987, p. 88.

80. Gibson, "The Sale of Russian America," p. 31.

81. In dollars, Soviet national income is perhaps 55 percent that of the United States, with the Far East accounting for a mere 2.8 percent of the total. Mozhin, Ekonomicheskoe razvitie Sibiri, p. 78. This would make the contribution of the region about $50 billion, the same as that of Taiwan in 1983. Taiwan's yearly export from 1981 to 1983 approximated $22.6 billion Keiji Furuya, "Taiwan: A Locomotive in Transition," Journal of Japanese Trade and Industry, 1984, November/December, pp. 50-52 and Keizai Koho Center, Japan Institute for Social and Economic Affairs, Japan 1984: An International Comparison (Tokyo, 1984), p. 11. The one-fifth of Soviet export to East and Southeast Asia plus Oceania which originated from the Far East amounted to a meager 1.13 billion rubles in 1983 or $1.45 at the official exchange rate. Vneshniaia torgovlia SSSR v 1983 godu (Moscow: Finansy i statistika, 1984), pp. 8-14.

5

Central Asia:
Manpower and Economic Policy
for the Soviet "Middle East"

In contrast to the Siberian and Far Eastern hinterlands which are firmly part of the Russian ethno-cultural
domain, Central Asia–Southern Kazakhstan represents an
entirely different problem of socio-economic integration
for the Soviet leadership. Its place in the Soviet
regional system is the legacy of imperial colonial conquest
and it remains an undigested and indigestibly separate
realm of the USSR. The region has remained overwhelmingly
Asian in ethnic composition. In addition, because of a
much higher rate of population growth and--since 1980--the
virtual cessation of <u>net</u> immigration, the share of the
Slavic <u>colons</u>, which was increasing until 1970, began to
drop steadily after the latter date. In 1970 Slavs
composed 20.9 percent of the population in Central Asia and
the five oblasts of Kazakhstan south of Lake Balkhash and
the Aral Sea; nine years later this share dropped to 18
percent. In Central Asia alone, the proportion of Russians
and Ukrainians declined from 16.6 to 14.2 percent during
the 1970s and, judging by different rates of natural
increase, to 12 to 14 percent today.[1] The inclusion of
other European populations with the Slavs changes the
figures only very slightly.

Not only has the region become even more Asian than in
previous decades, but the autochthonous and European
population continue to remain largely separate geographically. In Central Asia as a whole, for example, 88
percent of the 628,600 Russian families enumerated in 1979
were urban, and in the Uzbek, Tadzhik, and Turkmen republics they were from 94 to 98 percent so. Only in Kirghizia
(containing part of the historic Semirech'e, with its
Cossack settlements) did the share of rural families among
the Russian population reach 30 percent at the time of the

121

last census.[2] In addition, the bulk of the Slavic families were further concentrated in the few large industrial cities and a number of new workers settlements of the regions, with very few of them living in the ancient small towns. By contrast, 74 percent of the indigenous families and, therefore, over three-quarters of the native population lived in the countryside where family size is even larger.[3] As a result, contact between the large majority of the autochthonous nationalities on the one hand, and Russians and other Europeans on the other inevitably must be limited.

The cities of Central Asia can and do serve as instruments and local control points for the political and economic integration of the area with the metropolis. However, they have been much less successful so far in effecting more than a very partial socio-cultural integration of the native countryside into the Soviet mainstream. The structure of social relations and organization in rural Central Asia, of course, has become mostly socialist in form. Nor has the value system of the indigenous population avoided change under decades of Soviet rule. Such a cultural transformation, however, is proceeding not through direct "metropolitan" influence, but through the influence of an increasingly sophisticated, culturally complex, and often ambivalent native elite. This modern elite is essentially the creation of the Russian dominated-Soviet regime, but is by no means a replica of its Slavic counterpart. As Teresa Rakowska-Harmstone noted over a decade ago, members of this elite "must seek sources of legitimacy in their own unique national heritage and in establishing ties with people of their national group" and in pursuing the latter's interest and objectives. The forces of modernization and modern techniques of communication may actually have intensified and facilitated indigenous resistance to pressures to be molded to official, Moscow-defined cultural models and social norms.[4]

ECONOMIC INTEGRATION AND PROFILE

Even in the strictly economic realm, integration into the Soviet mainstream is narrowly channeled and one-sided. Economic interdependence with the metropolis has grown sharply since early Soviet times, as land in Central Asia was turned increasingly from food to industrial crops (especially cotton for the mills of the Moscow region), while the widening food deficiency was covered from West

Siberia, the Volga Valley and, more recently, North
Kazakhstan. Although the area's mineral wealth is not
outstanding, several key minerals play significant roles in
Soviet economic policy. Central Asia rivals or exceeds the
Yakut ASSR as the largest gold-producing region in the
USSR, accounts for over one-sixth of Soviet gas output and
probably an even larger share of Soviet copper. Central
Asia is the leading producer of antimony, the second
largest producer of mercury, and a very important supplier
of uranium, tungsten, lead, and nonmetallic minerals as
well.[5] Yet, for many years now, Central Asia has been
piping to the RSFSR (Russian Republic) and the Ukraine more
than three-fourths of its gas output, with gold and nonferrous metals also going overwhelmingly elsewhere.[6] At the
same time, while notable progress has been made in the
development of manufacturing, that sector too has become
strongly dependent on raw and semifinished materials hauled
in from Slavic provinces.

The economy of Central Asia has, in large measure,
remained colonial to this day. It has by far the least
manufacturing per capita, with the relative level actually
declining in every republic because of the burgeoning
population growth rates. Soviet Central Asia–Southern
Kazakhstan contributes over nine-tenths of the nation's
cotton fiber output, accounting for almost 16 percent of
all ginned cotton in the world in 1985 (nearly one-fifth in
1980, before the doubling of China's production sharply
reduced its world's share).[7] Yet in 1975, the last year
official data were released, the region manufactured 6.5
percent of Soviet cotton textiles (up from 5.2 percent in
1965).[8] Judging from the experience of Uzbekistan, by far
the most populous republic of Central Asia, the increase in
output since that time has barely kept ahead of population
growth.[9] From 1970 on, Central Asia produced an unchanged
5.0 to 5.2 percent of Soviet intimate apparel, though the
inclusion of Southern Kazakhstan adds another 3 percent to
that share. The region's contribution to the manufacture
of outerwear, hosiery, and leather footwear is very
similar.[10] These shares are far too small to satisfy even
half the demand of the region itself, especially since per
capita consumption of textiles here is 15 percent above the
Soviet average, synthetics being less popular than elsewhere. Altogether, the value of light industry products
shipped into the region more than twice exceeded the value
of such products shipped out.[11]

Nor are the four republics of Central Asia self-
sufficient in food products, with per capita output of the

food industries being less than half the Soviet average and
less than the mean for every major branch of these industries.[12] Although, as will be shown, private subsidiary
agriculture plays proportionately a much greater role in
the economy than in the Slavic north, products of the food
industries composed almost a fifth of all interregional
imports into Central Asia's most populous republic,
Uzbekistan, in 1972. At the same time, such products
represented only a negligible portion of interregional
exports.[13] The Uzbek SSR satisfied over 46 percent of its
meat consumption and over 48 percent of its pastry and
confectionery demand through inshipment from other republics. Although significant advance in industrial food
processing has been made since at that time, the rapid
population growth allowed for only modest improvement on a
per capita basis.[14]

As of 1982, Uzbekistan still consumed only 54 percent
as much meat per person as the Soviet average, 59 percent
as much dairy products, 39 percent as many eggs, and 39
percent as much fish. Only in the cases of vegetables and
melons, vegetable oils and, interestingly, bread and pastry
(since they are largely made of imported grain) does per
capita consumption surpass significantly the national mean.
In the Kirghiz SSR, per capita consumption of meat, vegetables, and potatoes reached only a third of the Soviet
average in 1985, of eggs and milk 50 and 44 percent
respectively. Even fish consumption is well below the
Soviet mean, despite the presence of Issyk-Kul', the USSR's
fourth largest fresh water lake.[15] In the smaller and
weaker Tadzhik SSR, the situation appears still worse. In
value terms, agricultural "imports" from other republics
exceeded such "exports" by 3.1 times. This is a far
greater relative deficit than experienced by that underdeveloped republic in its exchange of industrial products,
for which interregional imports surpassed exports by only
1.21 times.[16]

It is also noteworthy that the downstream stage of the
agro-industrial complex (storage, refrigeration facilities,
and similar infrastructure) is far more underdeveloped than
in other regions, though the USSR as a whole is well behind
Western countries in this field. The share of Central Asia
in such agricultural infrastructure is under 8 percent.
Yet the natural endowment of the region suggests a comparative advantage in the supply of fruits, melons, vegetables,
and lamb. Despite heavy investment in irrigation, the
ratio of infrastructural investment to total allocation in
agriculture has dropped markedly over the years and

declined in all republics of the region, except Turkmenia.[17]

Heavy dependence on raw materials, machinery, grain,
and consumer goods railed in from elsewhere is shown by the
dominance of incoming over outgoing freight. For Uzbekistan, the former exceeds the latter a full twofold by
weight. In addition, freight ties with distant regions
tend to be very strong. In the case of the Uzbek SSR, for
example, inshipment from the European USSR, Siberia, and
the Far East slightly exceeded inshipment from the three
other republics of the region.[18] For Central Asia as a
whole, over four-fifths of incoming freight originates from
noncontiguous regions, and most of that railed in from
Kazakhstan is also shipped in from the more distant
northern parts of this republic.[19] The interregional ties
of this Moslem periphery is, therefore, more like that of a
"plantation economy" than of a mineral, forest, and grain-
growing frontier, which is characteristic of Siberia.

Over the past decade, a small number of Western
studies have focused or touched on the complex relationship
of Central Asia to the commanding Slavic core.[20] Such
inquiries have become possible by a growing number of
analytical sophisticated monographs and articles of
surprising frankness appearing from the capitals of these
republics. These studies that lament the slow growth of
processing industries in the region, which leads to an
excessive degree of import dependence on the RSFSR in food
and light industry products, cautiously question the wisdom
of the massive export of natural gas and raw cotton and of
an investment policy still geared more to such resource
exports than to the expansion of employment in the area.[21]
Since the share of federal outlays in the region's industries have risen through the decades (reaching almost three-
fourths of all industrial investment in Kirghizia during
the Tenth FYP), the latter are inevitably serving and are
responsive to outside interests, not primarily to those of
these republics.[22]

The development of the South Tadzhik TPC (territorial
production complex) combining the construction of huge
hydrostations with big aluminum, other nonferrous, and
electrochemical projects that require vast amounts of
electricity is perhaps the best example of the dominance of
national, "metropolitan" interest regarding much industrial
investment in Central Asia over the past decades. It is
true that light and food industries are also to be part of
the TPC, and plans envisage the irrigation of almost two
million additional hectares (made possible by the new

reservoirs) "in the next 10 to 15 years."[23] Yet far more
efforts have been preempted by the power and heavy
industrial projects. From 1965 through 1980, yearly investment in the Tadzhik light and food industries combined
fluctuated from 27 to 37 million rubles, rising to 43
million in 1981. Meanwhile, investment in all industries
soared from 155 to 320 million, with two-thirds of fixed
assets, output, and labor force represented by the South
Tadzhik Complex.[24] However, much of that labor force is in
chemical and metallurgical enterprises unattractive to
native labor (see below). Although population in the
Southern Tadzhik TPC increased by almost 90 percent between
1965 and 1980, much faster than either in Tadzhikistan or
Central Asia as a whole, in 1983 only a fifth of all
persons employed in all the enterprises of the Complex were
Tadzhiks.[25]

SURPLUS LABOR AND EMPLOYMENT PARTICIPATION
IN THE COUNTRYSIDE

From January 1959 through January 1979, official
employment in Central Asia increased from 5,538,500 to
10,325,800 or an average of 3.2 percent per annum.[26] This
rate almost exactly matched that of population growth and
slightly surpassed the 3.1 percent yearly average increase
of the working-age population.[27] Yet the participation
rate of the expanding adult population remains much lower
than elsewhere. In 1979, for example, the ratio of the
population officially employed (outside the home and
private plot) to the total population within the 15 to 60-
year age group was 78.1 percent in Uzbekistan versus 90.4
percent in the Russian Republic.[28] At the end of 1986,
only three-fourths of the able-bodied population of Tadzhikistan was employed in the socialist sector and national
income per capita was roughly half the USSR average.[29]
Since 1970, the growth of the working-age population in
Central Asia has accelerated sharply. During the 1970s,
the average annual increase was almost double that for the
1959-1970 period (Table 5.1) and the problem of expanding
employment to match it is looming ever larger.

In addition, the geographic distribution of population
and employment assumes critical importance. Fifty-nine
percent of all Central Asians are still rural (versus
almost two-thirds in 1959), and at the end of the 1970s 86
percent of all rural families were composed of the indigenous nationalities of Turkestan.[30] During the past thirty

TABLE 5.1 Average Yearly Growth of Total Population and
Population of Working Age[a] in USSR, Central Asia and
Kirghiz SSR (1959-1970 and 1970-1979)

	Average Yearly Growth (percent)	
	1959-1970	1970-1979
1. Total Population		
USSR	1.3	0.9
Central Asia	3.5	2.8
Kirghiz SSR	3.0	2.1
2. Population of Working Age[a]		
USSR	0.8	1.8
Central Asia	2.1	4.1
Kirghiz SSR	2.4	3.7

[a]16 to 59 for men, 16 to 54 for women.

Source: E.P. Chernova, Narodonaselenie Kirgizskoi SSR v
usloviiakh razvitogo sotsializma (Frunze: Kyrgyzstan,
9184), p. 39.

years, outmigration has siphoned off no more than 15
percent of the natural increase in the countryside.[31] This
rural mass still depends overwhelmingly on agriculture for
its livelihood, but official figures for agricultural
employment and its growth are very deceptive. The evidence
is overwhelming that both in the socialist sector as a
whole, but even more on collective farms, alone the ratio
of those officially employed (i.e., nominal employment) to
actual yearly average employment rose sharply through the
1970s in all four republics of Central Asia. It is
especially high in the Tadzhik SSR, but is so in the Uzbek
SSR as well. Even in the Kirghiz SSR, where agricultural
overpopulation is somehat less severe, the participation
rate of kholkhozniki during the 1970s declined by almost
one-third according to Soviet data, the decline affecting
males and females almost equally (Table 5.2). The growth
of nominal employment through the 1970s exceeded that of
actual employment by a considerable margin throughout
Central Asia and both were topped by the expansion of the
population in working age (Table 5.3). By contrast in

TABLE 5.2 Participation of <u>Kolkhozniki</u> in Socialist
Production of Kirghiz Collective Farms

Age Groups and Sex	Participating in the Socialist Sector (Percentages)		
	1970	1975	1980
Population of Working Age	93.2	86.8	66.6
Males	93.9	87.6	66.9
Females	92.5	85.8	66.3
	Share of Participants Not of Working Age as Percent of Those of Working Age		
Youngsters	39.9	33.1	29.0
Over Retirement Age	21.2	15.2	15.5
Youngsters and Retirees Combined	37.5	26.2	35.7

Source: V.V. Bushman, <u>Prognozirovanie i razmeshchenie
sel'skogo khoziaistva Kirgizskoi SSR</u> (Frunze: Ilim,
1982), p. 121.

Kazakhstan, because of growing demand for labor in the week
northern two-thirds of this republic, the ratio of nominal
to actual average employment now approximates that of the
RSFSR. Yet, on Kazakh collective farms alone, which are
concentrated in the southern portion of the republic where
strong native majorities prevail, this ratio continues to
be somewhat higher (Table 5.3).

Besides the rapid increase of the working-age population, the sharp seasonality of agricultural work and the
lack of alternative activities on the farm contribute
greatly to this state of affairs. On Uzbek state and
collective farms, for example, only 18 to 20 percent of the
adult population not yet on pension can be fully engaged
throughout the year. Aside from those in administration
and animal husbandry even permanent farm workers are
utilized only 60 to 65 percent of the time.[32] Cotton
growing, in particular, is especially seasonal despite long-
time efforts to mechanize harvesting, its most labor-
intensive phase. Because of the perpetual problem with

TABLE 5.3 Ratio of Nominal Employment Over Actual Average Yearly Employment in the State and Collective Farm Sectors (actual average yearly employment = 100)

	1970[a]		1979[a]		1984
	In Entire Socialist Sector	On Collective Farms	In Entire Socialist Sector	On Collective Farms	On Collective Farms (estimates)[b]
Uzbek SSR	112.5	122.4	124.6	141.4	140
Kirghiz SSR	112.2	117.4	118.4	127.5	127
Tadzhik SSR	117.5	135.6	129.7	156.0	166
Turkmen SSR	109.4	108.4	115.5	119.2	121
Central Asian Republics	112.8	121.8	123.3	138.1	146
Kazakh SSR	110.9	111.7	106.2	112.0	116
RSFSR	106.6	101.2	106.5	102.6	110
USSR	107.4	107.1	108.5	109.3	115

[a]Nominal employment is according to the January censuses of 1970 and 1979; average annual employment according to these corresponding years.

[b]Estimates made by applying the growth rate of collective farm households from 1979 through 1984 to the 1979 number of collective farmers. The estimated 1984 figures for collective farmers were then divided by the official yearly average employment of kolkhozniki in the socialist sector.

Sources: Number of state employees and collective farmers from TsSU, Itogi vsesoiuznoi pere-pisi..., Tom. 5 (Moscow: Statistika, 1973), pp. 26–45 and TsSU, Chislennost' i sostav nase-leniia SSSR (Moscow: Finansy i statistika, 1984), p. 156. Yearly average employment and number of collective farm households from Narodnoe khoziaistvo SSSR v 1970 godu, pp. 405 and 514–515; Nar. khoz. SSSR v 1979 godu, pp. 290 and 390; Nar. khoz. SSSR v 1984 godu, pp. 300–301.

machine breakdown and spare parts, the bulk of harvesters
are in use on only one shift, with 200 to 300 idling every
per farm in many parts of the Tadzhik SSR alone. In
addition, harvesters currently in use leave 15 to 20
percent of the crop on the ground to be gathered manu-
ally.[33] The ineffectiveness of mechanization is shown by
the following comparison. The 1985 normative for cotton
harvest fixes labor expenditure as 3.3 man-hours per
hectare for mechanized systems and 337.3 man-hours for
manual picking, a hundredfold difference in productivity.
At present, the actual advantage in favor of machine
picking is merely 2.3-fold. As a result, more than half
the cotton in Uzbekistan and over three-fourths of that in
Tadzhikistan today is harvested by hand, and this work
makes up 40 to 50 percent of all labor input in the growing
of that crop.[34] Ironically, manpower needs at harvest time
are so great that outside labor (school-age youths, industrial workers, etc.) is regularly commandeered to the
countryside for several weeks. The Central Party Committee
of the Tadzhik SSR reportedly commandeers over 300,000
outsiders each year for the farms, as a rule for a month
and a half to two months.[35] Reportedly, 1986 was the first
year in the history of the republic, when the cotton
harvest was gathered without taking students and children
away from their schoolwork.[36]

As of now, kolkhoz and state farm auxiliary activities
have been too insignificant to make an impact on that sharp
seasonality. They have been even less effective in
increasing average yearly employment relative to nominal
employment throughout the Central Asian countryside. A
recent monograph, for example, reveals that in the Kirghiz
SSR the contribution of such activities to the value of
total farm output increased from a mere 0.5 percent in 1970
to only 1.2 percent a decade later. Ironically, the chief
reason given for this state of affairs is the lack of local
agricultural raw materials. In the interest of the quality
of the final product and of greater economies in processing
and the avoidance of spoilage (and pilfering?), the great
bulk of farm output is claimed by state purchasing organizations.[37] The availability of materials, therefore, allows
the operation of only small workshops (mills, bakeries, oil
presses, and sausage shops) for utilizing scrap. These are
useful for improving the provisioning of the local population but can make little headway towards solving the
problem of rural surplus labor."[38] Clearly, the Soviet
predilection for centralized planning and control over
resources appears as an obstacle to diversification and

increased employment in locally managed enterprises in the Central Asian countryside. To make matters worse, inter-collective agro-industrial enterprises are also poorly developed. In 1980, they employed only 9,200 persons on the territory of the strongest republic, Uzbekistan, which represented less than 0.2 percent of the labor force and a mere 0.14 percent of the working-age population.[39]

A careful German study by Anna-Jutta Pietsch and Reinhold Uffhausen has attempted to gauge the extent of the labor surplus in Central Asia, both as evidenced by those in the working-age group that remains outside the social-ized sector (excluding students and members of the armed forces) and as it manifests itself in the overstaffing of collective and state farm operations.[40] Since the dependency burden (the ratio of underaged and pensioner population to that of working age) actually declined some-what during the 1970s throughout the region,[41] the 1970 employment ratios could be safely applied to the 1979 numbers of working age as computed in Baldwin's major report for the U.S. Bureau of Census. In addition to the manpower surplus outside the sphere of "socialized production," again located mostly in rural areas and smaller towns, Pietch and Uffhausen also estimate the upper limit of the hidden labor surplus within state and collective farm agriculture. This can be gauged from the decline of capital-labor elasticities during the decade. The authors come up with a total of 1.1 million surplus laborers in Central Asia in 1979, some three-fifths of whom were found outside socialized agriculture, two-fifths within it. The estimates for Kazakhstan yielded another 315,000 surplus laborers, almost equally divided between those within and without the "socialized sector." The authors also project these figures forward to 1990 on the basis of the anticipated population in the working-age category and on past trends in employment, expecting at most a surplus of 1.8 million in Central Asia and half as much in Kazakhstan.

After 1990, the situation will rapidly worsen, as massive cohorts of youth continue to swell the workforce. In 1985, the ratio of national income produced in Central Asia per person of working age was 70 percent of the USSR average. A Soviet study calculates that, in order to hold to this ratio until the year 2000 and employ the population locally, national income produced in the region would almost need to triple. To create jobs, investment would have to increase annually by 12 percent, clearly an impossible task. Barring such a development, a labor

surplus of 7 million would accumulate. If the economy of
Central Asia could grow 2.5 times by the turn of the
century, compared to a twofold increase for the country as
a whole, "only" a 3.5 million surplus should be expected.[42]
The problem of significant labor surpluses in the
Moslem countryside, juxtaposed with severe labor shortages
in many Slavic regions has been discussed and debated in
Soviet literature for some two decades. So far, the
natives of Central Asia show no inclination to migrate
elsewhere or even to move to the main industrial cities of
their own republics, which also struggle with manpower
shortages. The pull factor for migration is clearly absent
and, with cultural, linguistic, housing, and--in northern
republics--climatic barriers, it is almost certain to
remain so in the foreseeable future. Outmigration from the
Central Asian countryside hinges on a sufficiently strong
push factor, i.e., deteriorating economic conditions
brought about by relative overpopulation. It is on this
factor that Robert A. Lewis and associates base their
prediction of large-scale outmigration. More important,
the touchstone of Soviet policy towards Central Asia is and
will be the degree to which that push factor is deliber-
ately cushioned or reinforced or simply allowed to make its
impact. As Lewis himself writes, ". . . if for reasons of
policy or the welfare nature of Soviet society, wages and
employment are maintained, one reasonably cannot expect
significant outmigration."[43]

INCOME MAINTENANCE AND JOB CREATION:
GOVERNMENT POSTURE AND POLICIES

Despite endless discussion about the need to increase
the mobility of Central Asians, Soviet authorities have
shown no willingness so far to force outmigration by
permitting, let alone abetting, the decline of living
standards in the kishlak (village). However, one should·
properly separate welfare measures and passive arrangements
resulting in the safeguarding of living levels from
purposeful policies aimed at employment and job creation at
the source of surplus manpower. Evidence points to a
significant role of an economic cushion in blunting the
push factor, an economic cushion fostered both by active
welfare measures pursued by central planners and local
arrangements, lawful as well as sub-rosa, passively
supported or merely tolerated by them. On the other hand,
policy measures aimed at increasing employment within the

purview of planning authorities and at least roughly
congruent with their preference scale have so far had a
much more modest success.

The undeniable dependency relationship of Central Asia
in the Soviet regional system and its quasi-colonial
economic structure have been balanced by preferential
capital flows and social benefits. From official ratios of
national income produced and used in the Uzbek and Tadzhik
SSR since the period 1955-1960 (Tables 5.4 and 5.5) and
estimates by Western researchers, it is possible tenta-
tively to conclude that, since the 1960s at least, a
significant net transfer of resources towards Central Asia
has taken place.[44] Significantly, this interpretation is
openly challenged by an Uzbek scholar whose methodology,
however, seems to me somewhat dubious.[45] Be that as it
may, to the Central Asian republics (in contrast to most
others) are returned the overwhelming portion of federally
collected revenues from the socialist sector, which in 1980
accounted for 88 percent of all budgetary intake. Revenues
from personal income tax that make up the remainder are
also fully disbursed locally via the republic budgets.[46]
It is also notable that, despite the extremely rapid
population increase, the growth of social consumption funds
here between 1965 and 1979 managed to keep slightly ahead
of the Soviet mean even on a per capita basis (Table 5.6).

In 1980, the average monthly amount of such a transfer
payment per family in Uzbekistan reached 154.6 rubles, some
13 percent more than in the country as a whole.[47] It
reached about 170 rubles in Tadzhikistan, or almost one
quarter more than the Soviet mean.[48] Yet, per capita,
these payments trailed the Soviet mean by a large margin in
each of these republics. They were some 40 to 50 percent
lower than in Estonia and Latvia and more than 55 percent
lower than in the Far East (Table 5.7). More significant,
perhaps, is that since the late 1970s the per capita growth
of social consumption expenditures has fallen below the
rate of increase for the USSR as a whole, and the region
has been losing ground. Between 1979 and the end of 1982,
Uzbekistan dropped from 71 percent of the Soviet mean with
respect to these payments to 68.5 percent; Tadzhikistan
from 67 percent to 65 percent as early as 1981.[49]

As might be expected from the large number of
children, a much higher share of social consumption funds
go for education in Central Asia than in the entire USSR.
Yet schools in the region must work with a greater number
of shifts. Similarly, kindergartens and nurseries can
accommodate a much smaller share of preschoolers than in

134

TABLE 5.4 Produced and Utilized National Income in the Uzbek SSR, 1955–1982 (million rubles) (in current prices)

	1955	1965	1970	1976	1980 Plan	1980 Actual	1982
Utilized national income in Uzbek SSR	2,210	6,073 (6,023)[a]	9,545	14,005	16,010	18,432	20,310
Produced national income in Uzbek SSR	2,407	5,496	8,703	13,594	16,030	16,800	18,300[b]
Balance: (+) net inflow (−) net outflow	−197	+577 (+527)[a]	+842	+411	−20	+1,632	+2,010
Utilized national income as % of produced national income	92.2	110.5 (109.6)[a]	109.7	103.0	99.9	109.7	111

[a]Slightly different figure for utilized national income given in second source.
[b]Interpolated from 1980 and 1983 figrues.

Sources: Data from 1955 through 1976 and 1980 Plan from: K. Popadiuk, Obshchestvennyi pro-dukt i effektivnost' ego proizvodstva v period razvitogo sotsializma (Tashkent: Uzbekistan, 1979), p. 100. Data for 1980 and 1982 from A.U. Ul'masov, "Rost blagosostoianiia truzhenikov Uzbekistana," Obshchestvennye nauki v Uzbekistane, 1984, No. 6, pp. 3-4.

135

TABLE 5.5 Produced and Utilized National Income in the Tadzhik SSR, 1960–1980 (in percentages)

	1960	1965	1970	1975	1980
Utilized national income in Tadzhik SSR	100	100	100	100	100
Produced national income in Tadzhik SSR	86	92	89	94	96
Balance with other republics (net inflow)	14	8	11	6	4
Consumption	66[a]	67[a]	71	76	78
Accumulation	34[a]	33[a]	29	24	22

[a]Figures in original do not add up and are apparently in error. Those given here are computed from another table of the same source on page 43.

Source: R.K. Murzoev, Tempy, proportsii i effektivnost' obshchestvennogo proizvodstva v Tadzhikskoi SSR (Dushanbe: Donish, 1983), p. 45.

TABLE 5.6 Growth and Amount of Social Consumption Funds
in Central Asia

	Growth of Social Consumption Funds, 1965-1979 (in current prices; 1965 = 100)	
	Total	Per capita
Uzbek SSR	255.6	136.5
Kirghiz SSR	220.5	135.1
Tadzhik SSR	245.2	125.1
Turkmen SSR	231.3	125.4
Weighted per capita average for Central Asia (weighted by 1979 population shares)		133.4
USSR	163.0	129.7

Based on data in yearbooks of individual republics.

Source: Except for weighted average, Marie-Agnès Crosnier
and Michèle Kahn, "Développement et dépendance économique
de l'Asie Centrale Soviétique," Le Courrier des pays de
l'Est, No. 276, Septembre 1983, p. 27.

the country as a whole (less then 29 percent in Uzbekistan,
a little over 12 percent in Tadzhikistan, but 40 percent in
the USSR at the beginning of the 1980s).   On the other
hand, the portion of social consumption expenditures spent
on pensions was understandably much lower in the Central
Asian republics, and, though less glaringly, so was the
share of social insurance and "other social benefits"
(aside from health expenditures) because of the high
proportion of collective farm workers in the region.   Such
payments on collective farms are still notably smaller than
for workers and employees in other sectors and even on
state farms.[50]
    Despite the slow rise of labor productivity in Central
Asian agriculture (Table 5.8), the growth of collective
farm revenues, so far, has kept ahead of population
increase, resulting in a modest per capita expansion even
during the second half of the 1970s. Moreover, differences

TABLE 5.7 Per Capita and Relative Levels of Social Consumption Funds in Central Asia, Kazakhstan, Other Republics and the Far East in 1965, 1970 and 1980

Republics and Region	Rubles per Capita			Increment per Capita 1966–1980	Relative to USSR Average		
	1965	1970	1980		1965	1970	1980
Uzbek SSR	125	194	306	181	68.7	73.8	69.9
Kirghiz SSR	136	208	331	195	74.7	79.1	75.6
Tadzhik SSR	123	180	286	163	67.6	68.4	65.3
Turkmen SSR	137	196	317	180	75.3	74.5	72.6
Kazakh SSR	169	252	402	233	92.9	95.8	91.8
Estonian SSR	234	355	569	335	128.5	135.0	129.9
Latvian SSR	214	320	526	312	117.6	121.7	120.1
Lithuanian SSR	156	258	469	313	85.7	98.1	107.1
RSFSR	202	288	488	286	111.0	109.5	111.4
Ukrainian SSR	163	251	417	254	89.6	95.4	95.2
Belorussian SSR	148	231	415	267	81.3	87.8	94.7
Moldavian SSR	122	200	375	253	67.0	76.0	85.6
Georgian SSR	148	217	371	223	81.3	82.5	84.7
Armenian SSR	153	233	347	194	84.0	88.6	79.2
Azerbaidzhan SSR	133	190	293	160	73.0	72.2	66.9
Far East Economic Region	294	426	673	379	161.5	161.9	153.7
USSR	182	263	438	256	100.0	100.0	100.0

Source: A.S. Revaikin and T.V. Troshina, Regional'nye osobennosti formirovaniia i ispol'-zovaniia obshchestvennykh fondov potrebleniia (Moscow: Nauka, 1985), p. 64.

TABLE 5.8 Growth of Labor Productivity in Central Asian
Industry and Agriculture

	Industry	Agriculture (computed on basis of average yearly employment in socialist sector)	
	1985	1985	1981–1985 average
	(1970 = 100)	(1970 = 100)	(1976–1980 average = 100)
Uzbek SSR	150	102	93
Kirghiz SSR	170	99	94
Tadzhik SSR	137	106	97
Turkmen SSR	143	98	94
USSR	182	141	108

Source: Narodnoe khoziaistvo SSSR v 1985 g., pp. 113 and
316–317.

between industrial and agricultural wages, while varying
widely, diminished significantly in all Central Asian
republics, except Turkmenia. (In the latter the surge of
pipeline construction, gas production, and transport to
the RSFSR caused industrial wages to climb unusually fast
during the 1970s.) For the region as a whole, as for two
of its individual republics, the average wage gap between
agriculture and industry in 1980 was notably smaller than
in the entire country, or for the Russian republic and the
Ukraine.[51]

At any rate, the pay-scale disadvantage in agriculture
compared to industry was a mere 8.4 percent in Uzbekistan,
which accounts for about three-fifths of all farms in
Central Asia. The moderate extent of the wage gap between
the two sectors is all the more significant because the
region is also the beneficiary of an industrial wage
coefficient for 15 to 20 percent above the basic rate that
applies in the middle and southern zones of the European
USSR. This coefficient may be the historic legacy of past
needs to attract skilled Slavic migrants to the area rather

than a welfare measure.[52] Its effect, however, is again to raise living standards <u>inside</u> Central Asia in comparison to the outside, but it is not enough to spur greatly the migration of the native rural population to the cities. As will be shown, the relatively modest wage difference between agriculture and industry is more than counterbalanced by revenues from the private plot.

The rapid increase of wages in the agricultural sector of Central Asia, based largely on rising procurement prices for the region's agricultural products, explain the continued improvement in income from collective and state farm work. The increase in farm wages, in fact, have been way out of line with productivity growth, much more so than elsewhere in the USSR. From 1970 through 1982, labor productivity in Soviet agriculture as a whole improved by 28 percent but wages received per worker rose by 70 percent. In Uzbekistan, on the other hand, labor productivity improved by a mere 4 percent, while wages received rose by 45 percent. On Uzbek state farms, which today hold 62 percent of all arable land and almost half of all farm employment, productivity has, in fact, declined sharply in recent years.[53] (Table 5.9). The experience in the Kirghiz SSR was even more glaring. While, during the 1970s, each one percent increase of labor productivity in the republic's economy as a whole corresponded to a 1.2 percent rise in wages and salaries, in the agricultural sector it was matched by a staggering 8.7 percent wage improvement.[54] In the Eleventh FYP (1981-1985), labor productivity in Kirghiz agriculture fell by 5.5 percent.[55]

In recent works, Soviet demographic experts have cited the relatively high procurement prices for the region's agricultural products as one factor impeding outmigration from the Central Asian countryside. In view of that acknowledged link, the sharp new increase in the procurement price of cotton introduced in 1983 would suggest, in the words of a Western authority, that "however favorably the authorities look on outmigration, they are chary of antagonizing the Central Asians by allowing poverty and need to drive them out of rural areas." The new prices are expected to raise the profitability of the farms by as much as 77 percent, which should permit the rise of per capita income for the agricultural labor force at previous rates for perhaps the better part of another decade.[56]

In addition to socialized farming, private agriculture provides very substantial additional income to rural families, even when only legitimate activities are considered. Unfortunately, systematic regional data about the

TABLE 5.9 Growth of Wages, Labor Productivity, and Capitalization in Uzbek Agriculture, 1965–1983 (rubles per agricultural worker)

	1965	1970	1975	1980	1983
State Farms					
Wages and salaries	817.2	1,183.2	1,450.1	1,833.6	1,854.0
Labor productivity	2,162.8	2,610.0	2,835.2	3,013.3	2,670.2
Capitalization of labor (fondovooruzhennost')	2,274.4	4,220.8	5,811.2	6,712.7	7,546.3
Collective Farms					
Wages and salaries	844.9	1,104.0	1,156.8	1,560.0	1,624.8
Labor productivity	2,211.5	2,427.6	2,375.5	2,659.8	2,570.1
Capitalization of labor (fondovooruzhennost')	970.2	1,324.3	1,828.7	2,416.6	2,592.1

Source: I.B. Blinder, ed., Razvitie material'no-tekhnicheskoi bazy sel'skogo khoziaistva Uzbekistana (Tashkent: Fan, 1985), p. 123.

contribution of the private plot to farm income is unavailable. In the country as a whole, it amounted to 55.5 percent of the income earned by a collective farm (kholkhoz) family from the socialized sector in 1984, a share which has not varied much during the past decade.[57] However, Western research has shown that official figures for sales in urban kolkhoz markets and, consequently, income from urban sales of foodstuffs produced on the private plot through the USSR are grossly understated.[58] In the southern republics, among them those of Central Asia, the role of private agriculture in farmers' supplies and revenues is much higher than the Soviet average. In the Uzbek SSR, for example, the private plot in 1980 (with 4 percent of the arable land) produced almost half of all vegetables, over half of all melons, and 62 percent of all fruits. Fifty-four percent of all cattle and, more important, 68.5 percent of all cows were also kept privately, and the contribution of these plots to milk and meat output reached 61 and 45 percent respectively.[59]

Data from the Kirghiz SSR attest to the lucrative nature of private subsidiary agriculture in Central Asia. From 1969 through 1978, average labor productivity per unit of gross output on Kirghiz private plots amounted to two-thirds of that in socialized agriculture, when weighted by the higher prices for its products. Per value added, it rose to 94 percent of that prevailing in the socialized sector because of the lower material intensity of private agriculture. Finally, and most relevant for the topic at hand, personal income per unit of labor input on the private plot exceeded that derived from work on the collective farm by 48 percent, since in private agriculture all value added remained with the farmer.[60] A thriving network of farm markets is responsible for a substantial part of all food sales in the region--12 percent in Uzbekistan with its 464 markets, where during the 1970s the volume sold was expanding at an 8.1 percent annual rate, 2.3 times as fast as in government stores.[61] An important sociological study conducted recently also came to the conclusion that rural incomes in Central Asia are in fact higher than urban ones.[62]

Legal activities, however, do not exhaust opportunities to earn income in Central Asia. Nancy Lubin convincingly argues that semilegal and illegal enterprise seem to flourish more in this region than anywhere else in the country apart from Trans-Caucasia. She quotes an Uzbek source that lists "over eighty distinct methods of embezzling finances from industrial enterprises alone," with certain sectors providing greater opportunities than others. "Embezzlement and plundering in Uzbekistan are most prevalent in the cotton-cleaning industry, construction, government, trade and agriculture . . ., in the light and food industries and among . . . Party personnel." The bribes paid to facilitate entry to specific jobs and occupations correlate closely with opportunities for illegal income on the side. Indeed, the unpopularity of many types of industrial jobs with the native population (a theme that Lubin documents and analyzes at length) is largely related to the lack of opportunities for such gains. "Several heavy industrial enterprises in Uzbekistan (and elsewhere in the USSR) have earned the nickname nevynosimye," meaning unbearable or intolerable but also non-portable "because nothing can be carried out for resale or for additional profit elsewhere."[63]

Recent Soviet literature confirms the prevalence of embezzlement, pilfering, and the importance of illegal income. One such practice, detailed in a late-1985 article, concerns the collusion between regional feedlot centers and supplying farms in a systematic underreporting of the liveweight of animals and the falsification in the distribution of their weight categories. At one center in Kirghizia, the article reports extensive weight falsification for almost 60,000 small-horned cattle in the course of only four months. The weights of almost 2,200 hogs and untold numbers of large cattle were similarly misreported, with the practice continuing undetected for three years.[64] In Uzbekistan, the quantities of surplus vegetables and fruits sold by individuals to the state range from 72 to almost 100 percent of all state purchases. These shares far exceed aggregate production from private plots, proving that much, and sometimes most, of this produce is diverted from the socialist sector. The spontaneously developed and widely varying institution of gektarshchina (ranging from legitimate cultivation of small plots by individuals under lease and sundry contract work through grey and black market activities under a facade of authorized agreement with the collective farm) provides ample opportunities for such diversion. The institution itself is a highly controversial grey legal area: the chief of the agro-industrial complex at the Uzbek Gosplan estimates that two-thirds of all gektarshchiki, those working under that system, operate outside the law.[65]

When too blatant or extravagant, illegal activities do bring retribution. However, the attention that the extraordinary plenum of the Uzbek Communist Party Central

Committee (held in June 1984) devoted to the problem of corruption and embezzlement and the scale of the many examples cited suggest the magnitude of illegal earnings in Central Asia.[66] The recent unprecedented 12 percent decline in the volume of cotton deliveries in Uzbekistan (most of the decrease taking place between 1983 and 1984) may, in fact, indicate more accurate or honest accounting after years of reported gross padding at all levels of the cotton-growing and cotton-ginning complex.[67]

As the foregoing sections show, active welfare measures and passive arrangements, such as an even greater tolerance of the "second economy" than would be the case in the Slavic republics, have both been instrumental in providing a cushion against declining living standards, at least up until now. Yet in the longer term, these will not be adequate by themselves to cope with the rapid growth of population and labor force and the built-in demographic momentum. In addition, they probably will be much more closely controlled now under the Gorbachev leadership, judging from the harsh tone of the Soviet press with respect to widespread sub-rosa activities in Central Asia. Vigorous measures aimed at job creation and increasing employment outside the agricultural sector would thus appear imperative. An expansion of labor-intensive industries in the region has long been officially advocated. Central Asian scholars and Party functionaries have also lobbied energetically for a shift of emphasis from large integrated mills towards a greater number of small specialized plants in light industries, where labor intensity per unit value of fixed assets is the highest (Table 5.10). Dispersed, specialized plants are also advocated for the food industries and for some other branches.[68] To bring greater local influence over plant location and management, there is even an argument for transferring those enterprises which process Central Asian agricultural and mineral resources from the tutelage of Union ministries to republican and even local control.[69] Some scholars from the region also argue that the participation of their republics in the national planning process should be enhanced and their decision-making power over questions of territorial significance increased.[70]

Such pressure, particularly from the vocal and comparatively numerous Uzbek elite, may help to explain the relative progress of branch plant location in that republic in contrast to the weaker ones. During the Tenth FYP (1976-1980), 290 branch plants and shops were created in small towns and settlements of Uzbekistan, permitting the

144

TABLE 5.10   Employment per One Million Rubles of
Fixed Capital in Different Branches of Uzbek
Industry (about 1980)

Industrial Branches	Employment
Footwear	1,421
Sewn garments	1,182
Metal articles	648
Knitted garments	566
Textiles	458
Furniture	434
Instruments	345
Confectionary	290
Machine building	271
Electrotechnical	267
Conserves	226
Food industries not elsewhere noted	221
Building materials	120
Chemicals	40

Source: R.I. Khakimov, Effektivnost' sovershenstvovaniia proportsii promyshlennosti v soiuznoi respublike
(Tashkent: Uzbekistan, 1982), p. 119.

employment of almost 30,000 persons. A very ambitious plan
called for an additional 400 such plants with 130,000 new
jobs during the first half of the 1980s.[71]   Large
enterprises (most under central Union ministries) in major
urban centers of the republic are being pressed by Uzbek
Party officials to create filials (branch plants) in small
towns of overpopulated oases with overwhelming native
majorities.   However, even Central Asian specialists differ
on the extent to which such industrialization should
concentrate on the traditional cotton, wool, and food-
processing branches or be extended to more modern
industries.   They also disagree on the degree to which that
rural processing of raw materials can soak up surplus labor
on the farms.[72]
     Despite very significant industrial progress in
Central Asia, however, the efforts at job creation appear
modest when compared to the expansion of the labor force.
Today, out of every 100 new jobs in the USSR still only six
to seven are created in Central Asia.[73] Equally serious,

resistance to rural and small town location on the part of the Union ministries remains strong. They continue to prefer the large cities, while settlements under 50,000, which in Central Asia account for two-thirds of the growth of manpower, received only 30 percent of capital investment during the Tenth FYP (1976-1980).[74] In 1980, the city of Tashkent alone, with less than 12 percent of the republic's population, concentrated over 28 percent of all industrial employment in the Uzbek SSR and 18.4 percent of industrial fixed assets. Tashkent city and Oblast combined accounted for 45.6 percent of industrial employment and an almost identical share of fixed capital. If one adds the relatively developed Fergana Oblast, these three administrative units, with somewhat over a third of Uzbekistan's human resources, represented almost three-fifths of that republic's total industry (Table 5.11). Although some relative dispersion of manufacturing from the Tashkent node is undeniable, that city and oblast reduced its contribution to the industrial labor force by only 9 percentage points from 1965 through 1980.

In several branches of light industry, plant size is too large to benefit rural and small town inhabitants living in widely separated oases. Half of all footwear in the Uzbek SSR is produced by one factory in Kokand; almost three-fifths of knitted undergarments by another in Andizhan. Five large works account for 95 percent of all output of the republic's silk industry. About the only branch of the light industry well dispersed among farms and villages is cotton drying, cleaning, and ginning. Besides 120 large plants in 1980, Uzbekistan also counted 419 shops and 517 preparation points for the first-stage processing of the crop.[75]

In contrast to light industry, the food industry producing for the local population tends to be much more dispersed. It also tends to be under republic and local control to a far greater degree than any other industry (Table 5.12). Oil mills using mostly cotton seed and the manufacturing of preserves form the major exception. Here plant size is large, the technology more modern, and Union ministry control prevalent. Product specialization also seems excessive, given the need for small-scale, scattered shops producing for local use and given the nature of the labor force. About 60 percent of all preserves produced in Uzbekistan consist of tomato products.[76]

Besides a more radical move towards small plants and greater geographic dispersion, successful rural industrial-ization would require greater adjustment to the rhythm of

TABLE 5.11 Geographic Distribution of Population and Industry in the Uzbek SSR, 1965 and 1980 (in percent of total)

Republics and Oblasts	1965				1980			
	Population	Employment[a]	Industry Value of Fixed Assets	Value of Gross Output	Population	Employment[a]	Industry Value of Fixed Assets	Value of Gross Output
Uzbek SSR	100.0	100.0	100.0	100.0	100.0	100.0	100.0	100.0
Tashkent (city)	10.6	36.6	20.0	18.4	11.6	28.2	18.4	21.7
Tashkent Oblast	13.7	18.0	35.8	18.0	11.6	17.4	26.7	18.2
Syr Daria Oblast	2.8	1.4	1.2	2.1	2.9	2.2	4.0	3.0
Dzhizak Oblast	2.6	1.0	0.9	0.8	3.3	1.8	1.5	1.8
Fergana Oblast	14.0	14.5	13.5	16.2	11.0	12.6	11.1	12.8
Andizhan Oblast	9.5	5.0	6.3	8.0	8.8	6.5	4.6	5.5
Namangan Oblast	6.8	3.5	2.3	5.3	7.1	5.9	3.3	5.4
Samarkand Oblast	12.4	8.0	5.9	10.0	11.6	8.2	6.6	9.5
Kashkadar'ia Oblast	6.4	1.5	1.3	2.8	7.3	3.4	6.6	4.9
Bukhara Oblast	7.4	4.2	6.7	8.0	8.2	5.8	10.0	7.8
Khorezm Oblast	4.6	1.5	1.2	3.2	4.8	2.6	2.0	2.9
Surkhandar'ia Oblast	5.4	1.8	2.5	3.7	5.8	2.4	2.4	3.4
Karakalpak ASSR	5.8	3.0	2.4	3.5	5.9	3.0	2.8	3.1

[a]Industrial production personnel.

Source: R.I. Khakimov, Effektivnost' sovershenstvovaniia proportsii promyshlennosti v soiuznoi respublike (Tashkent: Uzbekistan, 1982), pp. 144-145.

village life and local cultural factors. Night-shift work, in particular, has little chance for attracting the indigenous population, especially women. Other adaptations to ethnic habits, family requirements, and climatic conditions would also be necessary. Contracted piece work inside the home (cf., "putting-out system" in the early days of the Industrial Revolution), for example, holds much greater attraction than factory labor to most women with families in Central Asia. Yet, at present, only about 16,000 women work on that system in the whole of Central Asia.[77] Iu. Bromlei and O. Shkaratan also pointed out the importance of the long noon siesta among the autochthonous nationalities in response to the summer heat. Conflicting goals and criteria concerning locational efficiency and economic benefits between central planning organs, on the one hand, and local or regional ones, on the other, are all but inevitable.[78]

The lack of enthusiasm by central ministries for Central Asian locations and, still more, a decentralized, dispersed strategy of industrialization is not surprising in light of their own management and organizational structure. Distressingly low labor productivity in these republics, and especially in the countryside, is another obvious factor. Finally, the very inadequate development of construction organizations and trusts outside the principal cities of Central Asia must be counted as a very significant disincentive for Union ministries. The lack of construction organizations through the Central Asian countryside result in much longer delays and higher capital costs to central planners of almost any project than elsewhere in the USSR, aside from the Siberian Northland.[79]

When plan fulfillment is in danger, enterprises routinely hire extra labor. This may be welcomed by Central Asian planners concerned about the burgeoning manpower pool, but it further depresses productivity indices for industry located in the region and raises the wage bill. Nor does serious underfulfillment of plans for productivity growth carry any penalty through reduction of the wages paid out. In Uzbek industry as a whole, labor productivity during the five years of the 1976-1980 Plan grew only 2.2 percent overall, while wages and salaries increased by almost 10 percent. In fact, in a number of ministries, such as those of the food industries, heavy machine building, and nonferrous metals, the average wage in the Uzbek SSR has risen, while labor productivity actually declined. During the Tenth FYP (1976-1980), the number of manual workers in that republic rose by more than

148

TABLE 5.12 Branch Distribution of Industrial Output and Employment in Uzbek SSR, 1982 (in percentages)

Industrial Branches	Uzbek SSR		USSR
	Value of Gross Output[a]	Employment	Value of Gross Output[a]
All industry	100.0	100.0	100.0
Electric power	3.7		3.9
Fuel industries	4.6		8.0
Machine building-metal working[b]	15.2	ca. 31	25.4
Of which: repairs[b]	3.5		
Chemical and petro-chemical industries	5.3		6.4
Of which: fertilizers	3.2		
Wood products and cellulose industries	1.7		4.5
Building materials industry	6.0		3.8
Light industries	39.2	ca. 30	15.7
(1) cottonginning	20.0	13.2	
(2) textiles, apparels footwear	16.7	ca. 16	
Food industries[c]	17.8		18.8
(1) state and republic jurisdiction	ca. 6[d]		
(2) local	ca. 12[d]		
Non-ferrous and ferrous metallurgy and other minor branches	6.5[e]		14.1[e]

149

[a]Value of output in current prices.
[b]1980 share of repair applied to the 1982 data. Percentage of repair from R.I. Khakimov, Effektivnost' sovershenstvovaniia proportsii promyshlennosti v soiuznoi respublike (Tashkent: Uzbekistan, 1982), p. 141.

[c]Includes grain milling and the production of complex animal feed.
[d]Rough estimate from statement of Ziiadullaev, pp. 169-170, that vegetable and animal fat and oil producing branches are one of the most technically advanced of the food industries and therefore account for over half of the state controlled food industries in that republic, i.e., republic jurisdiction or higher. Large-scale milling was also assumed to be under republic or Union jurisdiction. The breakdown of different branches of the food industry in Uzbekistan is given on page 169.

[e]Estimated as a residual. In Uzbekistan, the great bulk of that share is composed of nonferrous metallurgy. In the USSR as a whole, ferrous and nonferrous metallurgy contribute to gross value of output in roughly equal proportions.

Source: S.K. Ziiadullaev, Industriia Sovetskogo Uzbekistana (Tashkent: Uzbekistan, 1984), pp. 114-115, 139, 148, 159, 162 and 169-170.

31,000 and in a number of industries (textiles, machine
building, and metal working, for example) even their
relative share increased. The proportion of manual
laborers in Uzbek machine building reached 54 percent in
1980 and in the textile industry almost a full half.[80]

EDUCATION AND TECHNICAL TRAINING

The achievements of the Soviet regime in uplifting the
education level of Central Asian nationalities is indisput-
able and deserves the highest praise, whatever motive one
may ascribe to that effort. Moreover, as Vernon Aspaturian
has noted, "even in the most benevolent colonial empires,
educational opportunities were available almost exclusively
in the ruling language . . . and usually without a serious
concurrent effort to promote literacy and learning in the
indigenous languages." The Soviet leadership, on the other
hand, "chose the more complicated and expensive, but less
painful, way of promoting literacy through the medium of
the local language, and using that as a base from which to
switch to Russian."[81] While in 1926, literacy even for
young males of most Asian nationalities was very limited
(under 25 percent among the 15 to 34 age group versus 85
percent for Russian males of similar age).[82] By 1979, over
91 percent of Uzbeks of both sexes ten years or older, for
example, received at least primary schooling. Most of
those who did not were no doubt over sixty years of age, a
group that composed 7.2 percent of the Uzbek population and
one-tenth of those that passed their tenth birthdays.[83]
Similar ratios most probably prevail elsewhere in Central
Asia. It is also significant that, while the quality of
instruction may be somewhat lower than in more developed
regions, student-teacher ratios in the mid-1970s were only
marginally higher than in the Slavic republics and the
qualifications of the teaching staff, at least on paper,
were comparable.[81]
    Since the early or mid-1970s, however, the burgeoning
population growth and increasing capital constraints have
been threatening these impressive gains. By 1980, in
comparison to 1970, all Central Asian nationalities (and
most other Muslim groups as well) had lost ground relative
to Russians, other Slavs, and Balts in student enrollment.
That relative slippage was true for both specialized
secondary and higher education. This is not to deny
continued rapid growth in enrollment in Central Asia at a
rate well exceeding that in the European republics. Ellen

Jones and Fred Grupp have noted, however, that "in order to maintain the 1960 momentum in convergence in higher educa- tion and specialized secondary enrollment, the Soviet authorities would have had to phase out ongoing education programs in the European USSR and transfer a large portion of existing resources from this area to the Muslim southern tier". As it is, the number of Uzbek VUZ (higher educa- tional institute) students rose by 32 percent during the 1970s against only 11 percent for their Russian counter- parts but "the Uzbek enrollment score relative to the Russian decreased nearly 30 points from 96 to 69. Few school systems would find it easy to adjust immediately to such rapid shifts in 'client' population."[85] It is therefore not surprising that in Central Asia as a whole the share of physical workers declined by only one per- centage point (from 76.6 percent to 75.6 percent) during the 1970s. In the Turkmen SSR the share even rose slightly, while in the Tadzhik SSR it remained unchanged.[86] The proportion of intelligentsiia (apparently those with higher education working in professional jobs) among ethnic Turkmens and Tadzhiks stayed even at a low 13.5 and 12 percent respectively throughout the decade and only among the Kirghiz was a really substantial relative increase registered.[87]

This relative (though clearly not absolute) backslide bodes ill for increasing labor productivity, social mobility, and significant outmigration from the countryside even in the medium term. Although the desire among rural youths to raise their qualification apparently exists (with some two-thirds registering such a wish according to a sociological survey), lack of opportunities prevent such an upgrading of skills for the majority. Not unexpectedly, most stay put: over 60 percent of the graduates from rural schools stay in the village and go to work in agricul- ture.[88] Although the stage of economic development would probably call for a higher proportion of students in technical schools than in VUZy (plural of VUZ), the oppo- site is in fact the case. The number of students attending VUZy in Central Asia, as a whole, surpassed those in middle technical schools by almost 11 percent in the period 1984- 1985. In the Tadzhik SSR, the former exceeded the latter by some 44 percent.[89] The unavailability of technical- vocational training in many heavily rural districts is, therefore, a serious problem. At the end of 1982, only sixteen of Tadzhikistan's forty-one districts had any such schools.[90]

Perhaps more serious is the still very modest

proportion of women receiving vocational-technical training, with the Tadzhik republic again standing out with a
particularly low share. Here girls composed a mere 15
percent of all pupils admitted to vocational-technical
schools in 1985. Most females who do go to factories have
no skills and will thus have to be employed in low-paying,
unpleasant jobs.[91] An Uzbek woman writer complains about
the heavy, unhealthy work females are engaged in her
republic's industry. (Half of the employees of Uzbekistan's foundries are women, as are half of the workers at
brick plants, undoubtedly a large portion of these being
Slavs and other Europeans).[92] Not surprisingly, few rural
indigenous women find such an alternative to village life,
agricultural work, and domesticity particularly appealing.
A sociological survey conducted through the Uzbek countryside revealed that over nine-tenths of them are satisfied
with their lot. The average level of satisfaction
reportedly reached as high as 2.4 on a three point scale.[93]

KORENIZATSIIA (NATIVIZATION) AND SOCIO-ECONOMIC INTEGRATION

Western observers agree that the rapid growth of population and the labor force, combined with Moscow's own
stress on education had already resulted in major changes
in the relationship of indigenous and European communities
in Central Asia. The process of korenizatsiia (nativiza-
tion) of local and regional institutions, power structure,
and economic life is well under way. In the economic
sphere, this korenizatsiia is no doubt spurred by the
increasing pressure of manpower resources elsewhere in the
USSR, contributing to the cessation of net immigration from
the Slavic republics. Slavic cadres, indispensable in the
early stages of modernization, may still be more productive
than their indigenous counterparts. However, their
marginal productivity in labor-short regions of Siberia and
the European USSR today is almost certain to be higher than.
in Central Asia. In fact, a Russian reemigration may now
be emerging, spurred by the more assertive, nationalistic
attitude of the indigenous population and "a growing
psychological discomfort on the part of the Europeans."[94]
Outmigration of European nationalities from Kazakhstan
averaged 52,000 per year during 1979-1984 already, rising
to roughly 90,000 in 1986. However, much of that outmigration probably represents rural flight from the Virgin
Land provinces, rather than a response to ethnic conflicts.
Still, even the Kazakhs, long a minority in their republic,

have now overtaken the Russians there in sheer numbers.[95]

Western experts indeed report "that a type of 'affirmative action' has been implemented to meet quotas generally in favor of the indigenous nationalities. . . . Should an enterprise manager hire too many Russians, in fact, he will risk accountability for actions contrary to the spirit of Soviet cadre policy and may suffer unpleasant consequences. . . . Over the past several years, this type of 'implicit' affirmative action has slowly become a well-entrenched and often explicitly stated part of official Soviet policy."[96] These experts also note that in Uzbekistan, but also in Turkmenia, the management of enterprises even in industries subordinated to Union ministries are being entrusted increasingly to indigenous personnel.[97]

For the crucial leading Party positions the situation is also evolving. In his latest study of district Party officials in Uzbekistan, Michael Rywkin reports a significant, though regionally varying, increase in native control since the early 1980s. In the 1983–1984 period, almost three-fifths of Uzbek districts (raions) had Muslims in the position of first, second, and third secretaries. Nonetheless, second secretaries often are still Slavs and tend to be much more important persons than their counterparts in the RSFSR, Belorussia, and the Ukraine. Yet, unlike in the Stalin era, the second secretary today is clearly a junior partner besides the Uzbek first secretary, but one with much power "to intervene in case of nationalistic deviation or gross economic shortcomings." Other instruments of central control, or at least oversight, also exist and will no doubt remain. In 1980, the heads of the Department of Organizational Work (responsible for checking compliance with Party directives and selecting cadres for lower Party organs) were nonnatives in all Central Asian republics. Leadership of the "Special Section" (KGB liasons) and the military and defense apparatus remains and will continue to remain in Slavic hands.[98] In addition, Moscow will continue to guard against the threat of Central Asian regionalism by limiting the interaction of the native officials across republic boundaries. Elite mobility and transfer among these republics from the <u>nomenklatura</u> (Party appointments list for individuals eligible for important Party and government positions) is strikingly low and most probably will remain so.[99] Yet Rywkin sees further changes favoring the indigenous Party elite as inevitable. Russian Party officials will, of course, stay in key positions but not "as planted obstacles to local self-government, but rather as guardians of federal links and protectors of local European minorities."[100]

Whether Gorbachev's anticorruption campaign will slow the trend in the reduction of the political role of Russian cadres in Central Asia remains to be seen. Recent articles on shortcomings in Central Asia and Kazakhstan are marked by a particularly severe tone. While localism and mutual protection circles have been criticized in the past, the harsh language of these recent articles is noteworthy--especially in view of the 1984 massive purge that had already shake up the Uzbek Party apparatus. Two recent exposes, for example, excoriate the Mafia-like network throughout the Bukhara Party organization and judicial apparatus and the pervasive nepotism in Uzbekistan. Half of the members of Dzhizak Oblast's central Party apparatus are claimed in one source to be each other's relatives.[101] Still another recent disclosure about irregularities and illegal conduct pervading the Kazakh Ministry of Geology appears equally harsh.[102] Gorbachev may also be less willing to accept the same degree of cultural assertiveness, the attempts to rehabilitate much of the region's traditional heritage, and the tolerant attitude to Islam that was allowed to develop under his predecessors. In late 1986, the replacement of Dinmukhammed Kunaev, the first party secretary of Kazakhstan, by a native Russian sparked disturbances in Alma-Ata. In his November 24, 1986 Tashkent speech, Gorbachev called for a decisive and uncompromising struggle against religious manifestations and lashed out at indulgent Party cadres who themselves participate in such practices.[103] At the 1986 session of the Kirghiz Communist Party, First Secretary Masaliev also assailed the influence of Islamic preachers on women, children, leadership cadres, and the Young Communist League. He attacked religious ceremonies, the attempts by the "class enemy" to revive national-religious sentiments, the widespread bribery and the plunder of socialist property.[104] More recently, _Pravda_ excoriated the Kazakh press for neglecting "international education," and for proposing more Kazakh language schools in Alma-Ata and the Virgin Land provinces (where Russians have majorities). A Kazakh demographer was criticized for pointing out, with apparent gratification, that the Kazakhs in their republic now equal the Russians in number and will soon be the dominant nationality.[105]

As this chapter has shown, the disruptive potential of rapid population growth and growing ethnic assertiveness in Central Asia to date has been checked by both passive and active policies pursued on the national, as well as local, levels. Income maintenance through substantial transfer payments, the toleration of a vigorous private economy, both legal and sub-rosa, and more modest achievements in job creation with grossly suboptimal labor use suggest a sofar successful balancing act on the part of the authorities. At the same time, the process of <u>korenizatsiia</u>, giving much greater elbow room for the indigenous elite and increasing opportunities to run local affairs, have promoted stability up until now.

Yet, as a perceptive observer has noted, the same set of factors that work for political stability will also encourage restiveness, at least in the longer run. "The indigenous nationalities [today] do not regard themselves as a deprived social class in Central Asia, but rather as economically and culturally superior to the Slavs in their midst. They have not been excluded from the modern 'Russian World' as much as they have resisted Soviet efforts to integrate them into that world."[106] Even interethnic sexual conduct reflects this assertiveness on the part of the indigenous nationalities, according to an émigré source. Intermarriage between Central Asians and "Europeans" in any combination is extremely rare (a fact confirmed in Soviet sources), is sharply resented, and almost never happens with the female partner being from an autochthonous nationality. At the same time, sexual liaisons between Uzbek males and working class Slavic women are widespread. These liaisons rarely lead to marriage and carry strong overtones of ethnic retaliation and dominance.[107]

Only time will tell how serious an impact the growing capital constraint will have on stability and relations with the metropolis in the coming years. For at least a decade and perhaps longer, the resources Moscow can spare for the development of Central Asia simply cannot expand at a rate to keep up with the population increase. In the first half of the 1970s, for example, the four Central Asian republics still managed to obtain 2.5 times more investment than Tiumen' and Tomsk Oblasts, though the exploitation of oil and gas resources in the West Siberian North was already underway. By contrast, in the first half of the 1980s, the two regions received roughly equal volumes of capital, and the new Twelfth FYP (1986-1990) allocates some 25 percent more to the two West Siberian provinces than to Central Asia with nine times more population.[108] Nor will structural, institutional, and functional constraints in the Politburo, combined with a rising tide of Great Russian nationalism, permit a significant shift in the regional allocation of investment more in favor of Central Asia in the near future. Such a shift would not provide the Russian-dominated leadership either the immediate economic or the ethno-cultural and emotional rewards that emphasis on the country's Slavic territory can produce. Both the pro-European and pro-Siberian lobbies in the planning and Party hierarchy and even the non-Russian nationalities west of the Urals should find themselves in agreement on that point.

As Nancy Lubin has written: "In Soviet Central Asia, economic and social change is occurring, accompanied by the same frustration, questioning and dissatisfaction which has accompanied similar changes and upheavals in other areas of the world. . . . Pressures are growing [and] a lot of adjustments will soon have to be made in Soviet society at large." Yet the extent to which this society can make major adjustments in a period of growing resource constraints remains an open question. At the moment, in Lubin's opinion, "a balance appears to have been established, where competing currents will seemingly neutralize each other for some years to come."[109] It is a delicate balance, however, not reinforced by the patriotism and emotional loyalty to a Fatherland embodied in the Slavic heartland. It could be upset by a sudden surge of a powerful current from the outside. Or it could be upset on the inside, by sharply deteriorating economic conditions and unexpected political developments that threaten the gains of the new modernized native elite.

NOTES

1. Tsentral'noe statisticheskoe upravlenie (TsSU), Itogi vsesoiuznoi perepisi naseleniia 1970 goda, Tom 4 (Moscow: Statistika, 1978), pp. 13-15; TsSU, Chislennost' i sostav naseleniia SSSR (Moscow: Finansy i statistika, 1984), pp. 110-134. The Slavic population of Alma-Ata is not revealed in the 1979 census. It was computed as the difference between the Slavic population in Kazakhstan and the sum of their population in the nineteen oblasts of the republic without the capital, Alma-Ata. In that city, Slavs still composed 72.8 percent of the total in 1979 as compared to 75.1 percent in 1970.

2. TsSU, Chislennost' i sostav, pp. 298-319.

3. Idem.

4. Teresa Rakowska-Harmstone, "The Dialectics of Nationalism in the USSR," Problems of Communism, Vol. 23, No. 3 (May-June), 1974, pp. 10 and 14-15.

5. Michael Kaser, "The Soviet Gold-Mining Industry," in Robert G. Jensen, Theodore Shabad and Arthur W. Wright, eds., Soviet Natural Resources in the World Economy (Chicago, The University of Chicago Press, 1983), p. 559; Theodore Shabad, "News Notes," Soviet Geography, Vol. 27, No. 4 (April), 1986, p. 258 and 262-63 and Ian Matley, "Central Asia and Kazakhstan," in I.S. Koropeckyj and G.E. Schroeder, Economics of Soviet Regions (New York: Praeger, 1981), p. 422.

6. Leslie Dienes and Theodore Shabad, The Soviet Energy System: Resource Use and Policies (Washington, D.C.: Winston and Sons, 1979) pp. 80-84 and N.P. Mun'ko, Ekonomicheskaia effektivnost' vyravnivaniia energopotrebleniia v Srednei Azii (Tashkent: Fan, 1977), p. 54.

7. Narodnoe khoziaistvo SSSR v 1985 godu, p. 210 and U.S. CIA, Handbook of Economic Statistics. 1986 (Washington, D.C.: CPAS 85-10001, September 1986), p. 203.

8. Narodnoe khoziaistvo SSSR v 1975 godu, p. 285.

9. Narodnoe khoziaistvo Uzbekskoi SSR v 1982 godu, (Tashkent: Uzbekistan, 1982), pp. 41 and Narodnoe khoziaistvo SSSR v 1985 godu, pp. 8-9 and Narodnoe khoziaistvo SSSR v 1975 godu, p. 10.

10. Narodnoe khoziaistvo SSSR v 1985 godu, pp. 162-64 and A.K. Koshanov, ed., Vnutriraionnye problemy sotsial'no-ekonomicheskogo razvitiia soiuznoi respubliki (Alma-Ata: Nauka, 1983), p. 97.

11. V.F. Pavlenko, Mezhotraslevye kompleksy Srednei Azii (Moscow: Mysl', 1980), p. 69 and M.A. Abdusaliamov, Problemy ekonomicheskoi integratsii Srednei Azii i Sibiri (Tashkent: Fan, 1982), p. 129.

12. A.K. Zakumbaev, Ekonomicheskoe razvitie soiuznykh respublik i raionov (Alma-Ata: Nauka, 1977), p. 185.

13. K. Popadiuk, Obshchestvennyi produkt i effektivnost' ego proizvodstva v period razvitogo sotsializma (Tashkent: Uzbekistan, 1979), p. 61 and M.S. Mirsaidov, Formirovanie i razvitie promyshlennogo proizvodstva predmetov narodnogo potrebleniia v Uzbekistane (Tashkent: Fan, 1981), pp. 162-163.

14. In Uzbekistan, per capita production of meat increased from 19.3 kg. in 1975 to 22.8 kg. in 1982. Per capita production of confectionery rose from 7.3 to 9.2 kg., of preserves from 38.7 to 44.6 units, while that of vegetable oil actually declined below the 1965 level. On the other hand, the production of milk and eggs, which are

158

much more poorly transportable, and of fruits and vegetables registered significant improvements on a per capita basis. A.U. Ul'masov, "Rost blagosostoianiia truzhenikov Uzbekistana," Obshchestvennye nauki v Uzbekistane, 1984, No. 6, p. 6.
15. K. Popadiuk, "Potreblenie i nakoplenie v sotsialisticheskom obshchestve," Kommunist Uzbekistana, 1985, No. 9 (September), p. 26 and Sovetskaia Kirgiziia, January 24, 1986, pp. 1-2.
16. P.K. Murzoev, Tempy, proportsii i effektivnost' obshchestvennogo proizvodstva v Tadzhikskoi SSR (Dushanbe: Donish, 1983), p. 66.
17. V.V. Kotilko, Proizvodstvennaia infrastruktura (Moscow: Nauka, 1986), pp. 21 and 38-41.
18. M. Abdusaliamov, "Mezhraionnye aspekty dolgosrochnogo razvitiia Uzbekistana," Obshchestvennye nauki v Uzbekistane, 1981, No. 1, . 77.
19. S.K. Ziiadullaev, "Sredniaia Aziia: sovremennoe industrial'no-agrarnoe khoziaistvo," Ekonomika i organizatsiia promyshlennogo proizvodstva (EKO), 1982, No. 12, p. 86.
20. A most up-to-date, excellent treatment of the issue is found in the two-part study by Marie-Agnès Crosnier, Michèle Kahn, Part I and Hervé Gicquiau, Part II, "Développement et dépendances économique de l'Asie Centrale soviétique," Le Courrier des pays de l'Est, 1983, No. 276 (September), pp. 3-58 and 1983, No. 277 (October), pp. 3-34.
21. See, inter alia, Popadiuk, Obshcheshestvennyi produkt; R.A. Ubaidulaeva, ed., Sotsial'no-ekonomicheskie problemy ispol'zovaniia truda molodezhi v Uzbekistane (Tashkent: Fan, 1982); R.I. Khakimov, Effektivnost' sovershenstvovaniia promyshlennosti v soiuznoi respublike (Tashkent: Uzbekistan, 1982); R.A. Ubaidullaeva, ed., Regional'nyi aspekt osushchestvleniia ekonomicheskikh zakonov v usloviiakh razvitogo sotsializma (Tashkent: Fan, 1984); M.I. Murakaev, Trudovye resursy Uzbekistana (Tashkent: Uzbekistan, 1983); R. A. Ubaidullaeva, ed., Intensifikatsiia obshchestvennogo proizvodstva v Uzbekskoi SSR (Tashkent: Fan, 1984); V.V. Bushman, Prognozirovanie razvitiia i razmeshcheniia sel'skogo khoziaistva Kirgizskoi SSR (Frunze: Ilim, 1982), p. 124; A. Ismanov, Ispol'zovanie trudovykh resursov v sel'skom khoziaistve Kirgizii (Frunze: Ilim, 1983); Murzoev, Tempy, proportsii i effektivnost', pp. 176-177; E.P. Chernova, Narodonaselenie Kirgizskoi SSR v usloviiakh razvitogo sotsializma (Frunze: Kyrgyzstan, 1984) and P.K. Savchenko and A.R. Khodzhaev, Toplivno-

energeticheskii kompleks Sredneaziatskogo ekonomicheskogo
raiona (Tashkent: Uzbekistan, 1974), pp. 176-177; K.M. Kim,
Sovershenstvovanie struktury toplivno-energeticheskogo
balansa Srednei Azii (Tashkent: Fan, 1973), pp. 197-198,
and 208-209; and L.A. Melent'ev and A.A. Makarov, eds.,
Energeticheskii kompleks SSSR (Moscow: Ekonomika, 1983),
pp. 194-195.
    22. Akademiia nauk Kirgizskoi SSR, Institut ekonomiki,
Ekonomika Kirgizii--sostavnaia chast' narodnokhoziaistven-
nogo kompleksa SSR (Frunze, 1977), p. 88. Quoted in
Gicquiau, "Développement et dépendance," p. 32.
    23. N.N. Nekrasov and A.A. Adamesku, eds., Territo-
rial'no-proizvodstvennye kompleksy SSSR (Moscow: Ekonomika,
1981), pp. 154-166.
    24. Narodnoe khoziaistvo Tadzhikskoi SSR v 1981 godu
(Dushanbe: Irfon, 1983), pp. 166-167 and Nekrasov and
Adamesku, eds., Territorial'no-proizvodstvennye kompleksy,
p. 158.
    25. Nekrasov and Adamesku, eds., Territorial'no-
proizvodstvennye kompleksy, p. 158 and L.L. Rybakovskii and
N.V. Tarasova, "Vzaimodeistvie migratsionnykh i etnicheskikh protsessov," Sotsiologicheskie issledovania, 1982,
No. 4 (October-December), p. 31.
    26. R. Murtazina, "Trudovaia aktivnost' naseleniia,"
in Narodonaselenie, No. 47, pp. 50-54. Quoted in
Referativnyi zhurnal. Geografiia, 1985, No. 8, E194.
    27. TsSU, Itogi vsesoiuznoi perepisi, Tom. 2, pp.
28-69 and Godfrey S. Baldwin, Population Projections by Age
and Sex: For the Republics and Major Economic Regions of
the USSR. 1970 to 2000 (Washington, D.C.: U.S. Bureau of
the Census, U.S. Government Printing Office, 1979), p. 128.
Baldwin's projection is for January 1980 and the average
annual growth rate was computed for the 1959-1980 period.
    28. Employment from TsSU, Chislennost' i sostav, pp.
146-150. Numbers in the 15- to 60-year age group from
Murray Feshbach, "The Age Structure of Soviet Population:
Preliminary Analysis of Unpublished Data," Soviet Economy,
Vol. 1, No. 2 (April-June), 1985, p. 189.
    29. Radio Moscow, 12:00, January 17, 1987. Quoted in
Ann Sheehy, "Antinatal Policy for Tadzhikistan," Radio
Liberty Research Bulletin, RL56/87, 1987, No. 7 (February
18), p. 4.
    30. Narodnoe khoziaistvo SSSR v 1985 godu, pp. 8-9 and
TsSU, Chislennost' i sostav, pp. 298-319.
    31. Rybakovskii and Tarasova, "Vzaimodeistvie," p. 15.
    32. Z.Kh. Umarova, "K voprosu o povyshenii trudovoi
zaniatosti sel'skogo naseleniia Uzbekistana," in Sredne-

160

aziatskii nauchno-issledovatel'skii institut ekonomiki sel'skogo khoziaistva, Tashkent, Trudy, 1985, No. 27, pp. 139-146.

33. Murzoev, Tempy, proportsii i effektivnost', pp. 176-177 and F. Kaiumov, "Povyshat' proizvoditel'nost' truda v khlopkovodstve," Kommunist Uzbekistana, 1984, No. 9, p. 16.

34. Kaiumov, "Povyshat' proizvoditel'nost'," p. 16; Sel'skaia zhizn, 1985, September 27, p. 2 and Murzoev, Tempy, proportsii i effektivnost', p. 177.

35. Sel'skaia zhizn', 1985, September 27, p. 2.

36. Izvestiia, November 21, 1986, p. 5.

37. The expression "sokhrannost' syr'ia," judging from the context in which it is frequently used, also carries the nuance of preservation from pilfering as well.

38. Bushman, Prognozirovanie razvitiia, p. 127.

39. Ubaidullaeva, ed., Regional'nyi aspekt, p. 68.

40. Anna-Jutta Pietsch and Reinhard Uffhausen, Arbeitskraftepotential und Migrationverhalten in der zentralasiatischen Republiken und Kasachstan (Osteuropa-Institut, Munchen. Working Papers, No. 83, December 1981). Esp. pp. 21-38.

41. Dependents and pensioners formed 46.8 percent of the Central Asian population in 1979. TsSU, Chislennost' i sostav, pp. 146-150. In 1970, those out of working age, the latter defined as 16-59 for men and 16-54 for women, composed 57.2 percent of the region's population. TsSU, Itogi vsesoiuznoi perepisi, Tom. 2, pp. 28-69. Although the 1979 data may refer to a slightly different universe than the 1970 category, the decline in the dependency ratio seems clear. For Uzbekistan, Feshbach reports 48.4 percent of the population in the 0-14 and 60-plus age group in 1979 but 53.9 percent in 1970. Feshbach, "The Age Structure of Soviet Population:" p. 189.

42. D.I. Ziuzin, "Vozmozhnosti razvitiia Srednei Azii," Sotsiologicheskie issledovaniia, 1986, No. 4, pp. 17-25.

43. Robert A. Lewis and Richard Rowland, Population Redistribution in the USSR (New York: Praeger, 1979), pp. 416-417.

44. James W. Gillula, "The Economic Interdependence of Soviet Republics," in U.S. Congress, Joint Economic Committee, Soviet Economy in a Time of Change. Vol 1 (Washington, D.C., U.S. Government Printing Office, 1979), pp. 630-636 and Crosnier and Kahn, "Developpement et dependance," pp. 12-13 and 40.

45. The claim that much of the turnover tax collected

on the product of light industries elsewhere in the USSR
really originates in Central Asian agriculture (which, as
in Soviet agriculture as a whole, bears no turnover tax) is
certainly correct. It is also true that gold, uranium, and
nonferrous metals produced in the region benefit Slavic
areas more than these Moslem republics. On the other hand,
relative to its productivity and in comparison to other
regions, Central Asian farm labor appears overpaid, as
discussed later, and the huge capital cost of irrigation
projects are paid mostly from the All-Union budget.
Therefore, the author's attempt to employ the wage-bill to
apportion national income created among the major sectors
and to prove that the Uzbek SSR, for example, contributes
more to national income created than used, seems ques-
tionable. Z. Salokhiddinov, "Otsenka effektivnosti
kapital'nykh vlozhenii," Ekonomika i zhizn', 1985, No. 10
(October), pp. 15-19.

46. Crosnier and Kahn, "Développement et dépendance,"
pp. 13-16 and Gosudarstvennyi biudzhet SSSR i biudzhet
soiuznykh respublik. 1976-1980 gg. (Moscow: Finansy i
statistika, 1982) and Ekonomicheskaia gazeta, 1985, No. 48
(December), p. 9 and 1986, No. 48 (November), pp. 16-18.
47. Ubaidullaeva, ed., Regional'nyi aspekt, p. 128.
48. Narodnoe khoziaistvo Tadzhikskoi SSR v 1981 godu,
p. 180. The number of families were assumed to have the
same ratio to the total population at the end of 1980 as
recorded at the time of the January 17, 1979 census. TsSU,
Chislennost' i sostav, p. 346 and Narodnoe khoziaistvo
Tadzhikskoi SSR v 1981 godu, pp. 5 and 180.
49. Narodnoe khoziaistvo Uzbekskoi SSR v 1984 godu,
p. 5 and 233; Narodnoe khoziaistvo Tadzhikskoi SSR v 1981
godu, p. 180 and Narodnoe khoziaistvo SSSR v 1984 godu, pp.
14 and 427.
50. Ubaidullaeva, Regional'nyi aspekt, p. 128-131 and
Murzoev, Tempy, proportsii i effektivnost', p. 186.
51. Pietch and Uffhausen, Arbeitskraftepotential, pp.
44-48.
52. Crosnier and Kahn, "Développement et dépendance,"
p. 26.
53. Popadiuk, "Potreblenie i nakoplenie," pp. 26-27;
I.B. Blinder, ed., Razvitie material'no-tekhnicheskoi bazy
sel'skogo khoziaistva Uzbekistana (Tashkent: Fan, 1985),
pp. 88 and 123 and Narodnoe khoziaistvo SSSR v 1985 godu,
pp. 205, 283 and 290.
54. Bushman, Prognozirovanie razvitiia, p. 124. Labor
productivity has become virtually unresponsive to increase
in capitalization. During the 1965-1970 period, each 1

162

percent increase in the capitalization of the Tadzhik agricultural labor force led to a 0.32 percent growth of its productivity. During the 1970-1983 period, each 1 percent growth in the level of capitalization resulted in a mere 0.03 percent growth of productivity. Kh. Umarov, "Trudoizbytochnoe selo: problemy i resheniia," Voprosy ekonomiki, No. 9, 1986, p. 101.

Sovetskaia Kirgiziia, January 24, 1986, pp. 1-2.

56. Ann Sheehy, " Prospects for Early Outmigration of Rural Central Asians Remain Bleak," Radio Liberty Research Bulletin, RL360/83, 1983, September 28, p. 7-8.

57. Narodnoe khoziaistvo SSSR v 1985 godu, p. 419 and various earlier issues.

58. Vladimir Treml, Purchases of Food from Private Sources in Soviet Urban Areas (Berkeley-Duke Occasional Papers on the Second Economy in the USSR, Paper No. 3, September 1985). Treml's paper, part of a large project on the second economy is based on systematic surveys of Soviet emigres. It suggests that "actual sales in urban kolkhoz markets in 1977 were about 6 times higher than reported in official Soviet statistical sources." Citation on p. 12.

59. Z.I. Kalugina and T.P. Antonova, Lichnoe podsobnoe khoziaistvo sel'skogo naseleniia: problemy i perspektivy (Novosibirsk: Nauka, 1984), pp. 45-56.

60. Bushman, Prognozirovanie razvitiia, pp. 78-80.

61. V.K. Zhivaev and I. Ivatov, "Sotsial'no-ekono-micheskaia sushchnost' kolkhozno-rynochnoi torgovli," Obshchestvennye nauki v Uzbekistane, 1981, No. 5, p. 19.

62. D.I. Ziuzin, "Prichiny nizkoi mobil'nosti koren-nogo naseleniia respublik Srednei Azii," Sotsiologicheskie issledovaniia, 1983, No. 1, pp. 111-112.

63. Nancy Lubin, Labor and Nationality in Soviet Central Asia (Princeton: Princeton University Press, 1984), pp. 183-184, 190-195 and page 286, footnote 37.

64. Sel'skaia zhizn', 1985, October 31.

65. "'Gektarshchina': za ili protiv?" Ekonomika i zhizn', 1985, No. 5, pp. 66-77, especially 66-67 and 69-71.

66. Soviet Analyst, Vol 13, No. 16 (August 8), 1985.

67. Narodnoe khoziaistvo SSSR v 1985 godu, p. 210 and Ann Sheehy, "Problems in the Cotton Fields of Uzbekistan," Radio Liberty Research Bulletin, RL149/85, 1985, No. 20 (May 15), pp. 2-3. Some deception may still be taking place, however; Sheehy quotes a report in Pravda, March 15, 1985 which claims that in 1984 some 221,000 hectares shown in farm returns as being sown to fodder crops were in fact sown to cotton.

68. A.A. Asanova, Problemy nauchno-tekhnicheskogo

progressa i povysheniia effektivnosti promyshlennogo proizvodstva (Frunze: Kyrgyzstan, 1981) pp. 111-113 and 116 and Ubaidullaeva, ed., Intensifikatsiia obshchestvennogo proizvodstva v Uzbekskoi SSR (Tashkent: Fan, 1984), pp. 33-34.
69. Pravda, May 5, 1983 and Bushman, Prognozirovanie razvitiia, pp. 129-130.
70. V. Osminin, "Territorial'noe planirovanie na sluzhbu intensifikatsii," Ekonomika i zhizn', 1986, No. 8 (August), pp. 14-17.
71. Khakimov, Effektivnost' sovershenstvovaniia, p. 118 and Ubaidullaeva, Intensifikatsiia obshchestvennogo proizvodstva, p. 33. See also Theodore Shabad, "Some Aspects of Central Asian Manpower and Urbanization," Soviet Geography, Vol. 20, No. 2 (February), 1979, pp. 127-128.
72. Khakimov, Effektivnost' sovershenstvovaniia, pp. 120-122 and Bushman, Prognozirovanie razvitiia, pp. 127-128.
73. G. Kopanev et al., "Segodnia i v budushchem," Ekonomika i zhizn', 1982, No. 2 (February), p. 23.
74. Pravda, June 18, 1984, p. 2 and Kopanev, et al., "Segodnia i v budushchem," pp. 23-24.
75. S.K. Ziiadullaev, Industriia Sovetskogo Uzbekistana (Tashkent: Uzbekistan, 1984), pp. 163, 165-167.
76. Ibid., pp. 170 and 172.
77. S. Ziiadullaev and R. Ubaidullaeva, "Aktual'nye problemy ratsional'nogo ispol'zovaniia trudovykh resursov v trudoobespechennykh regionakh," Planovoe khoziaistvo, 1985, No. 5, p. 103.
78. Iu. Bromlei and O. Shkaratan, "Natsional'nye traditsii v sotsialisticheskoi ekonomike," Voprosy ekonomiki, 1983, No. 4, pp. 40-46.
79. I.I. Iskanderov, ed., Voprosy povysheniia effektivnosti obshchestvennogo proizvodstva v Uzbekistane (Tashkent: Fan, 1982), p. 113; Kopanev et al., "Segodnia i v budushchem," pp. 24-25 and Ekonomika i zhizn', 1980, No. 11, pp. 74-75; and A.Kh. Khikmatov et al., Problemy povysheniia effektivnosti kapital'nykh vlozhenii v Uzbekskoi SSR (Tashkent: Fan, 1978), pp. 111-112.
80. Ubaidullaeva, ed., Intensifikatsiia obshchestvennogo proizvodstva, pp. 120, 123, 125-126 and 130-131.
81. Vernon V. Aspaturian, "The Non-Russian Nationalities," in Allen Kassof, ed., Prospects for Soviet Society (New York: Praeger, 1968), pp. 162 and 164.
82. Ellen Jones and Fred W. Grupp, "Modernization and Ethnic Equalization in the USSR," Soviet Studies, Vol. 26, No. 2 (April), 1984, p. 168.
83. Total population and numbers with primary educa

164

tion from TsSU, Chislennost' i sostav, pp. 7, 24-25. Age group percentages from Feshbach, "The Age Structure of Soviet Population," p. 189.

84. Jones and Grupp, "Modernization and Ethnic Equalization," pp. 166-167.

85. Ibid., pp. 163 and 168-169.

86. TsSU, Chislennost' i sostav, p. 181.

87. Iu.V. Arutiunian, "Natsional'nye osobennosti sotsial'nogo razvitiia," Sotsiologicheskie issledovaniia, 1985, No. 3, p. 29.

88. Ziuzin, "Prichiny nizkoi mobil'nosti," p. 117.

89. Computed from Narodnoe khoziaistvo SSSR v 1984 godu, pp. 8-9 and 524-525.

90. Report by Iu.P. Belov, Second Secretary of the Tadzhik Communist Party Central Committee. Kommunist Tadzhikistana, October 19, 1986, pp. 2-3 and Molodoi kommunist, 1982, No. 9 (September), pp. 62-72.

91. Report by Iu.P. Belov. See footnote 87.

92. Trud, August 1, 1984, p. 2.

93. R.A. Ubaidullaeva, "K probleme povysheniia effektivnosti ispol'zovaniia zhenskogo truda v UzSSR," Obshchestvennye nauki v Uzbekistane, 1980, No. 10, p. 48.

94. Michael Rywkin, "The Impact of Socio-Economic Change and Demographic Growth on National Identity and Socialization," Central Asian Survey, Vol. 3, No. 3, 1984, p. 89.

95. Ann Sheehy, "Do Kazakhs Now Outnumber Russians in Kazakhstan?" Radio Liberty Research Bulletin, RL65/87, 1987, No. 8 (February 25), pp. 1-6.

96. Lubin, Labor and Nationality, pp. 154-170 (citation on pp. 154-155), and Rywkin, "The Impact of Socio-Economic Change," p. 89.

97. Gicquiau, "Développement et dépendance," p. 32 and Lubin, Labor and Nationality, pp. 84-85. Lubin, however, notes that if such an enterprise is part of a strategically important sector of the economy, the deputies of the director--"and often their entire staffs--are almost always non-indigenous."

98. Michael Rywkin, Moscow's Muslim Challenge: Central Asia (New York: M.E. Sharp Inc., 1982), pp. 125-136.

99. John Miller, Nomenklatura: Check on Localism (London: Allan and Unwin Ltd, 1983), pp. 62-97.

100. Rywkin, "The Impact of Socio-Economic Change," pp. 5-7 and 10.

101. Pravda, January 4, 1986, p. 2 and Izvestiia, December 30, 1985, p. 2. For the 1984 purges see Soviet Analyst, Vol. 13, No. 16 (August 8), 1984, pp. 6-8 and Ann

Sheehy, "Major Anti-corruption Drive in Uzbekistan," Radio Liberty Research Bulletin, RL324/84, 1984, No. 36 (September 5), pp. 1-17.

102. E.A. Kozlovskii, "Nakazanie," Literaturnaia gazeta, 1985, December 11, p. 12.

103. Pravda Vostoka, November 25, 1986, p. 1.

104. Sovetskaia Kirgiziia, January 24, 1986, pp. 3-5.

105. Sheehy, "Do Kazakhs Now Outnumber Russians in Kazakhstan?", pp. 1-6 and Pravda, February 11, 1987, p. 2.

106. Lubin, Labor and Nationality, p. 231.

107. Mark Popovsky, Tretii lishnii (London: Overseas Publication Interchange Ltd., 1985), pp. 374-375.

108. Chapter 3; Narodnoe khoziaistvo RSFSR v 1975 godu, p. 329 and Narodnoe khoziaistvo SSSR v 1985 godu, pp. 12-17 and 370. Planned investment for Central Asia in the Twelfth FYP is not yet known. I assumed a planned growth approximating the Soviet average of 18-21 percent (Ekonomicheskaia gazeta, 1985, No. 46 [November], 1985, p. 11), an assumption which may be overly optimistic.

109. Lubin, Labor and Nationality, pp. 241-242.

PART THREE

Population, Settlement, and Regional Planning

6

Population, Employment, and Settlement Policy in Siberia and Kazakhstan

Idite vse, idite na Ural,
My ochishchaem mesto boiu
Stal'nykh mashin, gde dyshit integral,
S mongol'skoi dikoiu ordoiu.
(Go to the Urals, there we clear the place,
Machines of steel herald the coming age.
Against the hordes of a brute alien race
Go ye all, join the struggle we wage.
(<u>Skify.</u> Translation by Leslie Dienes)

So wrote Alexander Blok in 1919. This Russian call to "Go east, young man" is but the most poetic expression of that quasi-mystical belief in the value and potential of the vast eastern reaches echoed throughout Russian history from Radishchev to Solzhenitsyn. This <u>zapasnaia strana</u> (a country in reserve) has also been the bulwark of the Western world "against the hordes of a brute alien [Mongol] race." Yet, despite its mystical lure, the development of Siberia has been frustrated by the permanently operating factor of manpower shortage. The natural increase of the area has never been sufficient to satisfy the required increment to the labor force; economic growth always depended on substantial immigration. From the days of the first Kuznetsk iron and steel plant in the early 1930s to the second Kuznetsk (West Siberian) mill, the Tiumen' oil and gas complexes, and the BAM (Baikal-Amur Mainline), migrants from outside Siberia and the Far East supplied one-third to over half of the manpower for such construction projects.[1]

It is also clear that immigration does not represent long-term or permanent settlement any more than it did during the 1960s, when population mobility exceeded that in

169

the European USSR by two to four times and even more. In
fact, given the increased role of the "tour-of-duty" and
the "expedition" methods of employment, examined in Chapter
7, every sign points to still higher labor turnover and
instability today. The more rapid the immigration in
recent years, the greater manpower mobility seems to be,
because housing and social infrastructure are even less
able to keep pace with demand than elsewhere in Siberia.
In the oil and gas regions of Tiumen' Oblast, for example,
gross migration (arrivals plus departures) exceeds the
mechanical increase of the population by 7 to 7.5 times.
One third of all city dwellers in the oblast migrate each
year and, in the north of the province, one half of the
entire population does so. Along the central section of
the BAM, a mechanical growth of 78,000 in the population
was achieved through the gross migration and turnover of
half a million people.[2] Even in the long-established
Irkutsk area, with a favorable microclimate, only 42
percent of the urban population and 49 percent of the rural
population resided in the same region for more than a
decade at the beginning of the 1970s.[3]

I have shown elsewhere that the upsurge of migration
to Siberia, which took place in the 1970s after heavy net
losses through the previous decade and a half, is somewhat
deceptive and must be qualified. That upsurge was essentially limited to the Northland and to the Baikal-Amur area
along the Mongolian-Chinese border and the line of construction of the new railway. Elsewhere, population growth was
generally below the rate for the USSR as a whole, and the
West Siberian forest-steppe zone continues to suffer from
net outmigration. Since the mid-1970s, even adjoining
Kazakhstan is losing more migrants than it receives, especially from its northern and central provinces, where the
Slavic population predominates.[4] The zone of the BAM may
soon become one of net outmigration as well, with the rails
(though not yet two principal tunnels) finished but most of
the large projects along it postponed (see Chapter 4). On
its most important central section, only two-thirds of the
population is supplied with permanent housing, less than a
third with household services, and a mere tenth with clinic
and hospital space. Almost 90 percent of those polled are
dissatisfied with working and living conditions.[5]

WORKLOAD AND LABOR INTENSITY

As previous research revealed, the average time an

industrial and construction worker in Siberia spends on the job is strikingly low. For a worker in industry, this time on the job in 1975 amounted to a mere 163 days, only 70 percent as much as for his counterpart in Alaska. In construction, with more exposure to the elements, the number of days on the job was lower still, no more than 135 in West Siberia and 150 to 160 in East Siberia and the Far East.6

These figures support quantitatively the anecdotal information we have concerning the extreme instability of the labor force. Even allowing for harsher physical conditions and more undeveloped infrastructure than in Alaska, the comparison for Siberia is so unfavorable that only a very high labor turnover, punctuated by long periods without work, can explain it. The days of not working do not include idleness during work hours, whether through the worker's fault or not. Yet the widespread shortages of spare parts, delays, and snags in material supply that plague the Soviet economy are magnified in Siberia. The huge distances from suppliers, transshipments over several modes of transport, and the seasonality of all except railway transport guarantee that even more time is lost during the workday than elsewhere in the USSR. The extreme is reached in the Far Eastern North. Only 13 percent of all material goods arriving in the Yakut ASSR is shipped the year around; yet almost half of interindustry input comes in from the outside over thousands of kilometers. In Magadan Oblast, interprovince freight represents 95 percent of all freight turnover.7 Such extended and unreliable supply lines multiply idle time and raise the instability of the workforce.

This instability, combined with relative isolation and an inadequate support base, also accounts in part for the surprisingly high labor intensity of Siberian industries. As Table 6.1 shows, six of the ten major industrial branches require significantly more manpower input per unit value of output in Siberia than in the European regions of the Russian Republic. Four branches are less labor-intensive but, with one exception, their advantage over the European provinces is minor, and industry overall is more labor intensive than in the European provinces. Surprisingly, even the electric power, iron and steel, nonferrous metal, chemical, and petrochemical industries demand greater labor input in the Trans-Ural provinces, although the output mixes of the last three are certainly biased towards less finely processed products. One authority clearly states that Siberian workers do not work with more

172

TABLE 6.1 Labor Intensity of Industrial Branches in the European RSFSR and Siberia in 1977

| Industrial branches | Labor intensity of production (man-year per 10,000 rubles of gross output) | | Index of labor intensity in Siberia relative to European RSFSR (European RSFSR = 100) |
	European RSFSR (including Urals)	Siberia (including Far East)	
Fuel industries	0.35	0.34	97.1
Electric power	0.39	0.44	112.8
Iron and steel	0.42	0.47	111.9
Nonferrous metals	0.31	0.39	125.8
Chemicals and petrochemicals	0.45	0.47	104.4
Machine building and metal working	1.04	1.01	97.1
Wood products, pulp and paper	1.19	1.12	94.1
Building materials	1.00	0.89	89.0
Light industries	0.55	0.66	120.0
Food industries	0.29	0.33	113.8

Source: V.P. Mozhin, ed., Ekonomicheskoe razvitie Sibiri i Dal'nego Vostoka (Moscow, Mysl', 1980), p. 214.

advanced technical equipment, although statistically the
level of capitalization of labor in the region's industry
is one-fourth higher than the Soviet average. That phenomenon is simply due to the higher zonal evaluation of
buildings and structures in Siberia (resulting from the
higher cost of construction and shipment). In addition,
only 8 to 20 percent of the demand for specific northern
technology is met today, which lowers the effectiveness of
machines and equipment and, evidently, increases the labor
input.[8] Relative labor intensity in Kazakh industry and
construction (most of which is located in the central and
northeastern parts of the republic) is most likely still
higher, given the extremely low level of mechanization. In
the early 1980s, the share of manual laborers here reached
54 percent and 63 percent of production workers
respectively in the two sectors.[9]

RURAL MANPOWER, WORKLOAD, AND OUTMIGRATION

If instability and consequent low workload characterize manpower in industry and construction, very high
workload and consequent flight characterize the agricultural labor force. Siberia and northern Kazakhstan share
all the manpower woes that afflict the Slavic countryside
throughout the USSR with only a modest time lag. Over the
past decade, however, rural outmigration has accelerated
from most regions of northern Kazakhstan and Siberia
proper, though not yet from the Far East. By the time of
the 1979 census, West Siberia became one of the three Major
Economic Regions of the Russian Republic (out of a total of
ten) with the highest rate of net rural outmigration. Out
of every 10,000 rural inhabitants, annual net loss amounted
to 213 persons, 186 of which represented a net gain for
cities and twenty-one a net gain for rural areas outside
West Siberia. Almost one-half of those who leave the
region's villages are under twenty years of age and the
average age of the migrants is only twenty-six.[10]
    The negative impact of this outmigration for Siberian
agriculture is enhanced by the fact that, despite the much
larger arable land per agricultural worker than in the
Russian Republic as a whole (21.1 hectares in West and East
Siberia combined versus 13.4 hectares in the RSFSR in
1977),[11] the power capacity of equipment available to
Siberian farmers throughout the 1970s was less than the
mean for the whole republic. That capacity also increased
significantly more slowly in Siberia than in the RSFSR

during the decade not only per farm worker, but per hectare as well.[12] Ironically, the most fertile region of Siberia has become one of the most neglected. In Altai Krai, productive capital per hectare is barely over half that for the Russian Republic as a whole and per worker it is 8 percent below.[13] Nor was animal husbandry any more mechanized. The minor advantage of West Siberia was more than counterbalanced by the serious lag in the regions east of the Enisei.[14] In Kazakhstan, the mechanization of animal husbandry is more advanced, especially in the northern oblasts adjoining West Siberia, and work with most field crops, except vegetables, almost entirely mechanized. On the other hand, the work load in the northern half of Kazakhstan, at least, appears heavier than almost anywhere in the USSR--reaching almost 300 days per year in the socialist sector--and must be a factor in the significant rural outmigration of the last two decades.[15] According to specialists, it would take an increment of 3,600 rubles of fixed capital in Siberian agriculture just to compensate for each worker that leaves it and to keep production from declining.[16]

Siberian experts claim there are signs the manpower situation in the Siberian countryside is beginning to stabilize. As the smallest, most isolated villages that are unable to provide satisfactory living conditions lose inhabitants, with many of these places liquidated alto-gether, the rural population is being concentrated in larger, more viable settlements. The most viable of these represent the nodal village and headquarters of collective and state farms and enjoy some urban amenities (see below). In Novosibirsk Oblast, for example, they already concen-trated over 56 percent of the rural population in the 1970s, their dominance increasing. Net outmigration, both actual and potential, from such settlements is slight, according to a detailed survey. Well over half of their inhabitants already lived in cities before; yet only 6 percent of the population intends to move and almost nine-tenths are desirous of staying, although among those with high qualifications the intention to migrate remains much stronger.[17]

Despite such encouraging signs in recent years, the large-scale rural flight, combined with the relative undercapitalization of Siberian agriculture, had pushed the work load to very high levels during the 1970s. In the early years of that decade, a farm worker in Siberia spent an average of 271 days per year on the job, with the excep-tion of Altai Krai, where the workload then was lower. In some regions of the Far East and the whole of Northern Kazakhstan, a farm worker spent 297 days on the job, not including the private plot.[18] A 1977 survey shows 252 days a year in all of West Siberia per collective farm members of working age (including administrators) and 278 days per actual worker of both kolkhozy and sovkhozy (collective and state farms respectively) in Novosibirsk Oblast. Workers in animal husbandry put in around 300 days, though in their case the workload has declined slightly since the mid-1960s.[19] One must add labor on the private plot which, though decreasing, still averaged thirteen hours per week for farmers with full time work in the socialist sector.[20] The workload thus becomes almost equivalent to a seven-day, eight-hour work week throughout the year, nearly twice as high as the average for the Russian Republic.[21] Given the sharp seasonality imposed by the short growing season, the exertion must be utterly exhausting during the summer half of the year.

Dissatisfaction with such an unreasonable burden and with working conditions in general is one of the chief causes of the rapid flight from the land in Siberia. It was the most common complaint of respondents from 77 percent of the villages (accounting for 44 percent of the rural population) in the West Siberian survey, even exceeding dissatisfaction with the lack of industrial consumer goods ("Never any rest." "Always toiling in filth.")[22] In addition, the lack of official help in maintaining private subsidiary agriculture, particularly in providing supplementary feed, and the difficulties of continuing it, appeared as the chief motives for intended outmigration with almost a tenth of the respondents.[23]

THE RURAL SETTLEMENT STRUCTURE IN SIBERIA AND KAZAKHSTAN

In Marxist-Leninist thought, the industrialization of agriculture and the urbanization of rural areas (in the widest sense, meaning the diffusion of the urban way of life) has always been regarded as a crucial requirement for the full-scale socialist transformation of the countryside. This is the meaning of the oft-reported goal of overcoming the socio-economic distance existing between city and village. It is perhaps not surprising that, in a political system dominated by an essentially urban ideology, many (perhaps the majority) of experts have come to believe that this distance can be overcome not so much by directly

improving the condition of life in the villages, but rather
by functionally integrating the latter with the urban
network through improved communication. Accordingly, from
1918 through 1965 Soviet villages received eleven times
less government investment per capita on the development of
social infrastructure than cities.[24] Little was realized
then of the proposed improvement of communication between
city and country. As late as the mid-1970s, only 9 percent
of all rural settlements in the USSR were reached by hard-
surface roads,[25] and their isolation during much of the
year barely improved for over half a century.

Such a pro-urban bias has unquestionably helped
preserve the backwardness of the Soviet countryside, spur
the rural exodus and contribute to the nation's agricultural woes. More recently some scholars, with Tatiana
Zaslavskaia at their head, have expressed the view that
Soviet villages today are still a relatively distinct realm
and are destined to remain so for quite some time.   These
scholars are opposing the excessively urban bias in investment allocation for social infrastructure and hold that
efforts at the "urbanization" of rural life must have their
focus in the villages themselves. Zaslavskaia and her
Novosibirsk colleagues may have been instrumental in
lessening this urban bias, at least in West Siberia.   They
claim that, at present, the villages of this region are no
longer disadvantaged in the allocation of infrastructural
investment on a per capita basis, though the legacy of
neglect will take many years yet to overcome.[26]

In Siberia and the Far East, the obstacles to modernizing the rural infrastructure and fully integrate the
countryside into the nation's urbanized mainstream are even
greater than west of the Urals. It is true that the mean
settlement size is much larger than the average for the
Russian Republic as a whole (466 versus 240), not to
mention the Non-Black Earth Zone of the European RSFSR, and
that the share of villages with over 1,000 inhabitants is
considerably higher (Table 6.2). However, this is chiefly
the result of the lower proportion of the smallest-size
settlement category, those with up to 200 persons.
Siberia, including the Far East, has a far higher share of
villages in the 201 to 500 and 501 to 1,000-person categories than the RSFSR as a whole or its European Regions.
These are still very small settlements, those having
between 201 and 500 inhabitants especially so.   Although
the cost of improving the infrastructure and the quality of
life may be somewhat lower than in villages of less than
200 persons, this is certain to be counteracted by the much

greater isolation and far-flung nature of rural settlements east of the Urals. As Table 6.3 shows, even in the southern zone of Siberia and the Far East, mean distances between rural places in the different size categories exceed those in regions west of the Urals by several times. Average distances in the northern zone, which cover more than three-fourths of the territory of the trans-Ural part of the Russian Republic in turn exceed, correspondingly, those distances in the southern zone.[27] Throughout this huge territory, two-thirds of all rural settlements lack reliable year-round transport links to the outside world.[28]

In most of Kazakhstan the difficulties of improving living conditions through the countryside are not unlike those encountered across the agricultural belt of Siberia. However, environmental zonation strongly influences the size distribution of settlement and population and imparts some peculiarities to the Kazakh rural scene. In the steppe zone of North Kazakhstan, which was the focus of the Virgin Land Campaign and where 32.2 percent of the surface was sown to crops in 1984, the size distribution of rural places shows substantial similarities to that of adjacent West Siberia.[29] As in the West Siberian steppe and forest steppe zone, villages here tend to be somewhat larger than in the Non-Black Earth region of European Russia. The smallest hamlets compose only a third of all rural places and account for a mere 7 percent of the rural population, though here, too, the bulk of all settlements have less than 500 inhabitants (Table 6.4).

As the steppe gives way to semidesert and farming to extensive pasturalism, settlements with 70 to 100 persons overwhelmingly dominate the settlement pattern, though still accounting for a small share of the rural population. West, Central, and East Kazakhstan, occupying that semidesert belt between the Caspian Sea and the Altai Mountains, all show a strikingly similar pattern of rural settlements and were grouped in Table 6.5. The great majority of the approximately 11,000 rural places with less than 100 persons (some 81 percent of all rural settlements in the three grouped regions) are supporting an extensive pattern of stock raising in an environment unsuited for other kind of agricultrual activity. A substantial portion of the more than 1,600 settlements with less than 100 persons that are located in the dry margins of North Kazakhstan must also be of these type. These rural places form the outlying network of stations to huge stock-raising collectives and, still more, state farms. Most of them have twenty-five persons or less, the number of workers varying

178

TABLE 6.2 Average Population and Size Distribution of Rural
in 1979

Regions, Zones and RSFSR	Average Size of Settlements (Persons)	Categories of (In percent – Up to 200 Persons	
		% of all settlements	% of total rural population
Siberia and			
Far East	466	43.8	8.0
West Siberia	450	44.3	8.9
East Siberia	455	43.9	8.3
Far East	532	41.6	5.3
RSFSR	240	72.8	16.5
Non–Black Earth Zone of European RSFSR	122	86.1	32.4
European RSFSR without Non–Black Earth Zone	479	47.5	8.5

Source: A.R. Bernval'd, Regional'nye problemy tovarnogo

seasonally, according to the rhythm of pasturing and
wintering Kazakhstan's 35 to 36 million sheep, 1.4 million
horses, and 130,000 camels.[30] While over half of settlements with less than twenty-five persons disappeared in
Kazakhstan since 1959 with consolidation and the improvement of communications, their numbers still approached
9,000 at the beginning of the 1980s.[31]

In southern Kazakhstan, this pastural, stock-raising
economy remains strong, but is overshadowed by irrigated
agriculture, based on permanent rivers flowing north from
the Tien Shan. The settlement pattern conforms to the

Settlements in Siberia and the European Zone of the RSFSR

Settlements by Population Size ages, row totals = 100 percent)					
201 - 500 Persons		501 - 1000 Persons		Over 1000 Persons	
% of all settlements	% of total rural population	% of all settlements	% of total rural population	% of all settlements	% of total rural population
29.5	20.3	15.0	22.8	11.7	48.9
30.6	21.6	14.2	22.4	10.9	47.1
29.8	20.9	13.8	21.6	12.3	49.1
26.1	16.4	19.1	25.4	13.2	52.9
15.3	20.3	7.1	20.6	4.8	42.6
8.9	22.7	3.3	18.4	1.7	26.5
27.3	18.4	14.5	21.2	10.7	51.9

obrashcheniia (Novosibirsk: Nauka, 1984), pp. 49 and 50.

different environmental and economic conditions. Most of the rural places are again larger: the share of those in the size categories of over 501 inhabitants are higher even than in North Kazakhstan, with the difference most pronounced in the share of settlements greater than 2,000 persons. These villages concentrate 41 percent of the rural population, and villages over 1,001 persons 65 percent (Table 6.4). Clearly, the availability and distribution of water serves as an agglomerating force, making southern Kazakhstan a part of the Central Asian oasis world in settlement pattern as in most other aspects of the

TABLE 6.3 Average Distance Between Rural Settlements by
Categories of Population Size (in kilometers)

Regions and Zones	Population Size		
	200–500 Persons	501–1000 Persons	Over 1000 Persons
Siberia and Far East	32.1	50.0	79.9
Northern Zone	101.5	116.6	279.8
Southern Zone	22.1	35.3	54.7
European RSFSR	9.7	15.2	24.8
European USSR without RSFSR regions	5.4	7.5	11.0

Source: A.R. Bernval'd, Regional'nye problemy tovarnogo obrashcheniia (Novosibirsk: Nauka, 1984), p. 165.

socio–economic and cultural sphere as well.

The isolation of settlements in the Kazakh countryside is as great as in the southern zone of Siberia and the Far East. Even in the northernmost, best-settled oblasts, the average distance between all villages (89 percent of which have less than 1,000 inhabitants) tends to exceed those between the largest 10 to 11 percent of settlements in the steppe and forest steppe west of the Urals (Tables 6.5). This 20 to 30-kilometer mean distance in northern Kazakhstan doubles in oblasts of the semidesert zone, reaching 113 kilometers in the desert province of Mangyshlak. In southern Kazakhstan, along the irrigated foothills of the Tien Shan, the rural network is again somewhat more dense, though the extensive stretch of semidesert included in these large southern oblasts increases the average distance. The thinner the village distribution, the thinner the road network naturally tends to be. Kazakhstan as a whole, has only 80 percent as much hard surface road per 1,000 square kilometers as the entire USSR, whose average itself is severely depressed because of the vast roadless expanses of Siberia. Only two of the five major regions of Kazakhstan and eight of its nineteen oblasts boast a road network whose density equals the Soviet mean (Table 6.5). Presently even a host of raion centers and about 30 percent of the central headquarters of the roughly 2,500 huge state and collective farms in that republic lack proper hard–surface road connections to the existing

highway system.[32] (Raions are administrative units below
the oblasts. In 1970, there were 184 raions in the seventeen oblasts of Kazakhstan, an average of 10.8 per oblast.
Siberia and the Far East had 465 raions for eighteen
oblasts, krais, and ASSRs, i.e., 25.8 in each of these
basic higher-level administrative units.[33])

The organization of collective and state farms contributes to the problem of rural settlements in both Siberia
and Kazakhstan. In Siberia (with the Far East), somewhat
over 3,000 collective and state farms cultivate about 30
million hectares, and a total agricultural area is many
times larger still.[34] In Kazakhstan, a little more than
2,500 farms worked 35.7 million hectares of arable land in
1984 and held a total agricultural area, including grazing
land, of over 190 million hectares.[35] Throughout Siberia
and the Far East, an average farm comprises seven villages;
in Kazakhstan 8 to 9, although in the semidesert zone of
that republic some of these may be seasonal livestock-
rearing stations.[36] Nearly all social amenities and
infrastructure, all economic and political power and links
to the outside world on such a farm are concentrated in the
nodal village, the central usad'be (homestead or farm
headquarters). Aside from a tiny store, most outlying
settlements lack any service establishments and amenities.
Over a fifth of the villages lack a permanent store altogether or have one which is completely unsuitable for any
further utilization and must rely on periodic visits by
itinerant trucks. In addition, stores in 23 percent of the
settlements need major repair.[37] Under Siberian conditions, the isolation of these peripheral villages from the
central usad'be is severe. Over half of these are located
at a more than two-hour walk from the center, but 95
percent of the intrafarm roads in Siberia are unpaved and
public transportation is very inadequate. In a sociological survey conducted under Zaslavskaia's supervision, 63
percent of the respondents from such small villages were
extremely dissatisfied with the transport service, half of
them regarding it as the most important cause of their
dissatisfaction with life in the village.[38]

Current Soviet policy strives for the consolidation of
rural settlements, aided by the desire of many of its
inhabitants to move nearer to or into the village where the
farm headquarters is located. Between the 1970 and 1979
censuses, almost a quarter (24.1 percent) of the Siberian
and Far Eastern villages, with 7.1 percent of the rural
population, were liquidated and this process is doubtless

TABLE 6.4 Size and Population Distribution of Rural Settlements in Regions of Kazakhstan in 1979

	Categories of Settlements by Population Size in Percentages (row totals = 100)					
Regions of Kazakhstan	1-100 Persons		101-500 Persons		501-1000 Persons	
	% of all settlements	% of rural population	% of all settlements	% of rural population	% of all settlements	% of rural population
North Kazakhstan	33.9	6.9	38.2	22.3	16.6	24.5
West, Central, and East Kazakhstan	80.9	8.9	11.7	21.5	4.0	20.5
Southern Kazakhstan	27.0	1.3	33.4	14.3	20.0	19.5

Note: West, Central, and East Kazakhstan are almost entirely located in the semidesert zone. They exhibit very similar distribution of rural population and settlement size and were, therefore, grouped. For Central Kazakhstan, only the 1970 distribution was available and used.

183

TABLE 6.4 continued

Regions of Kazakhstan	Categories of Settlements by Population Size in Percentages (row totals = 100)				Totals	
	1001-2000 Persons		Over 2000 Persons			
	% of all settlements	% of rural population	% of all settlements	% of rural population	Number of settlements	Rural population
North Kazakhstan	9.7	27.8	1.6	18.5	4,831	2,272,398
West, Central, and East Kazakhstan	2.5	25.4	0.9	23.7	13,649	1,869,298
Southern Kazakhstan	12.3	24.2	7.3	40.7	3,410	2,437,539

Source: N.F. Golikov and A.I. Sedlovskii, Sotsial'no-ekonomicheskie aspekty sel'skogo rasseleniia Kazakhstana (Alma-Ata: Kainar, 1981), pp. 148, 160, 175 and 182.

TABLE 6.5 Density of Hard-surface Roads and Average
Distance Between Rural Settlements in Regions and Oblasts
of Kazakhstan, 1980

Regions and Oblasts	Network of Hard-surface Roads (kilo-meters per 1000 sq. km. of area)	Average Distance between Rural Settlements[a] (kilometers)
North Kazakhstan	42.3	
North Kazakhstan Oblast	49.6	17.3
Kustanai Oblast	41.0	27.7
Kokchetav Oblast	90.8	20.5
Turgai Oblast	26.9	30.8
Tselinograd Oblast	41.0	28.9
Pavlodar Oblast	26.6	29.1
Western Kazakhstan	13.3	
Ural Oblast	19.8	30.9
Aktiubinsk Oblast	12.8	45.1
Gur'ev Oblast	13.3	48.0
Mangyshlak Oblast	7.8	113.2
Central Kazakhstan	18.3	
Dzhezkazgan Oblast	10.2	74.2
Karaganda oblast	48.0	30.1
Eastern Kazakhstan	32.1	
Semipalatinsk Oblast	26.6	36.9
East Kazakhstan Oblast	42.0	31.5
Southern Kazakhstan	27.4	
Kzyl Orda Oblast	10.2	48.7
Chimkent Oblast	40.5	28.3
Dzhambul Oblast	33.1	33.0
Alma-Ata Oblast	41.0	32.9
Taldy Kurgan Oblast	29.5	32.4
Kazakhstan	26.1	
USSR	32.7	

[a]Apparently seasonal and semipermanent settlements are excluded. The total number of places considered are, therefore, much fewer than those noted in Table 6.4. They could
not be grouped by regions.
Source: A.K. Koshanov, ed., Vnutriraionnye problemy sotsial'no-ekonomicheskogo razvitiia soiuznoi respubliki (Alma-
Ata: Nauka, 1983), pp. 112-114 and 143.

continuing.[39] Yet this still leaves over two-fifths of all settlements with less than 200 persons and almost three-fourths with less then 500 (Table 6.2).

Soviet scholars acknowledge that, while providing amenities and infrastructure in the larger villages is significantly cheaper, the preservation of a network of smaller places is essential for the reasonably efficient functioning of agriculture, not to mention extensive stock raising. Villages over 1,000 inhabitants are not numerous enough for even one per state and collective farm in Siberia on the average (they suffice for little more than two-thirds of the farms) and, in Kazakhstan, even villages with 500 persons or more suffice for only two-thirds. Given the enormous size of these farms, the shortness of the growing season, and the poor road conditions, several settlements are needed to handle field work at sufficient levels of effectiveness. Studies in the Virgin Land region have shown that grain yields on state farms with three to five villages exceed yields on those with only one central settlement, while their cost of production is 20 percent lower. The fate of Soviet agricultural production, therefore, is inevitably decided in rural places of less than 500 persons, where over 70 percent of all labor is engaged in direct farm work and where most crop and stock-raising brigades live.[40]

The farm leadership and rural settlement planners thus face a dilemma. Improvements in rural amenities to help stabilize the depleted agrarian labor force can be most rapidly effected in the nodal villages of the farms. Yet in the rural conditions of Siberia and Kazakhstan, that is quite insufficient to really improve life at the very grass roots. In fact, the liquidation of outlying villages in the past has only intensified rural outmigration and may accelerate it further. In addition, given the much larger area of cultivation around settlements in Siberia (about 6,000 for each in Altai Krai versus less than 1,400 hectares as the average for the whole RSFSR), the disappearance of small villages since 1970 alone has raised the workload by 1.3 times. Farm administrators today are resisting further liquidation and want to retain all remaining peripheral settlements.[41]

THE NATIVE NATIONALITIES OF THE SIBERIAN NORTH:
POPULATION, EMPLOYMENT, SETTLEMENT STRUCTURE

Slavic immigration into Siberia and the Far East has

completely overwhelmed the native population today. Out of
a total population of over 30 million in the mid-1980s, the
more than thirty indigenous nationalities totaled little
more than 1.15 million.[42] Almost three-fifths of these
(some 670,000) lived in the southern border regions, the
overwhelming majority composed of Altaic and Mongol stock,
still inhabiting parts of their ancient heartland in the
very center of Eurasia. The huge Siberian North, com-
prising most of the Trans-Ural territory of the Russian
Republic, was thus home for about 482,000 indigenous
people. There were ten times as many Slavs throughout this
Northland in 1980, and the discrepancy is still greater
today.[43]

The Yakuts, themselves immigrant from the south some
700 years ago, represent more than two-thirds of the non-
Slavic population here. They are the only ones with an
Autonomous Republic (ASSR) and are, therefore, directly
subordinate to Moscow (as the capital of the RSFSR) in
administrative matters. Although much better-developed
than all other native groups, three-fourths of the Yakut
families were still rural at the time of the 1979 census.
Given the greater number of children than among the Slavs,
the rural component of the total Yakut population, therefore, was still higher.[44] By contrast, 73 percent of all
people inhabiting the Siberian Northlands were city dwellers.[45] Ninety-six percent of all Yakuts live in their own
ASSR, principally in its environmentally less-harsh central
portion, where the great bulk of their rural population is
also found.[46] More than a quarter of this rural population
lives in the administrative centers of rural raions and an
additional half or more in the centers of rural soviets
(councils).[47]

Relative concentration and numbers enable the Yakuts
to enjoy a certain political and economic weight unavailable to other indigenous nationalities in the Siberian
North. During the 1960s, the rate of natural increase
among the Yakuts also more than twice exceeded that registered by the Soviet population as a whole. While these
rates were halved during the 1970s, the Yakut population
still experienced a natural increase surpassing the rate
for the USSR or for the Russians in the country as a
whole.[48] Because of the heavy immigration of Slavs, this
did not prevent the Yakuts from becoming a minority in
their ASSR. Between 1959 and 1979, their share in the
population of Yakutia declined from 46.4 percent and 36.9,
while that of the Russians rose from 44.2 percent to over
half and, with Ukrainians added, to almost 56 percent.[49]

In fact, immigration contributed over half the population
growth of that ASSR during the 1970s.[50] The majority of
Yakuts today (over 55 percent at the time of the 1979
census) and most of those under forty years of age are
bilingual. Yet over 96 percent adhere to the native
language as the mother tongue, and national consciousness
seems to have strengthened rather than declined.[51] While
intermarriage between Yakuts and Russians increased sharply
during the 1970s (though still remaining well below the
theoretical percentage suggested by the population mix),
the large majority of children from such mixed marriages
declare themselves Yakuts. (The percentage is almost three-
fourths of the offspring when the father is of Yakut nation-
ality--much the more common case--but 45 percent even when
the father is Russian.[52])

While the national survival and political and economic
importance of the Yakuts, with their numbers and autonomous
republic, seem to be secure, prospects for the small
northern nationalities scattered over an area more than a
third of the entire USSR are far more uncertain. These
people, belonging to almost two dozen ethnic groups,
numbered 158,324 at the time of the 1979 census, with all
but some 9,000 of them found in Siberia.[53] Four-fifths of
them were living in rural areas engaged in reindeer
herding, hunting, fishing, and cottage industries. They
made up the overwhelming portion of the population in the
smallest settlements through the Siberian Northland: 75 to
80 percent in places with less than 200 persons and as much
as 95 percent of those with under 100. Some 18 to 20
percent (though by another source only 14 to 15 percent) of
these small northern tribes still lead a nomadic life,[54]
are on the move with at least part of their families and
have no fixed abode.[55] About 2.2 million reindeer, a
stable number for over a decade, are pastured over vast
areas; they account for over a quarter of all meat supply
in the northern regions of Siberia and the Far East and 65
percent of it in Magadan Oblast.[56]

The record of Soviet authorities towards these small,
remote nationalities has been quite praiseworthy. Yet, as
with the natives of the North American Arctic, the difficulties of adapting creatively to the intrusion of modern
technology are many and great. Youth, in particular, is
losing its attachment to the traditional way of life but
has not yet found a proper niche in the modern world. The
average age of reindeer herders today is forty. The
isolation, hardship, and frequent moves associated with
this work are no longer accepted by the younger age groups,

especially by those with some secondary education. Even a large portion of those settled permanently are dissatis- fied: according to surveys, 18 percent of the Evenki polled in the BAM zone are determined to leave, and among those under thirty this share is more than twice as high.[57] Well over a third are determined to change occupation. Divorce from the traditional way of life was not followed by a psychological adjustment to the more modern, sedentary agriculture or industry. The resettlements were carried out without regard to national traditions and customs. As a result, almost no members of the northern nationalities can be found today in milk, poultry, or crop production or even on fur farms throughout Siberia. Their numbers are similarly insignificant in industry, construction, trans- port, and communications, and they are represented only in service industries to some extent. Technical training for them, let alone more subtle help to ease adjustment to the new ways of life, is almost wholly absent.[58] In the 1970s, only some 65 percent of the Evenki of working age were actually employed, versus 83 percent of the Russians, and three-fourths of those employed were manual laborers with very low qualifications.[59]

Since the 1970 census, these small northern national- ities have barely increased in population. Their growth during the entire 1970s amounted to 3.3 percent, or well under 0.4 percent per annum compared to 16.1 percent (almost 1.4 percent per year) during the 1959-1970 inter- censal period. The rate of increase during the 1970s was 2.5 times lower than for the country as a whole, lower than for any of the East Slavic nations and half as low as for the Lithuanians (though not Latvians or Estonians) in the demographically mature Baltic.[60] About a third of the nationalities declined absolutely in numbers, even the Khanty and Mansi with an Autonomous District and the Nentsy within their own District (these being the scene of feverish oil and gas development since the late 1960s).[61]

Soviet scholars appear to find such decreases or extremely slow growth both rather embarrassing and econo- mically harmful.[62] Similarly, the loss of much of the traditional herding culture of the older generation is expected to be detrimental. Given the extreme labor shortages of northern Siberia and the very high cost of food supply, the demographic stagnation and the impending decline in the herding economy will only add to the difficulties of developing the region's resources. Rein- deer meat today is claimed to cost only half as much as beef or lamb and 45 percent as much as pork and, as mentioned, provides over a quarter of all meat supply in the Siberian North.[63] Soviet scholars view the potential loss of much of the native economic base with some concern. They urge greater investment in housing, infrastructure, and services for the autochthonous population, a shift to the outpost-brigade system in reindeer herding with regular helicopter visits to outposts, the construction of permanent shelters along herding routes, and specialized instruction in agricultural technical schools for the continuation and upgrading of traditional skills in the reindeer economy.[64]

Despite much effort and expense by the Soviet government to improve education and skill levels, these are still quite low among the natives of the Siberian North (Table 6.6). As a result, unskilled physical labor with low productivity is much more prevalent than among immigrant Slavs. In the mid-1970s, for example, 75.5 percent of the Evenki and Eveny of the Yakut ASSR were engaged in manual work. Even among the Yakuts, the most advanced and strongest of all the nationalities of the Siberian Arctic and Subarctic, the share of manual workers reached 63.4 percent. Since the average for the entire employed population of Yakutia was claimed to be under 53 percent, one can estimate the share of those engaged in physical hand labor among Russians and Ukrainians as not much over one-third.[65]

SECTORAL AND GEOGRAPHIC DISTRIBUTION OF LABOR

Resource-based industrialization is the principal course of Siberia's economic development. Over huge areas, however, development involves the prior or at least concurrent construction of the most essential transport facilities and supply bases almost from scratch. Accordingly, one should expect industrial and construction labor and an essential workforce in transportation to dominate employment. Construction associated with the military further swells employment in that sector, especially in the Pacific provinces. The natural environment reduces the role of agriculture to well below the Soviet average, while the service sector, aside from transportation, plays a generally very subordinate part. Nevertheless, both agriculture and services employ unusually high shares of the labor force in certain areas of this vast land. In first place, agriculture is still the primary occupation of Siberia's indigenous nationalities and three large native

TABLE 6.6 Changes in Educational Level Among Native Nationalities of the Siberian North, 1970 and 1979 (numbers
per 1,000 population aged 20 years and older)

Nationalities	With Higher Education		With Middle School Education	
	1970	1979	1970	1979
Eveny	n.d.	n.d.	46	270
Evenki	13	28	n.d.	n.d.
Khanty	7	13	19	82
Nentsy	8	15	14	69
Mansi	12	22	20	72
Dolgan	11	19	25	90
Koriaki	n.d.	n.d.	38	127
Chukchi	n.d.	n.d.	17	100

Source: V.N. Uvachan, Gody ravnye vekam. Stroitel'stvo
sotsializma na Sovetskom Severe (Moscow: Mysl', 1984)
p. 278.

groups, the Buriats, the Yakuts, and the Tuvinians, still
are a substantial population (in the last case a big
majority) of their autonomous republics.[66] In the second
place, the sparse and scattered population of these vast
areas, expecially in the Northland, results in an inflated
requirement for service personnel (in trade, health and
education, culture, the household and communal economy,
repair, etc.) despite the low level and quality of these
services. In Yakutia, for example, the proportion of the
total workforce employed in these brances is twice as high
as the national average.[67]
     As Table 6.7 shows, industry indeed had come to
dominate employment in the material-producing branches by
1970 in all but one of its eighteen administrative units.
An interesting reversal took place in Chita Oblast through
the 1970s, where the agricultural workforce during that
decade increased faster than that in industry, so that in
1980 the agricultural sector was the major employer in two
of the eighteen administrative divisions. In Siberia
overall, the share of industrial employment in the three
main material production branches rose by almost nine
percentage points to three-fifths of the total, while that
of agricultural employment dropped from one-third to less

than one-quarter.

The decline in the relative importance of the agricultural sector since 1960 was strongly differentiated geographically through the vast land of Siberia. The share of agricultural employment declines sharply in the forest steppe region of West Siberia (Altai Krai, Novosibirsk and Omsk Oblasts), where rural outmigration has been particularly heavy (supra). It also decreased significantly during both decades in the Yakut ASSR, where the rapid development of mineral resources and transportation attracted large numbers of immigrants and also took some of the dominant native nationality off the land. Interestingly, the proportion of agricultural employment dropped less precipitously in Tiumen' Oblast and hardly at all during the 1970s, while in a few provinces, including heavily industrialized Kemerovo Oblast, almost coterminous with the Kuzbas, it rose slightly after 1970. To improve the reliability of their food supply, a number of strong industrial and construction trusts have built up their own agricultural supply organizations, and this may have accounted for the reversal of the trend. Finally, the notable increase in the share of the agricultural work force in Chita Oblast and Khabarovsk Krai between 1970 and 1980 may be related to the large military build-up along the Chinese border and to the fact that these provinces contain the headquarters of the Transbaikal and Far Eastern Military Districts.

Overall, the Northlands of Siberia seem to account for about a tenth of all agricultural labor input, a portion not drastically smaller than its share in the total Siberian population. The difficulties of providing the North with food are obviously so great that special efforts are made to utilize local land resources, despite low fertility and high cost, wherever climatically possible. This northern agriculture (apart from traditional reindeer herding) is also quite highly capitalized. In 1980, the Near and Far North between the Urals and the Pacific accounted for 10.2 percent of productive capital in Siberian agriculture. The level of capitalization is, therefore, more than 60 percent above the Siberian mean per hectare of agricultural land, although higher construction costs and zonal prices inflate the figure. It is certain to be well above the average per unit of labor as well.[68] The Yakut ASSR, almost entirely in the Far North (Figure 3) but with relatively favorable conditions for its latitude, stands out as an important local agricultural base. In 1980, almost 49,000 workers were employed on Yakut state

TABLE 6.7 Distribution of Employment in Material Production i.e., sum of three sectors = 100%)

Regions and administrative units	Industry	1961 Agri-culture	Con-struc-tion
Siberia (including Far East)	50.7	33.0	16.3
West Siberia	47.8	37.5	14.7
Altai Krai	36.6	51.3	12.1
Kemerovo Oblast	63.9	16.5	19.6
Novosibirsk Oblast	48.9	36.1	15.0
Omsk Oblast	39.7	46.4	13.9
Tomsk Oblast	61.6	25.8	12.6
Tiumen' Oblast	38.7	49.2	12.1
East Siberia	49.9	32.3	17.8
Krasnoiarsk Krai	50.4	33.0	16.6
Irkutsk Oblast	54.6	24.3	21.1
Chita Oblast	45.3	39.8	14.9
Buriat ASSR	45.8	38.7	15.5
Tuva ASSR	20.1	57.8	22.1
Far East	59.9	21.6	18.5
Maritime Krai	58.9	23.1	18.0
Khabarovsk Krai	70.5	11.6	17.9
Amur Oblast	45.5	39.3	15.2
Kamchatka Oblast	65.8	14.7	19.5
Magadan Oblast	66.9	12.3	20.8
Sakhalin Oblast	69.1	9.1	21.8
Yakut ASSR	40.7	40.3	19.0[a]

in Siberian Provinces (percentages); (row totals by year,

	1970			1980	
Industry	Agri-culture	Con-struc-tion	Industry	Agri-culture	Con-struc-tion
56.6	25.9	17.5	59.5	24.1	16.4
55.0	29.4	15.6	57.3	27.6	15.1
47.5	41.3	11.2	53.8	35.7	10.5
69.7	12.8	17.5	68.7	13.3	18.0
55.8	29.4	14.8	60.1	25.0	14.9
49.2	37.6	13.2	49.8	38.5	11.7
62.6	19.4	18.0	58.8	20.7	20.5
41.2	34.3	24.5	48.2	33.1	18.7
55.8	26.1	18.1	58.9	24.4	16.7
57.9	24.7	17.4	60.8	22.3	16.9
62.0	18.4	19.6	66.9	16.5	16.6
44.4	37.4	18.2	39.9	42.5	17.6
50.0	34.8	15.2	55.0	31.1	13.9
25.6	53.8	20.6	29.6	51.3	19.1
61.2	17.3	21.5	65.5	15.4	19.1
63.0	16.9	20.1	68.0	15.5	16.5
69.6	8.8	21.6	71.5	9.9	18.6
46.0	34.7	19.3	51.5	31.2	17.3
65.4	11.5	23.1	72.6	8.3	19.1
65.4	11.3	23.1	67.5	9.3	23.2
67.9	8.7	23.4	68.9	7.9	23.2
43.2	33.0	23.8	49.8	25.0	25.2

Sources: For Siberian provinces, V.P. Mozhin, ed., Eko-nomicheskoe razvitie Sibiri i Dal'nego Vostoka (Moscow, Mysl', 1980), p. 79. Reprinted from L. Dienes, "The Development of Siberian Regions: Economic Profiles, Income Flow and Strategies for Growth," Soviet Geography, Vol. 23, No. 4 (April), 1982, p. 230.

194

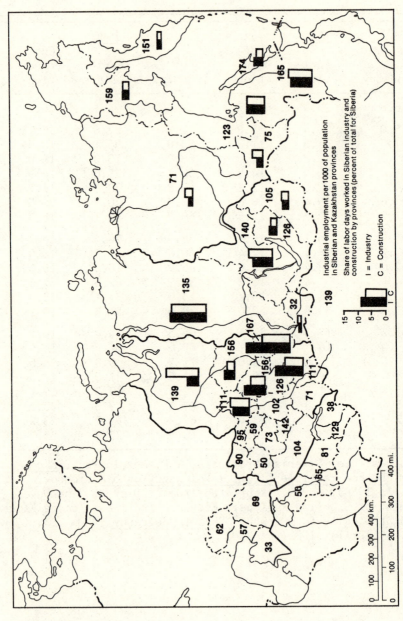

FIGURE 3 Level of Employment in the Provinces of Siberia and Kazakhstan.

farms (all collectives have been converted to state farms), a number which increased <u>absolutely</u> by 3,100 since 1975, when all collectives have already been converted.[69]

Whereas industry now dominates the work force, the index of industrial employment per 1,000 of population in Siberia as a whole is not particularly high. It barely exceeds the mean for the USSR in 1975 (with no <u>relative</u> improvement since 1960) and is considerably lower than this index for the Russian Republic at both dates (Table 6.8). Per 1,000 of population, only half of Siberia's eighteen provinces had significantly more workers in industry than the whole country. In all three macroregions, more industrialized provinces were flanked by an equal number of much less industrialized ones. As for construction, the geographic distribution of this activity was apparently strongly influenced by the huge efforts channeled into the Tiumen' oil and gas region, the work starting on the BAM (including the north-south spur line from Amur Oblast to southern Yakutia) and both civilian and military construction along the Pacific coast (Figure 3).

In contrast to Siberia and the Far East, Kazakhstan is still much less industrialized. In the mid-1970s, in only one oblast, Karaganda, did industrial employment per 1,000 of population surpass the Soviet average. Northern Kazakhstan produces about one-eighth of all Soviet grain, over one-sixth of all wheat, and a significant portion of Soviet livestock. Despite a relatively high level of mechanization, much hand labor is still the rule. This and high procurement prices have kept a large share of the work force on the farms. That rural workforce is augmented in some provinces by the high numbers of Kazakhs, whose preference for agriculture and a herding economy is greater than that among the Slavic majority. As Figure 3 shows, agriculture in 1980 employed more people than industry in the clear majority of provinces in the Kazakh SSR. The ratio of agricultural to industrial employment was especially high in some oblasts of the Virgin Lands and in parts of southern Kazakhstan.

In industry and construction, the Siberian North shows favorably in labor productivity when compared to the southern, more developed zone. Such favorable performance, however, is due entirely to the industry mix and the influence of the Soviet price system; were these distortions normalized, that lead would be wholly lost. In industry, for example, the provinces with the highest labor productivity, with 58 to 66 percent above the mean for Siberia in 1975, were the Yakut ASSR, Kamchatka, and Tiumen' Oblasts.

TABLE 6.8   Industrial Employment in Siberia and Kazakhstan

Regions and Republics	Industrial employ- ment (1000 persons)	1960 Per 1000 popu- lation	Index to USSR average (USSR = 100)
Siberia (incl. Far East)	2,405	108.5	105.2
West Siberia	1,145	109.1	105.8
East Siberia	734	101.1	98.1
Far East	526	119.4	115.8
Kazakhstan	562.5	54.2	52.6
RSFSR	15,139	125.6	121.8
USSR	22,291	103.1	100.0

[a]Estimated by assuming that the average number of days worked by industrial employees in the Far East as a whole is roughly similar to those in the two Siberian regions. Labor days worked from V.P. Mozhin (1980), p. 84.

[b]Weighted average.

[c]1974 data. Information for later years no longer available.

Yet, industrial labor in Yakutia is capitalized to a level less than half the Soviet average,[70] with conditions not much better in Kamchatka. The cause of superior labor productivity, therefore, must lie entirely in the preponderance of industries favored with especially high prices in the USSR. Precious metals and stones, with activities immediately serving their production, composed four-fifths of all industrial output in the Yakut ASSR.[71] Fishing and fish processing account for a probably similar share in Kamchatka, which contributes about 13 percent of all Soviet catch. In addition, the huge naval installation has some supply industries within the Kamchatka Oblast itself, and these industries are likely to receive above average prices. The dominance of the oil and gas industries, also with high-value commodities augmented by favorable geological conditions and tremendous capital investment, explains the high labor productivity in Tiumen' Oblast. By contrast, the poor showing of certain southern provinces, especially in West Siberia, may indicate no more than an

(1960 and 1975)

Industrial employ- ment (1000 persons	1975 Per 1000 popu- lation	Index to USSR average (USSR = 100)	Average number of days worked by industrial worker
3,650	136.3	102.3	163
1,788	145.5	109.2	163
1,012	128.0	96.0	163
850[a]	129.2	96.9	162
1,161	81.0	60.8	228
21,433	159.2	119.4	231[c]
34,054	133.3	100.0	231[c]

Sources: All 1960 figures from Nar. khoz. SSSR v 1960 godu, pp. 164-165. For 1975, industrial employment in USSR, RSFSR and Kazakhstan from Nar. khoz. SSSR v 1975 g., pp. 536-537; in West and East Siberia, computed from growth rates given to 1960 base in T.B. Baranova, "Dinamika zaniatosti, proizvoditel'nosti truda i osnovnykh promysh-lennykh fondov Sibiri," Akademiia nauk SSSR, Izvestiia SO AN SSSR, Seriia obshchestvennykh nauk, No. 6, 1980, p. 105. Number of days worked from Nar. khoz. SSSR v 1974 g., p. 189; Nar. khoz. RSFSR v 1974 g., p. 96; Nar. khoz. Kazakhstana v 1974 g., p. 35, and V.P. Mozhin, Ekonomika Sibiri i Dal'nego Vostoka (Moscow: Mysl', 1980), p. 84. Reprinted from L. Dienes, "The Development of Siberian Regions: Economic Profiles, Income Flow and Strategies for Growth," Soviet Geography, Vol. 23, No. 4 (April), 1982, p. 226.

industry mix dominated by low-price commodities and goods, such as coal, iron and steel, chemicals, and bulky forest products (e.g., Kemerovo, Novosibirsk and Tomsk Oblasts, and Altai Krai). Low prices, however, do not automatically signal low priority, nor high prices the opposite.

As for construction, the less glaring but still notice-able advantage of the North in the productivity of labor again lies in the high price put on the value of northern construction in the USSR. Among all economic sectors, the shift to the Arctic and Subarctic during the 1970s was most noticeable in construction, when measured by net value.

The geographic thrust of this activity, however, has been highly selective. Some 30 percent of all the growth (increment) in the net value of construction throughout Siberia and the Far East was accounted for by Tiumen' Oblast alone, whose share in Siberia's total soared from less than 10 percent in 1970 to over 18 percent ten years later. Another 32 percent of the increment was contributed by Krasnoiarsk Krai, Amur Oblast, and the Yakut ASSR,[72] all three sites of major construction projects during the 1970s associated with hydroelectric and mineral resource development and the BAM. Yet, between 1970 and 1980, the share of employment in the construction sector declined in Tiumen' Oblast, Krasnoiarsk Krai, and Amur Oblast and increased only modestly in the Yakut ASSR (Table 6.7). The high valuation of construction work in the northern zone, in which most major projects in these provinces except some large ones in Krasnoiarsk Krai, imparts an upward bias to output in the North. In addition, in Tiumen' Oblast at least, a very substantial part of construction is performed by labor flown in as help from other regions and thus not registered as employment in Siberia (supra). By the early 1980s, such "fly-in" brigades were building 30 percent of all new roads and 17 percent of all new housing in the province.[73]

POPULATION AND EMPLOYMENT STRUCTURE IN THE NORTH TIUMEN' OIL AND GAS REGION

The exceptional importance of the Tiumen' oil and gas region in Siberian development demands a more detailed examination of population and employment in the area. The disappearance of regional demographic and employment statistics has long frustrated researchers in their attempt to focus on geographic subunits of the huge Russian Republic. However, newly discovered data based on the 1979 census, almost none of which has been published, permits closer scrutiny of the labor force in this region so critical for the Soviet economy. In 1985, the north of Tiumen' Oblast provided 45 percent of all fuel produced in the USSR, based on heat content. (Neighboring Tomsk Oblast on the West Siberian Plain added another one percent.) It provided 60 percent of all Soviet hydrocarbons, i.e., oil and gas combined.[74] The region is essentially coterminous with the Khanty-Mansi and Yamal-Nenets Autonomous Districts. The two districts account for 97 percent of all hydrocarbon extraction in the whole of Siberia, the first yielding most of the petroleum, the second most of the gas.[75]

Since 1965, when oil production began, the population of the two districts multiplied by nearly fivefold, from 300,000 to over 1.43 million at the beginning of 1986. Employment, however, grew even faster--by roughly seven times--perhaps more. From less than 40 percent of the total population in 1965, the share of those employed rose to over 62 percent in 1979 and may, therefore, be 65 to 70 percent today (Table 6.9). In the early 1960s, the West Siberian North was still an economic backwater: fish and fish processing provided 44 percent of all industrial output of the Khanty-Mansi and 42 percent of the Yamal-Nenets District. A few sawmills, chiefly on the edges of the plain, provided most of the rest.[76] About 35 percent of the population in 1959 was under fifteen years of age (almost a third even nine years later)[77] and the indigenous non-Slavic nationalities, with relatively few women working outside the home, still composed close to a fifth of the total population.[78] Rapid immigration, dominated by the 20- to 40-year age group, radically transformed that low employment-population ratio, to one of the highest anywhere in the USSR today. Among the indigenous nationalities, employment is still low, under 40 percent of the population (Table 6.10), but they now make up less than 4 percent of those living in the two districts.[79]

A detailed breakdown of employment provides a rare glimpse of economic activity in each of these two districts, so crucial for Soviet energy prospects (Table 6.11). In 1979, construction commanded the largest workforce throughout the West Siberian North. This is certainly expected in the Yamal-Nenets District where, at that time, only one of the supergiant gas fields, Medvezh'e was fully on line and even Urengoi had barely begun production.[80] Yet it was also true, albeit less obviously, of the Khanty-Mansi District, where the oil industry was approaching maturity. As the few supergiant petroleum deposits, with Samotlor in the lead, were reaching peak capacity, the development of widely scattered oil fields in the roadless marshes have begun to produce new requirements for construction. In the 1980s, such needs only multiplied. Eighteen new fields were put on line during the Eleventh FYP (1981-1985), instead of the thirty demanded, but the Twelfth FYP (1986-1990) calls for seventy-two fields to begin production, forty in its first three years.[81] Most of these are quite small. Those put on line during the 1985-1986 period each yielded two to three million tons per year, though full capacity for some of these will probably be larger.[82]

TABLE 6.9 Growth of Total Population and Employment in
(in thousands and percentages)

Population and employment	1965 (end of year)		1970 (Jan. 1)	
	Kh–M[a]	Y–N[b]	Kh–M[a]	Y–N[b]
Total population	230	70	270.8	81.2
Employed population	87.3	n.d.	146.5	41.0
Workers and employees	83.5	29.3	141.5 (145.0)[c]	39.8 (40.7)[c]
Workers and employees as % of total population	36.3	41.9	52.3 (53.5)[c]	49.0 (50.1)[c]
Collective farmers	3.8	n.d.	1.3	negl.

[a]Khanty–Mansi Autonomous Okrug.
[b]Yamal–Nenets Autonomous Okrug.
[c]Figures in parenthesis are from Itogi vsesoiuznoi perepisi naseleniia 1970 goda, Vol. 5 (Moscow: Statistika, 1973), pp. 36–37.
[d]Estimate. Assumes a 65% employment to populatin ratio.
[d]Estimate. Assumes a 70% employment to population ratio.

Besides these exogenous pressures, however, departmental autarchy and the very high proportion of manual workers have swollen the labor force engaged in construction in northwest Siberia. About thirty separate ministries and state agencies (vedomstva) work on capital construction in the West Siberian oil and gas complex.[83] The old nemesis of "departmentalism," resulting in duplication, lack of coordination, and disunity of action has long plagued development in the region,[84] and the two interdepartmental commissions created recently to improve the situation (in part, perhaps, because of insufficient power granted to them) so far have not made much difference.[85] The share of manual workers is still extremely high, 47 percent on the average for the economy of Tiumen' as a whole. Since it is somewhat lower in industry, that proportion is certain to reach at least one-half in construction, further inflating the labor force requirement.[86]
    Industrial employment is small in the northern gas-

the Oil and Gas Regions of Tiumen' Oblast, 1965–1984

1975 (end of year)		1979 (Jan. 1)		1983 (end of year)	
Kh–M[a]	Y–N[b]	Kh–M[a]	Y–N[b]	Kh–M[a]	Y–N[b]
425	126	569.1	157.6	907	306
n.d.	n.d.	357	99.1		
237.4	60.4	355	98.7	590[d]	200[d]
				635[e]	215[e]
55.9	47.9	62.4	62.6	65[d]	65[d]
				70[e]	70[e]
n.d.	negl.	2	negl.		

Sources: V.V. Alekseev et al., eds. (Akademiia nauk SSSR, Sibirskoe otdelenie, Institut istorii, filologii i filosofii), Sotsial'nye aspekty industrial'nogo razvitiia Sibiri (Novosibirsk: Nauka, 1983), p. 174. Population figures are those of the 1970 and 1979 censuses or are official estimates from the appropriate years of Narodnoe khoziaistvo SSSR. Reprinted from L. Dienes, "Employment Structure, Settlement Policy and the Development of the North Tyumen' Oil and Gas Region," Soviet Geography, Vol. 26, No. 8 (October), 1985, p. 610.

producing district, but ten percentage points greater in the southern region, where most petroleum extraction and the processing of oil well gases take place. The huge gas fields of the north yield almost pure methane, which requires no processing before transport and thus generates virtually no forward (downstream) economic linkages in the area. The growing extraction of condensates has slightly increased forward linkages since 1979. At the same time, the extreme harshness of the environment keeps backward linkages and the employment multiplier to an absolute minimum, i.e., almost all supplies, both for the gas industry and the work force, are shipped in from the outside. Further south in the Khanty-Mansi District, oil extraction and the processing of associated gas generate a greater number of locationally associated forward and backward linkages, even though the refining of the crude oil

TABLE 6.10 Employed and Total Population in the Oil and Gas Regions of Tiumen' Oblast by Ethnic Group, 1979.

Ethnic groups	Khanty-Mansi Autonomous District			Yamal-Nenets Autonomous District		
	Total population	Employed population	Employed population as % of total population	Total population	Employed population	Employed population as % of total population
Indigenous nationalities[a]	18,378	7,438	40.5	25,481	9,338	36.6
Others (mostly Russians)	550,761	349,218	63.4	132,135	89,900	68.0

[a]In Kh-M Autonomous District: Khanty, Mansi and Nenets; in Y-N Autonomous District: Nenets, Khanty, and Sel'kup.

Sources: V.V. Alekseev et al., eds. (Akademiia nauk SSSR, Sibirskoe otdelenie, Institut istorii, filologii i filosofii), Sotsial'nye aspekty industrial'nogo razvitiia Sibiri (Novosibirsk: Nauka, 1983), pp. 176-177, and TsSU, Chislennost' i sostav naseleniia SSSR (Moscow: Finansy i statistika, 1984), pp. 12, 86 and 88. Reprinted from L. Dienes, "Employment Structure, Settlement Policy and the Development of the North Tyumen' Oil and Gas Region," Soviet Geography, Vol. 26, No. 8 (October), 1985, p. 612.

overwhelmingly takes place outside the region. The somewhat better physical environment has allowed the establishment of more supply industries, both of capital and
consumer goods, although here too the great bulk of demand,
by the basic industries as well as the population, is
satisfied from the outside.

It is interesting, therefore, that in agriculture the
contrast between the two districts is actually reversed.
Despite more marginal physical conditions, agriculture in
the gas region engages almost four-fifths as many workers
as the oil region further south, and its share in total
employment is almost three times as high. As Table 6.11
shows, this difference is mostly due to the much greater
absolute number of native nationalities practicing agriculture, chiefly reindeer herding in the Yamal-Nenets
Autonomous District. Still, even among the nonnatives, the
percentage of those employed in agriculture remains higher
in the northern than in the southern district (2.8 percent
versus 1.9 percent), though the absolute numbers are understandably small. Clearly, the difficulties of providing
the Far North with food are so great that industry, transport, and construction trusts make special efforts to
provide some vegetables, meat, and milk for their workers
from hothouses and acclimatized stables. Almost 2,500
persons were employed this way from nonindigenous nationalities on the territory of the Yamal-Nenets Autonomous
District in 1979.

As expected, the share of transport in total employment is very high in both the oil and gas regions, in the
latter even exceeding that in industry. The absolute
number in the Khanty-Mansi District, however, was four
times larger in 1979. The need for transport services has
grown sharply since that time in both districts. The full-
scale exploitation of Urengoi and the start in the development of Yamburg have multiplied such demand in the Far
North, while the dependence on evermore scattered, smaller
oil fields and the big rise in drilling activity have
greatly increased it farther south. At any rate, the 16.8
percent share of the labor force accounted for by transport
and communications in 1979 throughout the West Siberian
North contrasts to the 9 percent claimed by this sector
each year since 1975 in the Soviet economy as a whole.[87]

Trade and public catering, housing and the municipal
economy, health and social services, education, art, and
culture combined was responsible for less than a fifth of
all employment in each district, testifying to the severe
pressure on social infrastructure and to the diversion of

TABLE 6.11 Employment by Sectors in the Oil and Gas Regions of Tiumen' Oblast, 1979

| | Khanty-Mansi Autonomous District | | | |
| | All ethnic groups | | Indigenous ethnic groups[a] | |
Sectors of the economy	Numbers employed	Percent of total employment	Numbers employed	Percent of employment in sector
All Sectors	356,656	100.0	7,438	2.1
Industry	84,536	23.7	1,319	1.6
Agriculture	8,326	2.3	1,700	20.4
Forestry	2,428	0.7	69	2.8
Transport and Communication	61,267	17.2	303	0.5
Construction	86,715	24.3	320	0.4
Trade and public catering	27,724	7.8	457	1.6
Procurement and supply management	8,464	2.4	20	0.2
Other branches of material production	3,033	0.9	1,082	35.7
Housing and municipal economy	11,065	3.1	83	0.8
Health and social services	10,944	3.1	496	4.5
Education	18,452	5.2	901	4.9
Art and culture	2,427	0.7	157	6.5
Science (including supporting personnel)	14,973	4.2	140	0.9
Government insurance and credit	2,016	0.6	33	1.6
Management and party organization	6,767	1.9	134	2.0
Unable to specify plus residual	7,519	2.1	224	3.0

[a]Khanty and Mansi.
[b]Nenets, Khanty and Sel'kup.

TABLE 6.11 continued

| | Yamal–Nenets Autonomous District | | | |
| | All ethnic groups | | Indigenous ethnic groups[b] | |
Sectors of the economy	Numbers employed	Percent of total employment	Numbers employed	Percent of employment in sector
All Sectors	99,238	100.0	9,338	9.4
Industry	13,682	13.8	3,125	22.8
Agriculture	6,471	6.5	3,990	61.7
Forestry	80	negl.	3	3.8
Transport and communication	15,126	15.2	56	0.4
Construction	25,698	25.9	232	0.9
Trade and public catering	7,030	7.1	257	3.7
Procurement and supply management	2,278	2.3	257	11.3
Other branches of material production	491	0.5	194	39.5
Housing and municipal economy	2,305	2.3	92	4.0
Health and social services	3,377	3.4	261	7.7
Education	5,653	5.7	618	10.9
Art and culture	866	0.9	124	14.3
Science (including supporting personnel)	10,393	10.5	53	0.5
Government insurance and credit	690	0.7	5	0.7
Management and party organization	2,452	2.5	129	5.3
Unable to specify plus residual	2,646	2.7	199	2.1

Source: V.V. Alekseev et al., eds. (Akademiia nauk SSSR, Sibirskoe otdelenie, Institut istorii, filologii i filosofii), Sotsial'nye aspekty industrial'nogo razvitiia Sibiri (Novosibirsk: Nauka, 1983), pp. 176–177. Reprinted from L. Dienes, "Employment Structure, Settlement Policy and the Development of the North Tyumen Oil and Gas Region," Soviet Geography, Vol. 26, No. 8 (October), 1985, p. 614.

resources into the material production sphere. This relative neglect lies at the root of the high labor turnover. Interestingly, housing and the municipal economy fare the worst (labor in housing construction is excluded here); trade, public catering, education, and health fare somewhat better. Finally, science (with its supporting personnel) employs a surprisingly large labor force and in the Yamal-Nenets District a very high share as well—more than a tenth of all manpower used. Obviously, the development of West Siberian oil and gas is a science and technology-intensive activity. The very much greater proportion in the gas versus the oil region is at first surprising, but on reflection appears quite logical. The more mature state of the West Siberian oil industry probably requires highly sophisticated scientific work, most of which cannot be done in the Khanty–Mansi District. The bulk of science-related employment in Tiumen' Oblast is probably concentrated in the south of the province, especially in the oblast center of Tiumen' City, which boasts a university. Some thirty research and project-making institutes opened during the past two decades, with over 1,000 senior scientists with doctorates and candidate status.[88] The big gas deposits of the Far North, on the other hand, are located much farther from the oblast center than the Khanty–Mansi oil region. Their development and the transport of the gas also require the more straightforward, on-site application of scientific talent and improvisation in the field. This is also dictated by the permafrost and by the capacity and dimensions of equipment installed, for which no precedent exists anywhere in the world.

Table 6.11 highlights the role of the indigenous nationalities as well. The contribution of the Khanty and the Mansi to the labor force of their homeland is now negligible. In the Yamal-Nenets District, the native groups still accounted for close to one-tenth of all employment in 1979, but 43 percent of them were still engaged in agriculture, chiefly reindeer herding. Their fairly high representation in procurement and supply management probably also involves the acquisition of meat and hides from seminomadic herding collectives. Besides agriculture, the indigenous nationalities have large or significant representation only in the catchall category of "other branches of material production" (most likely unskilled, auxiliary work) and in education, art, culture, and social services (few of them would be engaged in health) occupations specifically tied to the native language and culture. They are also found in fair proportions in local party

organizations and management. This is the consequence of
the Soviet federal system, which expresses the multinational nature of the country, giving scope to diverse
ethnic groups on the local level. However, the influence
of these indigenous nationalities on such crucial issues as
energy policy would certainly be minimal, less even than of
the Eskimos in Alaska or the Canadian North.

The rapid immigration engendered by the oil and gas
boom consists mostly of young adults, able to cope with the
harsh environment and the physically demanding work. Yet
the expectation of a disproportionately high share of
single persons in the total population is only partially
supported by the data. In the two autonomous areas
combined, single persons composed only 14.3 percent of the
total in 1979, a mere 1.6 percentage point above their
share in the Russian Republic as a whole (12.7 percent).[89]
This small difference stems almost entirely from the significantly higher proportion of this demographic group in the
population of the Yamal-Nenets District (17.0 percent),
whose southernmost regions are climatically similar to
Yellowknife, Canada. In the Khanty-Mansi District farther
south, single persons accounted for no more than 13.6
percent of the population, only marginally greater than the
12.7 percent average for the RSFSR as a whole (Table 6.12).
The share of two-member families is actually much smaller
through the West Siberian North than in the Russian
Republic. In that case, however, such families in the
RSFSR make up a large portion of single women with one
child, while in northern Tiumen' this type of family would
be rare and most two-member families are probably composed
of childless couples. At any rate, 85.7 percent of all
people in the two districts (a little more in the Khanty-
Mansi, a little less in the Yamal-Nenets) were living as
families with three or more members in 1979 (Table 6.12).
Virtually all of these would seem to be couples with
children, for whom decent accommmodations would be more
critical than for singles or childless couples. Yet, the
Tenth and Eleventh FYPs (1976-1985) cumulatively allocated
only 5 billion rubles for housing and social
infrastructure, less than a tenth of total investment.[90]
As a result, at the close of the 1970s, only six square
meters of average housing space was available per capita in
the oil and gas regions of Tiumen'.[91] Given the huge (67
percent) growth of population in the following five years
(Table 6.9) and the report that by the end of 1983 Tiumengazprom fell 25 percent behind the goal set by the Eleventh
FYP for housing construction, it is almost certain that

TABLE 6.12 Breakdown of Population by Family Arrangement in the Oil and Gas Regions of Tiumen' Oblast, 1979

Population types	Khanty-Mansi Autonomous District		Yamal-Nenets Autonomous District	
	Number of people	Percent of total population	Number of people	Percent of total population
Total population	569,139	100	157,616	100
Number of people in families	491,996	86.4	130,755	83.0
Number of people in families with three or more members	419,534	73.7	110,327	70.0
Number of people in two-member families	72,462	12.7	20,428	13.0
Single persons	77,143	13.6	26,861	17.0
Singles and people in two-member families	149,606	26.3	47,289	30.0

Source: TsSU, Chislennost' i sostav naseleniia SSSR (Moscow: Finansy i statistika, 1984), pp. 12 and 238-239. Reprinted from L. Dienes, "Employment Structure, Settlement Policy and the Development of the North Tyumen' Oil and Gas Region," Soviet Geography, Vol. 26, No. 8 (October), 1985, p. 616.

there has been no improvement since.[92]

POPULATION POLICY AND EMPLOYMENT: THE NORTH
OF EAST SIBERIA AND THE FAR EAST

The burgeoning growth of population and employment in
the West Siberian oil and gas region is unmatched anywhere
else in Siberia even in the Northland. The rest of the
Siberian Arctic and Subarctic, with six to seven times the
population of the Yamalo-Nenets and Khanty-Mansi Autonomous
Districts in 1959, contributed only a little more to total
population growth since that time. Still, even this more
measured increase has been very rapid indeed and was
exceeded only by that experienced in the Moslem republics
and Armenia.[93] Here too, however, employment has grown at
a 50 to 60 percent faster rate, judging from available data
for most administrative units for the 1965-1976 period.[94]

From the lower Enisei River eastward to the Pacific
Ocean, the extraction and smelting of nonferrous and
precious metals employ the largest percentage of the labor
force.   To this must be added employment in fuel and power
industries, plus construction activities directly serving
that metal production complex. Only in Sakhalin and
Kamchatka Oblasts do mineral industries give way to
fishing, fish processing, and the forest industries in
their dominance of the employment structure. In addition,
transport, communication, and a residual category contribute very substantial shares of employment in both
Sakhalin and Kamchatka (over one-fourth and almost one-
third respectively in the two oblasts [Tables 6.13-6.15]).

The large transport shares are, in large part, related
to the maritime position of both these provinces, effectively cut off from the mainland by water. The big
residual categories, however, are clearly connected to the
military, and such needs may inflate employment in transport and communication as well. Petropavlovsk-Kamchatka is
the second largest submarine base and the third largest
naval base in the USSR. Three-fourths of all submarines
assigned to the Soviet Pacific Fleet are based here. The
city also serves as the headquarters of the Seventh Naval
Squadron and has airforce and naval aviation bases as well.
There also is a strong military presence on the southern
Kuriles, a part of Kamchatka Oblast but claimed by Japan.
Sakhalin lacks the huge naval concentration of Kamchatka,
but hosts six aviation and two army bases, including
artillery divisions, with the Fifteenth Army headquartered

TABLE 6.13 Workers and Employees in the Economy of Kamchatka Oblast (in percent of total)

Economic Sectors	1950	1970	1975
Total for Oblast	100.0	100.0	100.0
Industry (industrial production personnel)	45.9	27.6	27.5
State farms and agricultural production enterprises	4.7	5.1	5.1
Transport	9.5	13.2	14.6
Construction	2.9	10.2	7.6
Retail trade, public catering, procurement, and supply management	9.4	11.3	11.0
Housing and municipal economy	3.9	4.0	4.1
Health and social services	5.1	5.8	5.7
Science (including supporting personnel)	1.8	3.2	3.4
Government and Party organization	4.8	2.8	2.9
Other branches	12.0	16.8	18.1

Source: Narodnoe khoziaistvo Kamchatskoi Oblasti 1971–1975 gg. (Petropavlovsk-Kamchatskii, 1977), p. 84.

TABLE 6.14 Industrial Employment in Kamchatka Oblast in
Various Branches (in percent of total)

Industrial Branches	1970	1973	1975
All industries	100	100	100
Electric power	4.6	5.4	5.6
Machine building-			
metal working,	20.3	18.0	17.7
of which ship repair	14.7	13.1	12.8
Forest, wood product,			
pulp and paper industries	9.6	8.2	7.6
Building material industries	6.9	7.2	6.4
Light industries	8.1	8.8	8.8
Food industries	49.2	50.9	51.8
of which fishing			
and fish products	42.9	45.2	44.4

Source: Narodnoe khoziaistvo Kamchatskoi Oblasti 1971–
1975 gg. (Petrolpavlovsk-Kamchatskii, 1977), p. 23.

at Yuzhno-Sakhalinsk. In addition, both oblasts are saturated with early warning and intelligence-gathering electronic gear, with a large supporting infrastructure and
service personnel.[95]
    In this northern zone between the Enisei and the
Pacific, almost every mineral deposit opened up before
Stalin's death was first exploited by penal labor. Some of
the most important districts of nonferrous and precious
metal extraction today (Noril'sk, Kolyma) were also the
sites of the largest and most notorious labor camps. While
forced labor in the North is still present to a degree,
economic development during the past three decades has
hinged on the size, technological skill, and productivity
of a free population. Given the type of mineral resources
that demand not only more manpower for extraction than oil
and gas in the West Siberian North, but also local processing (and given the fixed nature of such deposits for
longer periods), the labor policies required here differ
appreciably from that applied in Tiumen' Oblast. The same
is true of labor policies required in Kamchatka and
Sakhalin, with their fish and forest industry-dominated
economy and huge defense infrastructure. A mobile labor
force flown in from the European USSR and from southern

TABLE 6.15 Workers and Employees in the Economy of Sakhalin Oblast (in thousands and percentages)

Economic Sectors	1975 In thousands	1975 In percentages	1978 In thousands	1978 In percentages
Total for Oblast	336.6	100.0	350.2	100.0
Industry	105.8	31.4	110.4	31.5
Agriculture	17.2	5.1	18.4	5.3
Construction	37.4	11.1	39.3	11.2
Transport and communication	47.2	14.0	47.6	13.6
Services related to the mater- ial production sphere	38.5	11.4	42.4	12.1
Non material production sphere	74.4	22.1	88.9	25.4
Discrepancy	16.1	4.8	3.2	0.9

Source: Computed from B.N. Zykin, Effektivnost' regional'noi ekonomiki (Moscow: Nauka, 1981), pp. 52–53.

bases in Siberia for a substantial part of resource extraction, housing construction, pipeline laying, etc., as in North Tiumen', is inapplicable here--and so are the large number of temporary and quasi-temporary settlements characteristic of that oil and gas region.

Labor and settlement policy in the East Siberian and Far Eastern Arctic-Subarctic zone, therefore, must emphasize the long term. "Workers here are less interested in delaying material gratification, as most expect to stay long enough to marry and begin raising families. Consequently, they are more interested in better housing and improved access to social services than in income for its own sake. The [main] problem becomes not making money, but finding ways of spending it to improve the standard of living."[96] This issue of providing a "family style" habitat for a large, permanent labor force at the world's biggest northernmost mining and smelting operation at Noril'sk has been ably analyzed by Andrew Bond. He has shown that "planners in Noril'sk did not achieve their labor goals easily and quickly...[but] started with a very poor understanding of the measures needed." A trial-and-error theme thus runs through the entire experience. Bond traces the demonstrable improvement in the physical base of social services and infrastructure through a massive building program. The positive results of such progress can be gauged by the fact that, during the 1970s, a full half of the city's growth was attributed to natural increase. While a goodly portion of the young who are native to Noril'sk have indicated a desire to leave, a much smaller share have actually done so.[97] Even in the small cities of the East Siberian Arctic, where (after Noril'sk) the bulk of the immigrant Slavic population live, families with children thoroughly dominate. In Dudinka (with about 30,000 inhabitants), Dikson, and Talnakh, families with three and more members composed over 71 percent of the population in 1979 and those with two members 15.2 percent. The share of single persons is under 14 percent, only one percentage point higher than the average for the Russian Republic.[98]

Yet Bond also shows that the massive construction effort to expand housing, physical infrastructure, and social services has until very recently remained primarily a mechanical exercise. It has concerned itself with fulfilling quantitative targets, with "little in-depth analysis of what people want or what their real needs are," as perceived by those actually involved. And "only during the last few years has the major concern of labor planning

in the city shifted from one of quantity, or size of the
work force, to quality, or more precisely productivity."
However, further population growth now tends to be opposed,
lest per capita provision of social services deteriorate
and the quality of life be lowered. In turn, significant
labor-saving technologies have been introduced. According
to Bond, "the problems with labor recruitment and retention
essentially have been resolved . . . [and] planners no
longer believe that labor shortages compromise the feasibility of mining and metallurgical operations."[99]
     One additional point about development at Noril'sk in
worth noting. The almost total absence of farming in the
northern half of East Siberia and the extraordinary
variety, size, and richness of ore bodies in the Putorana
Mountain-Taimyr area[100] (requiring fairly complex processing before outshipment) have resulted in a geographic
concentration of population and development plus a degree
of urbanization unmatched almost anywhere else in the USSR.
The whole northern half of East Siberia (north of the 60th
parallel), with its roughly 2,000,000 square kilometers,
has only some 280,000 inhabitants. Over 76 percent of
these live in the Noril'sk-Dudinka area on less than 0.3
percent of the huge territory, almost two-thirds in
Noril'sk alone.[101] Some nine-tenths of the population is
urban and this share is still higher among the overwhelmingly dominant Slavic population. By contrast, in the
Yakut ASSR to the east 31.5 percent of the inhabitants were
still rural in 1985, and in Magadan and Kamchatka Oblast 19
and 18 percent respectively.[102]
     This northern "family style" development must also be
qualified. The Noril'sk region and some of the high-
priority gold-, diamond-, and tin-mining areas indeed seem
to have been quite successful in providing accommodations
and services for a permanent labor force. As the foregoing
paragraph shows, however, the North of the Far East still
includes a substantial rural population scattered over a
vast territory engaged in agriculture, herding, forestry
and, especially along the coast, fishing. A good portion
of that population is also composed of Yakuts and small
northern nationalities. For them and for the Slavs in
forestry, fishing, and other relatively low-priority industries successful development "family style" hardly applies.
In the Yakut ASSR and Kamchatka Oblast, for example, the
mean per capita housing space today falls 35 percent (!)
below the average for the Russian Republic.[103] This is
despite the fact that the Yakut ASSR is a crucial diamond-,
gold-, and tin-mining province and that Kamchatka contains

the third largest naval base in the USSR. Even though there are the huge gas reserves of the Yakut ASSR, only a quarter of its urban housing stock has access to gas, and the volume of housing space with gas supply is actually declining. Yakutgazstroi (Yakut Gas Construction Trust) is unable to cope even with industrial demand and will not, in the foreseeable future, engage in new hook-ups or, apparently, expand the distribution of bottled gas. The reliability of supply to users already connected has worsened greatly in recent years, especially through the winter months.[104]

Accommodations and services are not much better in most of the BAM zone, where the railway and coal and power production in the Neriungri-Chul'man complex have proved so costly that resources for the necessary infrastructure simply could not be found. In the entire central section of the BAM, only 67 percent of the population is provided with housing, and a far smaller fraction has access to household and hospital services.[105] The March 1985 session of the Yakut Supreme Soviet made clear that the average level of supply of consumer goods and services in the ASSR is in last place among provinces of the Russian Republic. Per ruble of wages paid out, the Yakut ASSR produces seven times less consumer goods than the RSFSR average and six times less even than Kamchatka Oblast. Most goods have to be shipped in via rivers during the short navigation season. The shops in Yakutia, therefore, lack the most elementary provisions (sugar, flour, vinegar, soap, tooth-paste, kitchen utensils, shovels, baby food, children's footwear, felt boots, etc.) for many months, in some cases, and in outlying districts, for even years.[106]

COASTAL SETTLEMENTS IN THE FAR EAST

Compared to most other nations, the share of coastal settlements in the total Soviet population is low. Moreover, the share of maritime population was actually declining until very recently, in line with the essentially autarchic, inward-oriented development of the USSR through most of Soviet history. Among large cities of 100,000 and over, for example, the proportion of those situated on the coast declined from a full third in 1926 to 15 percent in 1979, with a slight rise since. Lately, investigators have noted a more active development on the Soviet littoral, "linked to the increasing foreign trade of the USSR and to greater involvement in ocean affairs in general." Still, overall maritime urban growth remained slightly below the rate of total urban growth for the entire Soviet population both during the 1960s and in the 1970–1983 period.[107]

The Far Eastern littoral, however, proved an exception to that inward orientation even during the Stalin era. The strategic vulnerability of that coast and fear of Japan induced considerable activity along it during the 1930s, and especially during the second half of the decade. Then the period of World War II and the early postwar years saw intensive development, particularly fisheries and the incorporation of southern Sakhalin and the Kurile Islands into the Soviet economy and the replacement of the former Japanese population. If the Caspian Sea is excluded, where most coastal development has been associated with the oil industry and inland fisheries, 27 percent of all urban places founded on Soviet seashores during the 1933–1941 period were along the Pacific. (Only on the Arctic coast, where the development of the Northern Sea Route was under-way were more urban settlements founded.) Then from 1942 through 1950, fifty-one of the eighty new urban places on Soviet coasts, and of a total of seventy-two without the Caspian, arose along the Pacific. Urban growth on the Far Eastern coast slackened during the 1960s, falling behind the Soviet average, but a renewed spurt took place in the following decade. From 1970 through 1983, maritime urban growth in the Far East overtook overall urban increase and ran well ahead of the growth of such settlements elsewhere in the USSR, except along the Black Sea.[108]

As Chapter 4 showed, the activities propelling that coastal development were largely associated with increased foreign trade (especially with Japan), the huge naval build-up, and the strengthening of maritime links to Magadan Oblast, with its crucial gold- and tin-mining industry. Several port cities (e.g., Nakhodka, Magadan, Petropavlovsk-Kamchatka) grew from 47 to 61 percent between January 1970 and January 1986,[109] while the small town of Wrangel, with its new, massive container terminal of Vostochnyi, appar-ently multiplied its population and was given city status. The rapid growth of Yuzhno-Sakhalinsk, near but not on the coast, also must have been partly military-related. The Soya (La Perouse) Strait between southern Sakhalin and the Wakkanai Penninsula of Hokkaido is the principal supply route between Vladivostok and Petropavlovsk-Kamchatka (the second largest submarine base in the USSR) and also to Korsakov, the port for Yuzhno-Sakhalinsk.[110] Not only is the Soya Strait the shortest passage to Petropavlovsk, the USSR is also forced to use it, since the entirely Soviet

Tatar Strait is too shallow and freezes solid during the winter. Besides these major ocean activities, the fishing industry has continued to be significant for population increase on the littoral. Sixty-nine out of the ninety-four urban places on the Pacific coast (i.e., 73 percent) did not have city status in 1983 but were called "settlements of urban type." The great bulk of these must be fishing settlements, though some should also be military-related. Thirteen of them have been newly established since 1959.[111]

The vast coastal zone from the Chukchi Peninsula to the Chinese-Korean border has effective access to the interior and the Soviet core areas only from its southernmost section. That portion composes less than one-eighth of the coastal zone and, even here, access is provided only through two portals, i.e., that between Vladivostok and Wrangel Bay in the extreme south and through Vanino-Sovetskaia Gavan'. Before the construction of the BAM, traffic from both portals had to funnel into the Trans-Siberian Railway. BAM provides an alternative route. Although it is destined to remain single-track for the foreseeable future, its present capabilities (when fully in service) will increase transport capacity between the seaboard and the Enisei-Angara region by 30 percent--from 80 million tons per year to 115 million. Eventually, the throughput capacity of BAM may double, almost equaling that of the Trans-Siberian.[112]

The implication of this crucial position for the southern littoral is that the transport sector, which in the Far East as a whole claims 19 percent of all workers and employees (30 percent of fixed assets and 23 percent of all investment),[113] must play an equally important or even bigger role. Within the transport sector, a very large part of the work force is engaged in ocean transport and in port operations related to the break in bulk between two different transport media handling large amounts of heavy freight. This traffic concerns not only export-import shipment and cargo through the Trans-Siberian land bridge, but even more domestic freight, since three of the Far Eastern provinces can be supplied only by water. A very substantial part of all shipment to and from the two portals (by rail from the interior and by sea to Kamchatka, Sakhalin, Viet Nam, and Cambodia) consists of military and related goods.

Not surprisingly, the share of employment related to maritime transport and the naval bases is unavailable. Even the relative share of the work force in the fishing industry was found only for Kamchatka Oblast, located in the northern zone, and only for 1975 (Table 6.14). Yet the significance of sea transport and of the naval bases for population and labor may be judged by the fact that the Pacific commercial fleet represents about 20 percent of Soviet civilian tonnage[114] and military ships and submarines based at Far Eastern bases account for almost 40 percent of all Soviet naval strength. Almost three-fourths of the surface ships and one-fourth of the submarines are stationed along the southern coast.[115] A rare Soviet monograph reveals that the number of sailors registered at Vladivostok exceeds 10 percent of the permanent population of that city and those registered at Nakhodka amount to some two-fifths of the population of the latter. This implies numbers of around 60,000 for each city.[116] Although the source is not entirely clear, these numbers seem to refer to sailors in the commercial fleet. The total number of _uniformed_ personnel in the Soviet Far East naval forces must approximate 180,000 since the Soviet navy as a whole claims some 467,000 men.[117] At least 120,000 of these must be based along the southern littoral.

Although the large ports, such as Vladivostok, Nakhodka, and, farther north, Petropavlovsk-Kamchatka, have multifunctional roles, their economic structures are still biased towards physically demanding, male-dominated activities. For the smaller cities of the coast, this is even more true. In maritime transport, even according to the broadest definition, men outnumber women three to one, a ratio that rises to nine to one in actual ship operations. In ship repair, 65 percent of all employed are male, and in the fishing industry it is 80 percent. Even in Vladivostok, by far the largest and most diversified city along the Soviet Pacific, 9 percent of the population of working age consists of women not employed outside the home. This means that around 19 percent of adult women not yet of pension age remain outside the work force--a very high share in the USSR, where 93 percent of all women of working age are gainfully employed outside the home.[118] In the Russian Republic this share must be even higher. The coastal provinces of the Far East, even in the extreme south, thus fully share the problem of occupational imbalance between the sexes that is so characteristic of Siberia, and especially of its northern zone. In addition, employment by women is probably biased towards heavy physical work even more than elsewhere in the USSR.

The large percentage of seamen forming the registered but not permanent population of Pacific coastal cities and the male-female imbalance in employment exacerbate the shortage of communal services, housing-municipal infrastructure, and the labor problem. When demand for housing, social-municipal services, and infrastructure is determined and forecast in investment allocation, the registered population that spends most of its time at sea is not counted in the projections of the planning authorities. The consequent pressure on the housing and tertiary sector and the resultant severe deficiencies are claimed to be one of the chief causes of the high labor turnover complicating the formation of a permanent population and the economic development of the Far East.[119] Very large numbers of people, especially fishermen and sailors, live in hostels, even those with families. In addition, the strongly seasonal nature of the fishing and fish-processing industries result in an influx of temporary labor to coastal settlements at peak times, which further aggravates the pressure on infrastructure.[120] The housing pressure on the coast must be a significant factor in pushing the Far East to last place among the eleven major economic regions of the Russian Republic in the availability of per capita housing space.[121]

The rugged topography and the shortage of level land along the littoral sharply increases construction and urban development costs even in the extreme south, where the climate is least severe. Yet two-fifths of the population of Maritime Krai and 30 percent of Sakhalin, 1,050,000 out of a total of almost 2.8 million in these two provinces, live on the immediate coast. Further north in Kamchatka, this share is as high as 70 percent, though the total coastal population amounts to less than 300,000.[122] As shown, Kamchatka depends entirely on the Vladivostok-Nakhodka portal for links with the rest of the USSR and for supplies not available on that rugged, remote, and sparsely inhabited peninsula. This connection, together with somewhat less intensive linkages with Sakhalin, Magadan Oblast, and the northern coast of Khabarovsk Krai, put further strain on the overloaded infrastructure of the southern littoral, especially at its two portals at Vladivostok-Wrangel Bay and Vanino-Sovetskaia Gavan'.[123]

NOTES

1. S.N. Zhelezko, Sotsial'no-demograficheskie prob-lemy v zone BAMa (Moscow: Statistika, 1980), pp. 42 and 113.

2. A.D. Khaitun, Ekspeditsionno-vakhtovoe stroitel'-stvo v Zapadnoi Sibiri (Leningrad: Stroiizdat, 1982), pp. 8-9 and Ekonomicheskaia gazeta, 1986, No. 28 (July), p. 8.

3. A.G. Aganbegian et al., eds., Sibir' v edinom narodno-khoziaistvennom komplekse (Novosibirsk: Nauka, 1980), p. 69.

4. Leslie Dienes, "The Development of Siberian Regions: Economic Profiles, Income Flows and Strategies for Growth," Soviet Geography, Vol. 23, No. 4 (April), 1982, p. 224.

5. Ekonomicheskaia gazeta, 1986, No. 28 (July), p. 8. As it is, the more than 500,000 immigrants over the past decade contributed only a 78,000 net addition to the population, the rest returned. Dissatisfied returnees are increasing in number, especially since a large percentage of women, qualified in medical, pedogogical, etc., professions cannot find work in their occupations, given the undeveloped social infrastructure, and must work as unskilled laborers. Nikolai Tkachenko, "Uroki Neriungri," Molodaia gvardiia, 1986, No. 3, pp. 267-68.

6. Dienes, "The Development of Siberian Regions," p. 225.

7. A.D. Kirillin, ed., Mezhotraslevye sviazi v Iakut-skoi ASSR (Iakutsk: Iakutskii filial AN SSSR, SO, 1985), p. 37 and V.N. Bugromenko, ed., Territorial'nye aspekty razvitiia transportnoi infrastruktury (Vladivostok: AN Dal'nevostochnyi nauchnyi tsentr and Institut geografii, 1984), p. 57. The first source reveals that, in five major branches of Yakut industry, over 80 percent, and in another three branches, from 50 to 70 percent of material inputs are shipped in from the outside. Only four major industrial branches shipped in less than a third of their inputs.

8. Iu.G. Benderskii and V.L. Kvint, eds., Ekonomi-cheskie problemy nauchno-tekhnicheskogo progressa v regione (Novosibirsk: AN SSSR SO, IEOPP, 1985), pp. 7 and 73.

9. L.A. Kvon, Zaniatost' naseleniia v usloviiakh sotsialisticheskogo rasshirennogo proizvodstva (Alma-Ata: Nauka, 1982), p. 111.

10. L.V. Korel', Peremeshcheniia naseleniia mezhdu gorodom i selom v usloviiakh urbanizatsii (Novosibirsk: Nauka, 1982), pp. 63-64 and 84.

11. For arable land 1975 figures had to be used, since data in later years are unavailable for Siberia. Narodnoe khoziaistvo RSFSR v 1975 godu, pp. 162-163; V.A. Artemov, ed., Problemy sotsial'no-ekonomicheskogo razvitiia zapadno-sibirskoi derevni (Novosibirsk: Nauka, 1981), p. 55.

221

12. A.N. Lifanchikov and A.D. Nastenko, Prodovol'-
stvennyi kompleks Sibiri i Dal'nego Vostoka (Moscow: Ekonomika, 1982), p. 25.
13. A.G. Granberg, ed., Ekonomika Sibiri v razreze
shirotnykh zon (Novosibirsk: Nauka, 1985), p. 158.
14. Lifanchikov and Nastenko, Prodovol'stvennyi kompleks, p. 42 and Narodnoe khoziaistvo RSFSR v 1980 godu,
p. 42.
15. A.K. Zakumbaev, Regional'nye aspekty ispol'zovaniia truda (Alma-Ata: Nauka, 1983), pp. 156-58; T.I.
Zaslavskaia and I.B. Muchnik, eds., Sotsial'no-demografi-
cheskoe razvitie sela (Moscow: Statistika, 1980), pp. 140
and 250-51 and Narodnoe khoziaistvo Kazakhstana v 1984 godu
(Alma-Ata: Kazakhstan, 1985), pp. 23-24.
16. Korel', Peremeshcheniia naseleniia, p. 63.
17. Ibid., pp. 66-75, 107-109 and 144-177.
18. Zaslavskaia and Muchnik, Sotsial'no-demografi-
cheskoe razvitie sela, pp. 250-251.
19. Artemov, ed., Problemy sotsial'no-ekonomicheskogo
razvitiia, pp. 69-71.
20. Z.I. Kalugina and T.P. Antonova, Lichnoe podsobnoe
khoziaistvo sel'skogo naseleniia: problemy i perspektivy
(Novosibirsk: Nauka, 1984), p. 108.
21. O.P. Kochetkov, chief ed., Trudovye resursy v
realizatsii prodovol'stvennoi programmy (Moscow: Tsentral'nyi-nauchnyi institut pri Goskomitete RSFSR, 1984),
p. 92.
22. Korel', Peremeshcheniia naseleniia, pp. 131-138.
23. Kalugina and Antonova, Lichnoe podsobnoe khoziaistvo, p. 68.
24. T.I. Zaslavskaia, V.I. Fedoseev and A.Ia. Trotskovskii, "K voprosu o sotsial'no-territorial'noi strukture
ekonomicheskogo raiona. Chast' 1," AN SSSR, SO, Seriia
ekonomiki i prikladnoi sotsiologii, Izvestiia, 1985, No. 1,
p. 7.
25. I. Buzdalov, "Perevod sel'skogo khoziaistva na
industrial'nuiu bazu," Voprosy ekonomiki, 1976, No. 12,
p. 82-93.
26. Zaslavskaia, Fedoseev and Trotskovskii, "K voprosu
o sotsial'no-territorial'noi strukture," pp. 7-8.
27. S.V. Slavin, Osvoenie Severa Sovetskogo Soiuza
(Moscow: Nauka, 1982), p. 22 and Narodnoe khoziaistvo RSFSR
v 1973 godu, pp. 9-10.
28. A.R. Bernval'd, Regional'nye problemy tovarnogo
obrashcheniia (Novosibirsk: Nauka, 1984), p. 39.
29. Narodnoe khoziaistvo Kazakhstana v 1984 godu, pp.
5 and 85 and N.F. Golikov and A.I. Sedlovskii, Sotsial'no-

ekonomicheskie aspekty sel'skogo rasseleniia Kazakhstana (Alma-Ata: Kainar, 1981), pp. 139-155.
30. Narodnoe khoziaistvo Kazakhstana v 1984 godu, pp. 105-107.
31. Golikov and Sedlovskii, Sotsial'no-ekonomicheskie aspekty, pp. 130-31.
32. Ibid., p. 75.
33. TsSU, Itogi vsesoiuznoi perepisi naseleniia 1970 goda Tom. 1 (Moscow: Statistika, 1972), pp. 135-139.
34. V.I. Bogatov, "Prodovol'stvennaia programma i problemy agrokhimicheskogo syr'ia Sibiri," AN SSSR, SO, Seriia ekonomiki i prikladnoi sotsiologii, Izvestiia, 1984, No. 12, p. 16.
35. Narodnoe khoziaistvo Kazakhstana v 1984 godu, pp. 121-22 and 125-26.
36. The total number of villages in Siberia and the Far East at the time of the 1979 census is computed to be about 18,300, which divided by 3,000 gives more than six villages per farm. Bernval'd, Regional'nye problemy, p. 127. Number of settlements in Kazakhstan is from Table 6.4.
37. Ibid., pp. 142-143.
38. E.E. Goriachenko, Sotsial'nye problemy razvitiia malykh sel'skikh poselenii. Preprint. (Novosibirsk: AN SSSR, SO, IEOPP, 1986), pp. 20-21 and A.A. Vershinin, ed., Napravleniia razvitiia prodovol'stvennogo kompleksa Sibiri. Sbornik nauchnykh trudov (Novosibirsk: Akademiia sel'skokhoziaistvennykh nauk, Sib. otdel., Sib. nauchno-issled. inst. ekon. sel'skogo khoziaistva, 1985), p. 29. Through the vast Northland, not even regular mail service may be available to many rural settlements. Ten to fifteen years ago, almost 45 percent of rural population points in the Yakut ASSR were without regular mail delivery or pickup, though the situation must have improved since that time. K.P. Kosmachov and V.P. Mosunov, "Ob otsenke prostranstvennykh razlichii v formirovanii normativnoi bazy," in AN SSSR, Institut Geografii Sibiri i Dal'nego Vostoka (Irkutsk), Doklady, 1976, No. 50, p. 8.
39. Bernval'd, Regional'nye problemy, p. 137.
40. Ibid., pp. 54-55, 130 and 137-138 and Goriachenko, Sotsial'nye problemy, pp. 4, 11-13 and 26-27.
41. Goriachenko, Sotsial'nye problemy, p. 11 and interview with Tatiana Zaslavskaia, Novosibirsk, July 1986.
42. Narodnoe khoziaistvo SSSR v 1985 godu, pp. 12-14; M.M. Traskunova, "Problemy i perspektivy ekonomicheskogo i sotsial'nogo razvitiia narodnostei Severa," AN SSSR, SO, Seriia ekonomiki i prikladnoi sotsiologii, Izvestiia, 1984,

223

No. 7, pp. 72-73 and V.I. Boiko, chief ed., Narodnosti Severa: problemy i perspektivy ekonomicheskogo i sotsial'nogo razvitiia (Novosibirsk: All-Union Conference, October 4-6, 1983. Proceedings), p. 60.

43. Narodnoe khoziaistvo SSSR. 1922-1982, p. 34 and Slavin, Osvoenie Severa, p. 22.

44. The urban-rural distribution from the 1979 census was not released by nationalities, except for families. From the number of families, average family size, and total population, one may compute that Yakut singles composed about 23 percent of the population and more of them were likely to have been urban. TsSU, Chislennost' i sostav naseleniia SSSR (Moscow: Finansy i statistika, 1984), pp. 288-293.

45. Slavin, Osvoenie Severa, p. 22.

46. TsSU, Chislennost' i sostav, pp. 74 and 82 and Atlas SSSR (Moscow: Glavnoe upravlenie geodezii i kartografii, 1985), p. 129.

47. D.G. Bragina, "O nekotorykh aspektakh sovremennykh etnicheskikh protsessov u Iakutov v tsentral'noi Iakutii," in I.S. Gurvich, ed., Etnokulturnye processy u narodov Sibiri i Severa (Moscow: Nauka, 1985), p. 37.

48. Computed from 1959, 1970 and 1979 census figures.

49. V.I. Kozlov, Natsional'nosti SSSR (Moscow: Statistika, 1975), p. 109 and TsSU, Chislennost' i sostav, p. 82

50. I.I. Poisev, ed., Otraslevye osobennosti ekonomicheskogo razvitiia IaASSR v razreze shirotnykh zon (Iakutsk: AN SSSR, SO, Iakutskii filial, 1985), p. 13.

51. TsSU, Chislennost' i sostav, pp. 82-83 and Bragina, "O nekotorykh aspektakh," pp. 32-33.

52. Bragina, "O nekotorykh aspektakh," p. 36.

53. TsSU, Chislennost' i sostav, pp. 72-73, 92 and 96.

54. B.V. Lashov and O.P. Litovka, Sotsial'no-ekonomicheskie problemy razvitiia narodnostei Krainego Severa (Leningrad: Nauka, 1982), p. 50 and M.A. Kolesnikov, "Traditsionnyi severnyi kompleks otraslei khoziaistva kak sfera zaniatosti narodnostei Severa," in Boiko, chief ed., Narodnosti Severa, p. 16.

55. AN SSSR, SO, Institut istorii, filologii i filosofii, BAM i narody Severa (Novosibirsk: Nauka, 1979), pp. 11 and 85 and 165 and Boiko, chief ed., Narodnosti Severa, pp. 18-19.

56. A.N. Kashtanov, et al., Razvitie sel'skogo khoziaistva Sibiri i Dal'nego Vostoka (Moscow: Kolos, 1980), pp. 97 and 270-271 and Narodnoe khoziaistvo RSFSR v 1984 godu, p. 29.

57. AN SSSR, SO, BAM i narody Severa, pp. 85, 93 and

224

130-138 and V.I. Boiko and N.V. Vasil'ev, Sotsial'no-professional'naia mobil'nost' evenkov i evenov Iakutii (Novosibirsk: Nauka, 1981), pp. 104-105.

58. Boiko, Narodnosti Severa, p. 59 and 61-62.

59. AN SSSR, SO, BAM i narody Severa, pp. 157 and 159.

60. Lashov and Litovka, Sotsial'no-ekonomicheskie problemy, p. 50; TsSU, Chislennost' i sostav, p. 71 and TsSU, Itogi vsesoiuznoi perepisi Tom. 4, p. 20.

61. TsSU Chislennost' i sostav, pp. 72-73 and 86-87 and TsSU, Itogi vsesoiuznoi perepisi, Tom. 4, pp. 21 and 123-24.

62. Boiko, Narodnosti Severa, pp. 35-36, 70-86.

63. AN SSSR, SO, BAM i narody Severa, p. 158 and Kashtanov et al., Razvitie sel'skogo khoziaistva Sibiri, pp. 97 and 270-71.

64. AN SSSR, SO, BAM i narody Severa, pp. 165-67.

65. Boiko and Vasil'ev, Sotsial'no-professional'naia mobil'nost', pp. 161, pp. 161-62.

66. TsSU, Chislennost' i sostav, pp. 76, 80 and 82.

67. V.M. Miakinenkov, Ekonomicheskie problemy rasseleniia i raionov planirovki na Severe (Leningrad: Stroiizdat, 1983), p. 20.

68. Granberg, Ekonomika Sibiri, p. 23.

69. Narodnoe khoziaistvo Iakutskoi ASSR v Desiatoi Piatiletke. 1976-1980 (Iakutsk, 1981), p. 30.

70. V.P. Mozhin, ed., Ekonomicheskoe razvitie Sibiri i Dal'nego Vostoka (Moscow: Mysl', 1980), p. 84 and E.G. Egorov, Problemy regional'noi ekonomiki (Novosibirsk: Nauka, 1979), p. 193.

71. Slavin, Osvoenie Severa, p. 127.

72. Computed from percentages of net value of output given in Mozhin, ed., Ekonomicheskoe razvitie Sibiri, pp. 76-77.

73. B.P. Orlov and V.N. Kharitonova, "Zapadno-Sibirskii Neftegazovyi Kompleks v Odinnadtsatoi Piatiletke," Ekonomika i organizatsiia promyshlennogo proizvodstva (EKO), 1985, No. 6, p. 43.

74. Leslie Dienes and Theodore Shabad, The Soviet Energy System: Resource Use and Policies (Washington, D.C.: Winston & Sons, 1979), pp. 46-47 and 70-71; Theodore Shabad, "News Notes," Soviet Geography, Vol. 27, No. 4 (April), 1986, pp. 248, 252 and 258.

75. Theodore Shabad, "News Notes," Soviet Geography, Vol 27, No. 4 (April), 1986, pp. 252 and 258.

76. V.V. Veselkina, "Sotsial'noe razvitie narodov Obskogo Severa v usloviiakh intensivnogo promyshlennogo osvoeniia," in V.V. Alekseev, S.S. Bukin, A.A. Dolgoliuk

and I.M. Savitskii, eds., Sotsial'nye aspekty industrial'-nogo razvitiia Sibiri (Novosibirsk: Nauka, 1983), p. 168 and Robert N. North, "Soviet Northern Development: the Case of NW Siberia," Soviet Studies, Vol. 24, No. 2 (October), 1972, p. 173.

77. Estimated by assigning half of the 10- to 19-year (inclusive) age group to the 10- to 14-year age category. TsSU, Itogi vsesoiuznoi perepisi, Tom. 2, pp. 140-141.

78. Veselkina, "Sotsial'noe razvitie," p. 172 and Narodnoe khoziaistvo SSSR v 1958 godu, p. 14.

79. They formed 6 percent of the population in January 1979. However, since the native population actually declined during the 1970s by 3.6 percent (Table 6.10 and TsSU, Itogi vsesoiuznoi perepisi, Tom. 4, pp. 123-124), it is unlikely to have increased between 1979 and the end of 1983 either. Meanwhile total population grew by 703,000 from January 1, 1979 through January 1, 1986. Narodnoe khoziaistvo SSSR v 1978 godu, pp. 14 and Narodnoe khoziaistvo v 1985 godu, p. 14.

80. Dienes and Shabad, The Soviet Energy System, p. 87.

81. Theodore Shabad, "News Notes," Soviet Geography, Vol. 27, No. 4 (April), 1986, pp. 251-52 and "S zasedaniia kollegii Minnefteproma" (no author), Neftianoe khoziaistvo, 1985, No. 2, p. 69.

82. Izvestiia, September 4, 1986.

83. S.N. Starovoitov, ed., Problemy razvitiia Zapadno-Sibirskogo neftegazovogo kompleksa (Novosibirsk: Nauka, 1983), p. 33. If one excludes Tomsk Oblast and the south of Tiumen', this number is somewhat smaller. The CIA, USSR Energy Atlas Washington, D.C., U.S. Government Printing Office, 1985), p. 18, claims twenty-six ministries and state agencies involved in the build-up of oil and gas producing region.

84. Pravda, February 27, 1977, p. 2; May 7, 1978, p. 3 and June 5, 1978, p. 2.

85. A.G. Aganbegian, ed., Territorial'no-proizvod-stvennye kompleksy: planirovanie i upravlenie (Novosibirsk: Nauka, 1984), pp. 54 and 57 and Thane Gustafson, The Soviet Gas Campaign. Politics and Policy in Soviet Decision Making (Santa Monica: Rand Corporation, 1983), pp. 23-26.

86. Starovoitov, Problemy razvitiia, p. 214. In the USSR as a whole, approximately three-fifths of all workers employed by the Ministry of Construction are manual laborers. Pravda, November 25, 1983, p. 2. However, in the Ministry of Construction of Petroleum and Gas Industry Enterprises, the Ministries of the Gas, Petroleum,

Petroleum Refining Industries, which are much more prominent in Tiumen' Oblast, this portion is certainly lower than 60 percent.

87. Narodnoe khoziaistvo SSSR v 1979 godu, p. 385 and Narodnoe khoziaistvo SSSR v 1985 godu, p. 389.

88. V.V. Trushkov, Naselenie goroda i prigoroda (Moscow: Finansy i statistika, 1983), p. 32.

89. Calculated from TsSU, Chislennost' i sostav, pp. 220-21.

90. Ekonomicheskaia gazeta, 1984, No. 36 (September), p. 9. For total investment see, Khaitun, Ekspeditsionno-vakhtovoe stroitel'stvo, p. 7; Leningradskaia Pravda, January 8, 1981, p. 1; N. Kazanskiy and N. Singur, "Sibir' i Dal'nii Vostok v narodnokhoziaistvennom komplekse strany," Planovoe khoziaistvo, 1984, No. 4, pp. 99-100; and D.V. Belorusov, "Zapadno-Sibirskii Territorial'no-Proizvodstvennyi Kompleks," Problemy Severa, 1983, No. 21, p. 76. Public health fairs even worse. Only 0.5 percent of the monies allocated for "nonproductive" construction have gone to public health. That is one-eighth of the norm. Sovetskaia Rossiia, December 9, 1983, p. 3.

91. S.N. Zhelezko, Sotsial'no-demograficheskie problemy v zone BAMa (Moscow: Statistika, 1980), p. 40.

92. Ekonomicheskaia gazeta, 1984, No. 36 (September), p. 9.

93. Official data available for the Taimyr and Evenki Autonomous Districts of Krasnoiarsk Krai, the Yakut ASSR, Magadan and Kamchatka Oblasts. Figures for the small population living in the northern zone of the remaining administrative units cannot be calculated. Narodnoe khoziaistvo SSSR v 1985 godu, pp. 12-14 and TsSU, Itogi vsesoiuznoi perepisi, Tom 1, pp. 12-14.

94. Narodnoe khoziaistvo SSSR za 60 let, pp. 49-51 and 468; Narodnoe khoziaistvo Magadanskoi oblasti v Deviatoi Piatiletke (Magadan, 1976), p. 80.

95. Jane's Defence Weekly, 1984, April 14, pp. 560-61.

96. Andrew R. Bond, "Northern Settlement Family-Style: Labor Planning and Population Policy in Noril'sk," Soviet Geography, Vol. 26, No. 1 (January), 1985, pp. 27-29.

97. Ibid., pp. 26-47.

98. Computed from TsSU, Chislennost' i sostav, pp. 230-231.

99. Bond, "Northern Settlement," pp. 40-43.

100. Some 60 percent of all the elements of the periodic table are present in the region. Over 100 of the approximately 2,000 minerals known have been uncovered in the Noril'sk deposits, with its nickel and platinum

reserves being among the largest in the world. More recently, a large deposit of copper in almost pure form has been discovered in the Taimyr Peninsula. At present, nickel, copper, platinum, gold, silver, tellurium, selenium, and cobalt are produced at Noril'sk on a large or substantial scale. Bond, "Northern Settlement," p. 27; "Gorod za Poliarnym Krugom," EKO, 1982, No. 4, pp. 77-78 and Paul Lydolph, Geography of the USSR (New York: John Wiley and Sons. Third Edition, 1977), p. 416.

101. Atlas SSSR, pp. 10-11, 50-51 and 186-87 and Theodore Shabad, "Population Trends of Soviet Cities, 1970-1984," Soviet Geography, Vol. 26, No. 2 (February), 1985, p. 138.

102. Narodnoe khoziaistvo RSFSR v 1985 godu, pp. 12-14.

103. A.G. Popov, "Industriia u okeana," Dal'nii Vostok, 1985, No. 9, p. 104.

104. Zasedaniia Verkhovnogo Soveta Iakutskoi ASSR odinnadtsatogo sozyva. Pervaia sessia. Stenograficheskii otchet (Iakutsk: Iakutskoe knizhnoe izdatel'stvo, 1985). Speeches by I.P. Tolmachev and M.P. Gubkin, pp. 76 and 88-89.

105. Ekonomicheskaia gazeta, 1986, No. 28 (July), p. 8.

106 Zasedaniia Verkhovnogo Soveta Iakutskoi ASSR. Speech by N.P. Iskanova, pp. 18-20 and 27-28.

107. V.A. Dergachev, "Peculiarities in the Formation of Populated Places on the Seaboard of the USSR," Soviet Geography, Vol. 27, No. 3 (March), 1986, pp. 143, 145 and 150.

108. Ibid., pp. 144-145 and 150.

109. Shabad, "Population Trends," p. 139 and Narodnoe khoziaistvo SSSR v 1985 godu, pp. 18-23 and TsSU, Itogi vsesoiuznoi perepisi naseleniia, Tom. 1, pp. 41-42.

110. I.V. Nikol'skii, V.I. Toniaev and V.G. Krasheninnikov, Geografiia vodnogo transporta SSSR (Moscow: Transport, 1975), p. 211 and Atlas SSSR, pp. 167 and 187.

111. Dergachev, "Peculiarities," p. 152.

112. Shan Cheng, "Second Siberian Provides Vital Links," Beijing Review, Vol. 28, No. 12 (March 25), 1985, pp. 12-13.

113. A.G. Proskuriakova, "Regional'nye ekonomicheskie problemy razvitiia transportnoi sistemy Dal'nego Vostoka," in Osobennosti i tendentsii formirovaniia i razvitiia regional'nogo transporta Dal'nego Vostoka (Vladivostok, 1982), pp. 9-19. Quoted in Referativnyi zhurnal'.

228

Geografiia, 1983, No. 8, E178.
114. V.I. Ivanov and K.V. Malakhovskii, eds., Tikho-okeanskii regionalizm: kontseptsii i real'nost' (Moscow: Nauka, 1983), p. 243.
115. Jane's Defence Weekly, 1984, April 14, pp. 560-561.
116. V.D. Tsareva, "Proizvodstvennaia spetsializatsiia i struktura rasseleniia Dal'nevostochnogo regiona," in P.Ia. Baklanov and V. N. Bugromenko, eds., Territorial'no-khoziaistvennye struktury Dal'nego Vostoka (Vladivostok, 1982), p. 139 and Narodnoe khoziaistvo SSSR v 1983 godu, pp. 18 and 21.
117. Soviet Military Power 1984 (Washington, D.C.: U.S. Government Printing Office, 1984), p. 61.
118. I.I. Sigov, Urbanizatsiia i razvitie gorodov v SSSR (Leningrad: Nauka, 1985), pp. 120-121.
119. A.I. Baibakov, Povyshenie nauchnogo urovnia upravleniia trudom (Moscow: Profizdat, 1980), p. 43.
120. S.S. Zykov, ed., Regional'nye osobennosti povysheniia effektivnosti obshchestvennogo proizvodstva na Dal'nem Vostoke (Khabarovsk: Khabarovskii politekhnicheskii institut and Khabarovskii institut narodnogo khoziaistva, 1984), p. 28 and Dal'nevostochnyi gosudarstvennyi universitet, Dal'nii Vostok za 60 let sovetskoi vlasti. Part 1, Sbornik. Manuscript (Vladivostok, 1985), p. 192.
121. Popov, "Industriia u okeana," p. 104.
122. Sigov, Urbanizatsiia, pp. 121.
123. I.I. Bartkova, "Portovye goroda Dal'nego Vostoka," in Baklanov and Bugromenko, Territorial'no-khoziaistvennye struktury, p. 146, and Nikol'skii, Toniaev and Krasheninnikov, Geografiia vodnogo transporta SSSR, pp. 211-12.

7

Regional Planning in the USSR
and the Development
of Soviet Asia

The Soviet leadership has long been explicitly involved with issues of regional development, though the intensity of this involvement has waxed and waned through time. Similarly, these issues have provided the theme for much geographic and economic research, even if strictly circumscribed and channeled by the prevailing guidelines of Party and state. One can discern both exogenous (objective) and systemic factors behind that prominence of regional issues. In the first category are the immense size of the country; its very uneven population, resource distribution, and environmental conditions; its multinational nature, with the clear historical and cultural association of most ethnic groups with specific geographic areas; and, finally, its adjacent strategic position to three of the great geopolitical world regions, Europe, East Asia, and the Middle East. The leadership of no other country is confronted by so many exogenous regional factors simultaneously and on so large a scale.

The systemic factors relate to the institutional environment, organization, and management of the economy. The institutional environment of the Soviet economy is overwhelmingly a hierarchical, administratively directed one. This contrasts with market economies, where production and distribution processes are coordinated primarily by "lateral communication, which entails negotiation and mutual accommodation between the controllers of the interrelated processes." In the latter system, information is decentralized and the need for it kept to a minimum by the impersonal market: the origin, destination, and quantity of resource flows need <u>not</u> be determined <u>ex ante</u>.[1] Regional problems, often severe, do in fact develop in market economies and may become a specific concern of the political leadership. They may, of course, be caused or exacerbated by a combination of exogenous factors, such as physical geography and racial, ethnic and educational disadvantages accumulated through time. Otherwise, however, they arise out of "market failures," just as externalities with respect to the environment or common property resources do (air, water, grazing land, etc.). Only by default then, and only when such problems are severe, do regional issues in market economies become the subject of decision making on the national level. In centrally planned economies, on the other hand, production processes are primarily coordinated through direct orders to each lower-level overseer involved in the particular production process. The vectors of principal resource flows (theoretically, all resource flows as to magnitude, origin, and destination) will have to be determined and coordinated administratively ex ante. The spatial dimension of resource allocation, therefore, must be confronted consciously at each level of the planning hierarchy.

We must press still further regarding that systemic difference. Resource allocation and combination is not a static but a dynamic process. Over the long term, the production possibilities of an economy themselves change, both with respect to technology and to the sectoral-geographic structure. The pattern of mineral endowment shifts with depletion of existing deposits, new discoveries and development, often in conjuntion with technological advance. The population distribution changes with differential natural increase and migration. All these guarantee that geographic changes are an organic part of the changing production possibilities of an economy. This is especially true of the USSR, with its huge undeveloped areas and territorially differentiated mix of European and non-European nationalities. It is, therefore, not enough that in the Soviet Union the existing spatial structure of the economy should form an integral ex ante part of the planning process. Modifications in the spatial structure itself must become conscious planning goals. They would have to become so even if the sole ultimate objective of system managers were to be dynamic efficiency, i.e., maximum long-term growth with least effort. In fact, other objectives, linked to strategic-military, political, or nationality policies, may be equally important. Koropeckyj has noted that the Soviet leadership attempts to maximize not total GNP, but GNP of a predetermined structure.[2] In such a system, the regional structure of the economy must also be predetermined at least to a large extent. Reality will, of

course, diverge from the plan. Incorporation of the
regional dimension, however, is a sine qua non of the
planning process itself.

Soviet sources emphasize the unabashedly centralized
nature of planning in the USSR, a process which, in fact,
has not changed radically since the later 1920s. Writing
in 1984 about the planning of territorial development of
the country, an authority stresses the following: (1) the
principle of democratic centralism (a term taken directly
from the political sphere of hierarchical one-party rule;
(2) the directiveness and obligatory nature of the plan;
and (3) the priority of national/state interest wherever
conflicts arise between branch and regional objectives or
between the goals of the Center and individual localities.[3]
In such a system, there can be no question of regional
autonomy in economic decision making and management.
Instead, the usefulness and importance of territorial
planning will hinge on whether geographic areas can provide
suitable primary blocks for the construction and disag-
gregation of centrally determined national plans. The
evidence so far indicates that they cannot. This weakness
explains the unsystematic, generally unsatisfactory nature
of Soviet regional planning and its subordination to
vertical branch planning through most of Soviet history.
Ironically, therefore, while the factors of geographic
space and regional differences loom large in the planning
process, this has not resulted in a comprehensive regional
approach or in the increased power of regional authorities,
except briefly during the Khrushchev period.

Centralized planning is a functional process that must
deal with the systemic interdependence of variables, themselves targeted for change. Clearly, even with high-speed
computers, only a restricted number of variables and their
functional linkages can be dealt with. The system that is
controllable by the Center must remain skeletal. The
functional linkages that can be quantified most reliably
are those among major industries and production processes.
The myriad of interrelationships that compose a hierarchical set of regions even in the purely economic sphere,
let alone in the ecological and social realm, are hardly
amenable to such centralized manipulation and control.
Consequently, even in theory, it is difficult to imagine
directive planning that starts with areas as building
blocks in attempting to achieve predetermined national
targets. In addition, despite some problems of overlap,
the boundaries of economic activities (i.e., industries)
present an easier task of definition than the boundaries of

areas, since the former is more or less a function of the production process itself. Not surprisingly, therefore, branch planning has remained the core of the Soviet planning process. The question is how can the interlinking interest of regions be represented in such a system and how can regional planning fit into that framework.

THE REGIONAL COUNCILS: THREAT TO CENTRAL CONTROL

The period of Khrushchev's sovnarkhozy or regional economic councils (1958-1965) was the only interval in Soviet history when territorial planning achieved an equal footing with branch planning. In its year-to-year operation, most of the economy was actually managed along regional lines. In 1961, 73 percent of all industry was subordinated to the sovnarkhozy and a full 93 percent to the fifteen Republics. The latter also managed four-fifths of all construction organizations and determined the allocation of 77 percent of all investment capital. Even in that period, however, transport, agriculture, and the bulk of the service sector were never put under the control of the regional councils--a decision economically justifiable in the case of transport, but hardly so with the other two.[4] An emigre scholar with a deep knowledge of the Soviet system recently had some kind words to say about the sovnarkhozy from the vantage point of one close to the grassroots. In his opinion, they were flexible, showed concern for local conditions, and thus enlivened the economy--at least in comparison with the system of branch management employed before and after. Moreover, under Soviet conditions, such a diffusion of power within the decision-making bureaucracy (through the better distribution and dispersal of that bureaucracy over the country's vast expanse) represents the only means of greater decentralization. Expectations of a radical revamping of the economy towards market principles are chimerical.[5] The last point about the diffusion of power expresses the dilemma of organically linking territorial and branch management in a balanced fashion. In any horizontal, regional structure, local institutions necessarily play a significant role in power arrangements, supervision, and the setting of priorities. Their meaningful participation is possible only if the Center abandons detailed planning, limits itself to the determination of large economic aggregates, and relinquishes control over the physical allocation of resources and more of the budget as well.[6]

Such a system would no longer be "directive planning," expressing the goals of system managers at the apex. While not reflecting individual consumer preferences either, such a system would organize production and consumption possibilities according to the preferences of regional constituencies. The evolving structure of the economy would thus represent the sum of these regional preferences.

As it happened, the Center never disengaged itself from detailed physical allocation even during the sovnarkhozy interlude. The attempt to maintain "directive planning," while allowing the devolution of management over much of the economy to regional and republican organs, was bound to lead to entanglements and gnarled and twisted lines of command. But more dangerous than these snags for those at the apex of Soviet society, the power and prerogatives of the fifteen Republic's Gosplans, of regional party secretaries, and other local institutions did increase significantly. Such threats to the whole concept of "democratic centralism" thus alarmed the top elite. The sovnarkhozy were being consolidated and some union branch ministries reestablished already under Khrushchev; upon his fall, the whole experiment of economic management along regional lines was abandoned completely. Branch planning by ministries, with the USSR Gosplan as the principal coordinating organ, was again supreme. A half-hearted attempt to increase enterprise autonomy within the reestablished vertical management structure has also failed. Gradually, the authorities reasserted central control over all important details of the production process. In the 1981 Plan, for example, the USSR Gosplan alone worked out about 2,000 material balances; ministries and their departments elaborated a total of 25,000.[7]

SPATIAL PLANNING: CURRENT EFFORTS AND SIBERIAN
ECONOMIC DEVELOPMENT

Soviet efforts at territorial planning, therefore, are essentially attempts at squaring the circle. Specialists implicitly admit that much when they distinguish two separate aspects of the task: (1) the areal profile (razrez) of industrial planning, i.e., the planned geographic distribution of economic activity and specific enterprises, and (2) complex regional planning, when the individual regions themselves comprise the subject of that endeavor. So far, no satisfactory theory exists of linking the two and ad hoc attempts in practice have produced rather indifferent results.

In the last fifteen years or so, the most intense intellectual effort to provide that systematic link was directed at mathematical modeling in a hierarchical approach: from national economic models without regional dimensions at the apex downward through regional interindustry (input-output) models to interregional programming models and regional programming models. These programming efforts are considered especially important for the vast Trans-Ural hinterland and have tended to focus on Siberia. "Because Siberia remains at an early stage of development, the range of possible choices for its future growth is great, and different proposals can be simulated and evaluated with these kind of economic models." Given this early stage of evolution and the narrower range of economic activities, data problems for this endeavor "are less severe in Siberia than in more highly developed regions characterized by more complex industrial structures." Yet these modeling approaches "are still in the experimental stages and are used in pre-planning and long-term projections rather than in operational planning."[8] Neither the inherent demand-driven nature of input-output forecasts, nor the aggregate character of technical coefficients, rendering them of little use once inevitable changes in plan targets are made, have endeared these models to Gosplan specialists.

Despite their shortcomings, these interregional and regional models do represent a significant achievement in economic analysis. They have also made possible the more systematic dovetailing of national and territorial plans for the major regions of Siberia and, since 1984, also for the Urals. Besides seven economic sectors planned in value terms, the 1981-1985 Plan drew up physical targets for more than fifty products for the Far East, seventy for East Siberia, almost eighty for West Siberia in a manner consistent with the national plan. Within these large economic regions, the plan was disaggregated and balanced by a smaller number of targets to the level of individual TPCs or territorial-production complexes (infra).[9] Planning efforts within smaller administrative units, even to the raion and city levels, have also proliferated in recent years. Unlike the interregional and large regional programming models, these small-area plans, drawn up by local bodies, aim at comprehensiveness, embracing the economic and social spheres, infrastructure, and the immediate physical environment. But, the local planning bodies suffer from great shortages of skilled manpower, computing facilities, and the like and work outside the framework of national and even the larger regional plans. For example, the planning work of municipalities are not coordinated with regional (raion, krai, oblast level) planning, and this in turn is seldom consonant with the larger interregional efforts. In general, each agency uses its own methodology. In particular, past experience throughout the whole Soviet period regarding individual Siberian cities has proved that not one of the economic hypotheses and forecasts would stand the test of time. The planning efforts of local organs, therefore, so far remains mostly an academic exercise, rich in detail but organically part of no larger system.[10]

There is also a deeper general problem underlying all Soviet attempts at comprehensive, rational management of the country's economic space. Planning is a goal-directed activity, but no single criterion of defining that goal has been accepted on any level, even in the purely economic sphere. Increasing the economic effectiveness of social production is vaguely held up as the goal of national economic planning, but the appraisal of this effectiveness is done by a multitude of coefficients and norms differentiated on at least four separate levels: national, regional (Union republics and geographic zones), sectoral, and enterprise.[11] For example, when comparing projects, some receive preferential treatment. Capital investment in heavy industries and geographically in the Trans-Ural provinces, especially the North, have tended to be artificially favored through lower putative interest charges (i.e., longer recoupment period), faster depreciation rates, omission of certain infrastructural costs, and the like.[12] The planning coefficients and norms thus reflect a composite of ideological convictions and political clout, compromises, and horsetrading among interest groups represented in the top leadership.

Similar opportunities in advancing regional and sectoral interests are afforded by programming models that attempt to circumvent the well-known distortions of the Soviet price system. It is generally accepted, for example, that Soviet domestic prices in the past greatly undervalued energy and raw materials, and even the 1982 price reform has not fully remedied this distortion. Energy economists, therefore, properly insist that in modeling the development of the energy complex some kind of shadow values must be used instead of prices. Since the late 1960s, the concept of the "marginal fuel" (zamykaiushchii vid topliva) has gained wide currency, although defining that margin in each region and by separate technological use, in view of great differences in opportunity costs, has remained controversial.[13]

The meteoric rise of world energy prices (and, much less consistently, those of other minerals) that followed the two oil shocks of the 1970s also gave Soviet energy economists and scholars concerned with the development of Siberia a powerful weapon. They have argued that, given the very high export value of Soviet fuels and some raw materials, they must be entered into the programming models on the basis of world prices. Researchers at Siberian institutes and regional planning agencies fully embraced this view and have been its most forceful advocates. Because of its importance in energy and raw material production, Siberia would greatly enhance its contribution to the national economy if its resources were valued at world prices prevailing until the debacle of the mid-1980s. The region would show a high return on total investment funneled into it, despite the harsh environment and sparse population, and would be in a strong position to ask for more. Academician Aganbegian and his colleagues at Novosibirsk thus stated that the roughly 1,700 million tons of hydrocarons (in oil equivalent) that West Siberia was expected to produce during the Tenth FYP was worth no less than 150 billion rubles at 1979 world prices, valued at offical foreign trade rubles.[14] The roughly 25 billion rubles of investment channeled directly into the West Siberian oil and gas complex in that five-year period thus repaid itself many times.[15]

The problem with these attempts at using shadow values or world prices in territorial and sectoral projections is that they apply only to restricted subsystems of the economy. They can point to partial and local optima of resource allocation, which are then used by regional and sectoral interest groups to buttress their demands, but these choices may turn out to be seriously suboptimal for the entire economic system. Recent Soviet works argue this point forcefully with respect to attempts at using some sort of marginal costs for energy and raw material inputs. One scholar declares unequivocally that "the concept of marginal costs [zamykaiushchie zatraty] is suitable for the solution of partial, local, though multifaceted tasks. . . . However, such problems as the future development of major industries and regions, the spatial dimension of production and the main direction of policy for technology cannot by their very scale be decided on that basis."[16]

In a similar vein, I have explained in an earlier

study that valuing all Siberian fuel and mineral production (and not just the portion destined for hard currency export) at world prices is unjustified and would lead to a strong and unwarranted bias in favor of Siberia. If the region's output destined for domestic use were to be reassessed at world prices, the inputs into the region, i.e., the investment, technology, and skills embodied in structures and equipment, would also need to be recomputed in similar fashion. Even allowing for the lower-than-world standard of Soviet construction and machinery, the development costs of Siberian resources at world prices would also be much higher.[17]

Very recently, two well-known Soviet economists expressed very similar ideas, pointing out that while Siberian products were indeed long underpriced, so were inputs used in the development of this huge territory. Some inputs, such as cement, have been strongly underpriced even relative to other Soviet regions, while capital costs were made to appear lower by more favorable recoupment norms and depreciation rates. They have taken issue with Aganbegian and his Novosibirsk group, who claimed that the huge subsidy to Siberia which showed up in regional input-output accounts of the 1970s was illusory and stemmed mostly from the improper underpricing of Siberian natural resources. In the view of these two experts at the Russian Republic Gosplan (central planning board) in Moscow, a large subsidy indeed existed uninterruptedly through the decades from 1960 to 1980. By extension, it exists today. The causes of these "regional differences between produced and utilized national income [i.e.,interregional subsidies] are found not in the specific anomalies of prices, but in the different territorial structures of material welfare and services and national priorities with respect to productive and nonproductive investment and consumption."[18] In plain words, the causes are found in Siberia's present state of underdevelopment; the reasons are in current national priorities associated with its development.

The use of world prices to justify Siberian resource development, of course, cuts both ways. The claim concerning a big net contribution to the rest of the country was sustainable when applied to West Siberia in the era of a $34 per barrel and even a $27 per barrel oil price. (The Far East was heavily subsidized even during that time; see Chapters 3 and 4.) In addition, the average cost of petroleum extraction in West Siberia was falling in the first half of the 1970s and so was the average cost of gas production through much of that decade. Given today's world fuel and metal prices, the peaking of Soviet oil output, and the sharp rise in both oil and gas costs in the USSR, the Siberian argument about the illusory nature of subsidies to this region becomes much more difficult to sustain.

The TPC and the Development of Siberia

The most intense intellectual effort of Soviet scholars to find a conceptual link between branch planning and territorial planning and to operationalize that linkage in the development of pioneer areas center on the TPC (territorial-production complex). The TPC concept is an old one. Like Western industrial complex and growth center theories, it has the appeal of synthesizing a range of technological, spatial economic, and developmental ideas. In the Soviet case, it has the advantage of doing so in an ideologically "safe" fashion. The TPC concept, therefore, has attracted a large number of investigators, each reworking the theory to his own taste and introducing new terminology so that over 100 more or less different definitions exist.[19] Terminological confusion, however, need not detain us here, since the essence of the notion concerns the locational association of technological linkages generated by a specific production cycle. In the original formulation of the concept, the stress on the technological form of the linkages resulted in the near-complete neglect of economic aspects and, consequently, also of the important role played by supporting services and infrastructure unless they were an integral part of the production cycle itself. More recently, however, Soviet scholars have come to admit the crucial and more than passive role of supporting services and infrastructure. "The industrial core determines the economic specialization of the TPC and its role in the national economy. These core industries provide the basis for a set of forward and backward interindustry linkages that tie the region together and generate further growth and development within the TPC."[20] The branch specializations of the TPCs are to reflect both their specific resource endowments and capabilities, the needs of the national economy, and the large macroregions in which they are located.

What is important here is that Soviet scholars clearly distinguish between traditional (classical) TPCs which have evolved over the decade in established, well-populated areas and the targeted-programming TPCs (programmnotselevye TPK) which are consciously created in the sparsely-populated pioneer hinterland. In the first case, the concept simply affords a framework for ex post analysis and the better management of existing relationships. In the second case, the TPC becomes the form of territorial organization for the realization of specific regional programs of development.[21] To be more precise, the new, programming TPCs would provide the needed coherence and unity in economic decision making for the development of new regions in two crucial ways. First, by providing a geographic demarcation of planned associated activities, the TPCs would help concentrate new development spatially. This would serve to counteract the lamentable tendency of scattering investment resources by Union ministries in Moscow, for which transport is simply a planned cost item and for which a whole huge oblast in Siberia may appear simply as a site for its enterprise. Second, these TPCs are to be defined by and around a problem, a development goal. "Their problem-solving capacity is to be delimited by the problem as such and not by traditional administative [departmental and geographic] boundaries." The TPC approach thus may provide a way of bypassing the autarchic, "empire-building" tendencies of the powerful ministries that has bedeviled Soviet planning for decades. The TPCs, geographically demarcated and subordinated directly to Gosplan and the Council of Ministries, thus may compel the development of regionally associated complex linkages through the very task of problem solving.[22] Mathematical modeling would delimit the areal extent of a complex, provide proportionality among its main elements, and the timing of their appearance (incorporating a necessary degree of indeterminacy) and would firmly integrate the complex into the long-range national plan. Influential scholars, with those from the Novosibirsk-based IEOPP (Institute of Economics and Organization of Industrial Production) in the lead, are pressing hard to make the TPCs one of the basic building blocks of national planning. The targets for the TPCs would strictly balance with the intersectoral plans concerning levels of output and timing and would be binding on ministries and enterprises.[23]

These academic concerns would, of course, remain entirely irrelevant without some high-level political support. Indeed, such support was gradually building up during the 1970s among planning and Party officials, reaching the top leadership by the second half of the decade. In 1976, Kosygin specified the development of a program for the formation of large TPCs as a top priority.

The formal identification of the TPCs in the Five-Year Plans, begun already in the first half of the 1970s, continued with further elaboration in the 1976-1980 Plan. The July 1979 planning reform "initiated by a joint CPSU Central Committee-USSR Council of Ministers decree . . . instructed Gosplan to prepare . . . a set of comprehensive target programs for the development of individual regions and TPCs." Gosplan was given explicit authority ". . . to exercise control over the fulfillments of these plans regardless of the departmental or local affiliation of the individual components involved," although the mechanics of this control was not explained.[24]

Another indication of the formal recognition of the TPCs as a unit of planning is provided by the USSR Central Statistical Administration. Since 1982, the latter regularly reports the percentage growth of industry in eight TPCs relative to a 1980 base for each year.[25] (Four TPCs mentioned in the previous [1976-1980] Plan, however, are not among these.) Only one of the eight, the zone of the Kursk Magnetic Anomaly, are found in well-populated, developed areas. Six lie east of the Urals (four in Siberia and the Far East) and one in the European North.

To what extent can the TPCs provide the needed coherence for the development of Siberia? Specifically, to what extent are they likely to concentrate investment and lessen the problem of "departmentalism"? It appears that the TPCs do indeed promote the geographic concentration of new investment earmarked for the Trans-Ural hinterland. In Siberia, at least, Gosplan does appear to reject new projects not within the area of TPCs. For example, of all industrial investment in new construction within East and West Siberia, 70 to 90 percent, depending on the branch, is now channeled into a few complexes.[26] For the rest of the century, the projected breakdown by major sectors and TPCs in the Angara-Enisei region, which composes the southern 30 percent of Krasnoiarsk Krai and Irkutsk Oblast is shown in Table 7.1. (Apart from the Noril'sk-Igarka node in the Arctic the Angara-Enisei region concentrates virtually all economic activity in these two huge administrative units.) The source indicates that the mature TPCs of Irkutsk-Cheremkhovo and Ust'-Ilimsk, plus other locations in the region, are slated to receive barely over a third of total investment allocated centrally into nationally significant projects, and almost two-thirds are funneled into three TPCs currently in process of formation. In some industrial sectors, the concentration is even greater. Eighty-four percent of investment to create new machine-building

TABLE 7.1 Projected Distribution of New Investment Connected with National Level Problems in the Angara–Enisei Region (percentages)

Industrial Sectors	Central Krasnoiarsk (Kansk-Achinsk) TPC	Saian TPC	Lower Angara TPC	Irkutsk-Cheremkhovo TPC	Bratsk Ust' Ilimsk TPC	Others	Total
All Capital Investment of which:							
Expansion of Fuel-Energy Base	35	13	18	7	7	20	100
Expansion of Energy Intensive Industries	42	7	31	4	1	15	100
New Machine Building Industries	13	18	24	5	7	33	100
Complex Industries	55	29	5	2	2	7	100
Processing of Timber	2	–	53	2	21	22	100

Source: A.G. Aganbegian ed., Territorial'no-proizvodstvennye kompleksy: planirovanie i upravlenie (Novosibirsk: Nauka, 1984), p. 10

242

branches in East Siberia will go to the Central Krasnoiarsk (Kansk-Achinsk) and Saian TPCs, 73 percent of new fuel-energy investment into the Kansk-Achinsk and Lower Angara complexes, and 74 percent of new capital for complex wood processing into the Lower Angara and Bratsk-Ust' Ilimsk TPCs. With the exception of the West Siberian oil-and-gas-dominated complex, the territorial extent of Siberian TPCs are fairly compact, at least on the scale of the Asian USSR. The combined area of the Bratsk--Ust'-Ilimsk, Saian and Lower Angara TPCs totals to about a quarter of Irkutsk Oblast and Krasnoiarsk Krai.[27]

If an official reliance on the TPC concept in planning is indeed prompting greater geographic concentration of investment, the same cannot be said so far of concentrating and sharing facilities among ministries. Nor have the TPCs lessened organizational autarchy in the management and utilization of infrastructure, repair capacity, and inputs. As before, each ministry, and even department, tends to plan separately for its own heat supply, warehouses, garages, repair shops, plants for prefab housing modules, and even railroad stations and roads if they are strong enough. The writer received a visual taste of this in 1983, while visiting the Ust'-Ilimsk part of the complex with a group of geographers under the aegis of the Soviet Academy of Sciences. Even though the Bratsk section of the TPC is now in a mature stage, with considerable accumulated experience, the whole complex continues to suffer from lack of internal balance and coherence. A recent source declares: "The future development of the Bratsk--Ust'-Ilimsk TPC is still not very clear; there is no comprehensive program for its development. This circumstance will not permit the liquidation of the lag in social infrastructure and agro-industrial enterprises, all of which increases the instability of labor and the outmigration of the most qualified specialists."[28] The duplication of power and heat supply capacity is almost beyond belief. In Tiumen' Oblast (West Siberian TPC), the hundreds of production departments, each anxious about its own supplies, have put up about 4,000 separate pygmy power stations, even though they generate a mere 6 percent of all electricity in Tiumen' Oblast. Besides a large heat and power plant, the city of Tiumen' (population 411,000 in 1984) counts some eighty separate industrial boilers; the city of Abakan (population 146,000 in 1984) within the compact and environmentally favorable Saian TPC counts 120.[29]

By Soviet admission, departmentalism in Siberia has penetrated even deeper down the industrial hierarchy east of the Urals than west of it. And the more remote the region, the worse the problem of departmental autarchy becomes.[30] Eight separate ministries and twenty-nine project-making institutes work on the Tomsk petrochemical complex alone, receiving supplies from sixty-three oblasts and krais and from all republics. Rampant departmentalism has resulted in enormous imbalances among the components of the huge project. Of these imbalances, the virtual unavailability of additional natural gas for the new 750,000-ton methanol installation (through the failure to plan for the doubling of the Nizhnevartovsk-Kuzbas pipline) is the most serious. "All the raw material [i.e., gas] has already been allocated. . . . The chemical industry which is rapidly moving closer to raw materials is not getting those materials."[31]

Elsewhere, I have described how conflicts between the Ministry of Coal Industry and the Ministry of Electric Power held up the development of the South Yakutian TPC in the later part of the 1970s. According to the First Secretary of the Yakut Party Committee, a similar conflict between the coal and electric power interests repeated itself in the 1980s, but was resolved through the urging and persuasion of the Yakut and local Party organizations.[32] A 1982 source reveals that the construction of the Bureia hydrostation in the Far East was, until very recently, held up for six years because of a dispute between Lengidroproekt and Zeiagresstroi (acronyms for two large construction trusts for power projects). Owing to the dispute, only one-tenth of the allocated funds could be spent, and nearly all the seasoned labor force assembled has left.[33] Tynda, the capital of the BAM zone, presented a crazy quilt of development in 1984, with fourteen separate sub-settlements. In this city of 56,000, as many as thirty-four ministries and departments are represented, each with its own river piers, workers' supply depots, and stores. Several telephone systems operate separately, and there are 104 departmental boiler houses.[34] Bureia and Tynda are not yet part of existing TPCs. However, they are focal points of prospective ones, whose areal extents have been roughly delineated but whose structure, level of complexity, and stages of development have not yet been agreed upon.

Some isolated attempts have been made to create supply organizations based regionally within a TPC, the most important example being KATEKsnab (Supply Organization for the Kansk-Achinsk Fuel-Energy Complex). In theory, such an organization could eliminate some of the duplication in

construction and material supply built up separately by
each ministry and department within the TPC, rationalize,
and save on transport costs. Yet even KATEKsnab is given
authority to furnish needed materials to only two ministries (those of coal and electric power) and cannot
redirect them to construction projects under other ministries. Clearly, the intention was to forestall material
shortages at the KATEK coal and electricity projects, the
industrial core of that TPC. Yet such restrictions on a
regional body regarding what enterprises it can supply
frustrate the entire attempt to promote geographically
concentrated horizontal linkages and shorten supply lines.
And it can defeat the possibility of the rational utilization of capacity at such a regionally based supply
organization, since the rational utilization of that capacity demands a high degree of fine tuning and avoidance of
slippages in construction among the enterprises that the
regional organization is permitted to supply.[35]

Departmental autarchy in Siberia has been clearly
strengthened by the sharp increase in the share of investment coming from the ministries' own resources as against
budgetary allocations, the other main source of centralized
investment (the third source, bank credit, has traditionally composed only a small share). Although funds coming
from the ministries' own resources is also included in the
Plan and, theoretically, controlled by the Presidium of the
Council of Ministers, reliance on their own financing does
give the ministries greater de facto influence over
allocation. In the USSR as a whole, their own funds were
the source of finance of some 58 percent of investment for
all industrial ministries already in the mid-1970s.[36]
However, in remote eastern regions, budgetary allocation
apparently dominated investment financing: in 1971, for
example, less than 21 percent of all investment for the
West Siberian TPC originated from the participating
ministries' own resources. Soviet scholars deem it
significant that, through the 1970s, the share of capital
allocation financed by ministries' own funds grew noticeably to almost one-third of the total by 1980. This has
strengthened the ministries' hand, enabling them to build
up their own construction organizations and even their
project-making bureaus in the region, increasing wasteful
duplications, and further aggravating the already severe
problem of departmentalism.[37]

Nor have the TPCs helped in the better planning of
manpower needs, labor supply, and consequent population
growth in the new regions of developments east of the

Urals. With respect to the most important TPC in Siberia, that of the Tiumen' or West Siberian complex, for example, one finds confusing and diametrically opposite statements. L.M. Kaplan and I.Iu. Murav'eva declare that scientific and project-making organizations have been in agreement in forecasting 1.3 to 1.5 million inhabitants in the Tiumen' TPC by the beginning of the Tenth FYP (1976-1980). In reality, the population reached only 800,000 persons because of the slower-than-planned development of other than strictly extractive branches, the failure to develop ancillary industries, and gross delays in the build-up of infrastructure.[38] On the other hand, A. Ananev and A. Silin claim, at about the same time, that the actual popu-lation in the West Siberian (Tiumen') Oil and Gas Complex during the Tenth FYP well surpassed the originally planned levels, despite the extensive reliance on the tour-of-duty method (workers flown into temporary settlements with minimum amenities from base towns and returned for rest and recreation). Already by 1979, the population of Surgut exceeded by two times the size originally envisaged, and that of Nizhnevartovsk by three, greatly exacerbating the pressure on housing and social infrastructure.[39] Although there appears to be a three to four year discrepancy in the time referred to in these two opposite statements, the difference in the claims are so huge that the short time difference cannot possibly explain it. (By 1979, Surgut and Nizhnevartovsk each had a population of close to 110,000 and were over 190,000 by the end of 1985.[40]) Clearly, the TPC concept has not made manpower planning noticeably more rigorous than before; nor has it helped much in harmonizing objectives among the various planning agencies, as the debate over the expedition and tour-of-duty methods, treated later, will further show.

The weaknesses and failure of the TPCs as instruments of rational and effective planning boil down to the question of power, formal and informal. To this day, the rights and position of the TPCs remain undefined either in the state or the Party apparatus; the complexes have no legal status. Nor do they have captains in command. As mentioned, the July 1979 planning decree by the Party Central Committee and Council of Ministries makes Gosplan responsible for the development of the TPCs. However, Gosplan itself is composed of representatives of the major ministries and is divided into departments along those lines, but has no representatives with authority for individual TPCs. So investment funds and all other resources for construction projects within the TPCs

continue to be disbursed through ministerial and departmental channels, and the problem of regional coherence and
synchronization remains.

In some previous large construction projects, later
declared to be part of TPCs, the problem of coordination
was tackled by creating a major construction organization
within the most appropriate ministry and making it into a
kind of general contractor (general'nyi podriadchik) responsible for all building work relevant to the project. As
Boris Rumer observed, however, such a trust becomes not so
much an organizer of the different construction work, which
in theory could be subcontracted to specialized organizations, but rather the universal performer itself of all
types of work to be done.[41] In consequence,

> The projected structure of production, both basic
> and auxiliary, the optimal number of population
> sites and the population distribution plan, the
> scale and development of the social infrastructure,
> and, above all, housing construction, are all
> deformed under the influence of the self generating,
> expanding construction complex. The real needs of
> the construction trust . . . often displace some of
> the requirement of basic producers. The development
> of cities, contrary to initial plans, is determined
> in such cases not by the functioning of future
> enterprises but by the level of construction
> activity at the time of the maximum scale of its
> work. In order to support this level, more and more
> new construction projects with no direct relation
> to their primary specialization are included in the
> scheme of the industrial center.

A recent work from Novosibirsk suggests such distortions by
organizations responsible for KATEK (Kansk-Achinsk TPC).
Projections of population and labor force for the city of
Chernenko, with the huge Berezovo lignite-fired power
plant, are inflated some 38 percent by construction and
project-making organs that pursue their own goals.[42]

The example of Bratskgresstroi (Bratsk Hydroelectric
Power Construction Trust), created in the early 1960s, also
supports Rumer's argument. Bratskgresstroi not only
constructed but has since managed a whole range of industrial and infrastructural facilities. It has grown into an
empire of its own, employing 80,000 workers[43] and extending
far beyond the Angara region. Experts now urge the
transfer of many of its long-functioning enterprises

serving the Bratsk area to the jurisdiction of the local
soviets (councils). The huge trust of Bratskgesstroi,
however, is able to pay higher wages and command better
equipment and material supplies than would the local
administrative organs. These discrepancies impede such
transfer and obstruct the balanced integrated territorial
management of infrastructure, services, and region-serving
industries.[44] In Tiumen' Oblast, too, the great industrial
and construction trusts show all the signs of self-serving,
self-perpetuating growth and empire building. Tiumengazprom (Tiumen' Gas Industry Trust) had reached the size of
43,000 workers by 1980; Glavtiumenneftegazstroi (Tiumen'
Oil and Gas Construction Trust) includes 170 construction,
industrial, transport, and other subordinate units,[45] and
is increasingly difficult to manage. Yet even with organizations of this size, the West Siberian TPC is so large
that Gosplan could not entrust its development to any one
general contractor.

As Thane Gustafson has pointed out, "the organization
that has traditionally provided the most effective horizontal coordination and local oversight is the Party
itself. The professional Party apparatus at the province
and district levels not only acts as expediter, overseer,
rescuer, and occasional knocker of heads, but it can also
intervene to advocate changes in policy, sometimes in
defense of the regional viewpoints."[46] Yet the tasks
associated with the synchronized, coherent development of
the large TPCs in Siberia appears beyond the capabilities
of local Party organs, although the Tiumen' obkom (oblast
party committee) has shown initiative and boldness in the
past. Academician Aganbegian, one of the foremost advocates of the vigorous, integrated development of Siberia,
no longer believes the obkom or kraikom (krai party
committee) to be the proper organs for that task. The
integrated development of the TPCs is a task of national
significance and, as such, it should be the responsibility
of an agency of the central government, endowed with full
authority (upolnomochennyi) and led by someone with
ministerial or vice-ministerial rank.[47]

During a recent roundtable discussion by well-known
scholars, Aganbegian's opinion was echoed by others, but
also opposed by a number of participants. The latter
believe that creating yet more administrative agencies to
cope with the myriad interindustry problems would further
complicate the already formidable problem of managing the
national economy. For these dissenters, the strengthening
of existing regional authorities (oblast and krai party

committees, local soviets) and/or the making the currently practiced supply-delivery agreements (dogovory) among enterprises legally binding (which they are not today) would seem to be the better way.[48] What none of these discussants appear ready or able to express, of course, is that, without essential enterprise independence from the "Plan" both as to inputs and output and independence from higher organs that transmit and modify that Plan in the course of its progress, such enterprise agreements must remain basically meaningless even if they officially have the force of law. Nor can the local party authorities do much more than cajole, press, and attempt to expedite; they cannot create intraregional coherence.

At present there exist two agencies for the West Siberian TPC, created in 1981, that are charged with the task of horizontal coordination: an agency within the staff of the USSR Council or Ministers in Moscow and a commission of Gosplan located directly in Tiumen', an on-site location never before attempted in the history of Gosplan, according to Gustafson. The powers of this thirty-six-member Gosplan commission are described in strikingly weak language; its staff is claimed to be small. It may actually have lost power since its establishment and it is evidently being undermined not only by the major ministries, but also by the Tiumen' "Party apparatus that does not welcome potential rivals."[49] Aganbegian, too, appears thoroughly unsatisfied with the functions of that commission (which he depicts mostly as the working-out of recommendations, proposals, and programs) and insists on the need for a fully empowered representative of the Council of Ministers and a large staff. He is even less charitable to the currently functioning commission in Moscow, which has neither the power of enforcement nor technical information and on-site expertise and must constantly turn to the Gosplan body in Tiumen' with inquiries, requests, and instructions. Catering to these requests consumes much of the time of the Tiumen' commission. Yet even Aganbegian seems hesitant to recommend a fully empowered permanent commission within the Council of Ministers for every TPC, and his strong recommendation is aimed only at the West Siberian oil and gas complex.[50]

Clearly, the concrete nature and management of TPCs as objects of planning and development remain unresolved even in theory and still more in practice. So far, they have failed to provide the needed mechanism for coordination between ministerial and territorial planning. Yet, by presenting clearly defined foci for regional objectives, the complexes furnish a stage for interindustry and interdepartmental conflicts. And it is just conceivable that in the Gorbachev era, under the pressure of a more aggressive and streamlined Party leadership, the actors so put on stage will feel more compelled to coordinate and synchronize their activities than formerly. In this way, the TPCs may possibly play a positive planning role even without an explicit mechanism for regional coordination.

Local-Municipal Planning and Administration

The functional role of the programming TPCs in long-range economic plans and in regional strategies for the Trans-Ural hinterland assures that their main structural profiles will develop and be determined according to exogenous factors. The search for greater horizontal coordination in planning and development purports to serve primarily the national interest through reduced cost and greater efficiency. However, on the microlevel, local interests surface. Soviet planning principles acknowledge the legitimacy of these local interests, to which adequate attention cannot be paid on the Union or republic level, and in theory provide a mechanism for their expression. In general, the law designates the local soviets as agents responsible for municipal and domestic services, infrastructure, and trade (water, sewage, housing, local transportation, repair facilities, food supply, culture, entertainment, etc.). However, the divisions of authority are not clear cut, and some of these functions also fall under the jurisdiction of other authorities at different levels of the hierarchy. Economic ministries in particular, with their ownership and control of a range of infrastructural and service facilities, have the power to influence regional development not only on the macro scale, but on the micro or municipal scale as well.[51] This influence is especially strong in Siberia, the Far East, and Kazakhstan, where the majority of cities are the results of the Soviet industrialization drive and where even those founded before the Revolution acquired their present morphology mostly in the Soviet era.

Lack of skilled personnel and a weak financial base of most municipalities and the fact that "the budget-planning process for the industrial ministries is entirely separate from that for the city (making coordination between the two virtually impossible)" have been identified as the chief reasons for the ineffectiveness of local and municipal planning. Since the latter 1950s, several decrees have been enacted to "strengthen the hand of the city soviets." Republic governments were instructed to facilitate "the transfer to city soviets of enterprise-owned housing and services and local, city-serving industry," and the soviets were granted "sole right to order the construction of housing, services and ancillary facilities."[52] City budgets rose. In the late 1970s, a new law ordered enterprises subordinated to republic authorities to transfer a set percentage of their profits to the raion (both urban and rural) budgets. Even if it had been rigorously applied, however, the impact of the decree in Siberia could only have been very limited: for many major branches of industry, especially those important east of the Urals, there are only Union, but not republic, ministries in the RSFSR.[53] The law was newly promulgated in 1984 and, in late 1986, decreed for all enterprises, regardless of subordination.[54]

One of the many decrees announced under Gorbachev's policy of restructuring aims at strengthening the territorial coordination of planning. It requires the preparation and approval of regional labor balances prior to the finalization of economic branch plans. It also attempts to strengthen the coordinating authority of local soviets over firms placed under republic and lower level jurisdiction by empowering the councils to create interbranch territorial-production associations of such enterprises. Yet the permission of republic ministries is needed for such a move, and firms under Union ministries can be included only with the expressed agreement of the given ministry in Moscow. Provincial councils may also unite enterprises in their territories into industrial nodes for better coordination but the decree gives them no additional legal or financial power to enforce their will.[55] It is clear that, despite Gorbachev's apparent desire to curb the prerogatives of the huge ministries and energize the grassroots, no major change in the centralized system of branch planning is in evidence so far.

At any rate, none of these decrees and laws improved the situation for the municipal and raion governments in Siberia. If, in the USSR as a whole, 61 percent of the urban housing stock belonged to ministries and other production organizations at the end of the 1970s, and in the RSFSR 72 percent, in Siberia on the average this share rose 10 percent higher still; only 18 percent of urban housing stock is administered by the city soviets.[56] In the city of Bratsk, twenty-four separate ministries hold jurisdiction over the housing stock; in Talmenka raion (Altai Krai) eighty different organizations, fifty of them in the small raion center. Here eighty-six boilers belong to seventy agencies, and none of the raion's three water filtration plants is under the direction of the raion soviet.[57] Only one-tenth of the investment devoted to housing construction and improvement in West Siberia is financed from local budgets.[58]

Such administrative dispersion often results in an urban landscape which is a chaotic assemblage of quasi-independent microcities, each of them tied to different ministries. Such an urban landscape is obvious in Bratsk and is taking place in Ust'-Ilimsk, Tynda, Saianogorsk, and elsewhere.[57] Besides such chaotic morphology, uncoordinated management, and high costs, such dispersion of responsibility also leads to great inequalities of infrastructure and services provided, both among cities of the same region and among microraions of the same city.[59] The amplitude of these infrastructural inequalities could sometimes match the worst in a Western market economy. For example, from 1965 through 1975, workers employed by the Ministry of Electrification (Minenergo) received three times as much housing as their counterparts in the iron and steel industry and 54 to 60 times as much as workers in the food and light industries.[60] In all the settlements of the Bratsk--Ust'-Ilimsk TPC, Minenergo alone employed 53 percent of all those engaged in trade and public catering at the close of the 1970s; Minenergo, the Ministry of Wood Processing, and the Ministry of Transport Construction combined almost 82 percent.[61] Clearly, the weaker ministries in the consumer-group industries were able to provide much less for their labor force than strong ministries, aggravating the rigors of life for the population, already more severe east of the Urals than in more settled western regions.

The ministries are also strongly involved in the financing of services throughout Siberia and may dominate in their provision in the newly formed TPCs. However, Table 7.2, shows that greater ministerial involvement, let alone preponderance, in the financing of services does not always guarantee better supply. According to this survey in fact, a negative correlation is manifest between the share of ministries in such financing and the degree of services provided in Siberian provinces compared to per capita levels in the European USSR. The higher the percentage of ministries and their departments in such financing, the more inadequately is the population provided with the

TABLE 7.2 Indices of Living Conditions in Siberia
(including Far East) and Share of Ministries and
Department in Their Financing (1971-1975)

Infrastructure and Service Indicators	Average Level of Supply Relative to European USSR (Mean for European USSR = 100)	Share of Ministries in Financing Service (% of Budget Channeled through Ministries)
Pupils per Classroom	114.8	8.2
Personnel in Retail Establishment per 100 Population	127.5	27.4
Number of Hospital Beds per 1000 Population	113.4	30.1
Sitting Place in Dining Halls and Cafeterias	95.4	43.2
Kindergarten and Nursery Places per 100 Pre-school Age Children	92.5	64.5
Mean Level of Urban Housing Space per Population	87.3	71.3

Source: V.P. Mozhin, ed., Ekonomicheskoe razvitie Sibiri i
Dal'nego Vostoka (Moscow: Mysl', 1980), p. 154.

particular service. That phenomenon is probably explained
by the fact that ministerial financing totally dominates in
the Arctic and Subarctic and other raw regions. By
contrast, in climatically less forbidding southern areas of
Siberia, larger population concentrations, longer development time, and more reliable supply lines have produced a
more satisfactory level of services under city control.
     The weakness of regional administrative organs against
departmental interest also shows up in the continued
concentration of industry in large cities. This concentration is even stronger in Siberia than west of the Urals.
Some twenty-eight cities, mostly centers of oblasts, krais,
and ASSRs already accounted for about 70 percent of
Siberia's population at the end of the 1970s and almost all
of its industry not tied to logging, fishing, and mineral

extraction.[62]   Yet during the Tenth FYP (1976-1980), about 100 new enterprises came on line in Omsk Oblast, all of it in the city of Omsk. Such preference helped to push the dominance of the city helped push to 82 percent of the urban and 54 percent of the total population of the oblast today. Similarly, the city of Novosibirsk continues to account for over four-fifths of all industrial production in that oblast and 51 percent of all its population.[63] In fact, the nonextractive industries of Siberia seem to be even more concentrated in cities over 100,000 than those of the USSR as a whole (where these large cities contribute about 75 percent of gross output).[64] At the same time, the importance of mineral extraction and logging has created a large number of new towns and so-called settlements of urban type during the last quarter of the century. Between 1959 and the end of 1977, for example, seventeen new cities and sixty-two urban type of settlements arose in the Siberian North alone (including that of the Far East).[65] New towns contributed almost half of the urban population growth of East Siberia through the 1960s and 1970s.[66]

Between the increasing dominance of large cities and the burgeoning growth of new towns and settlements of urban type, the long-established small towns stagnated or declined even more than elsewhere in the country. In Siberia, the number of cities with no growth or decline in their population from 1967 through 1976, for example, exceeded one-third of the total, a share 10 percent higher than in the huge Russian Republic as a whole.[67] (In West Siberia, half of the towns with population of up to 50,000 lost population during the 1970s.[68]) To a very large extent, the burgeoning development of new settlements (mostly in the northern zone) and the increasing concentration of population in the large cities throughout the southern zone was fed not by a net migration into the region, but took place at the expense of small and medium-size cities and the rural population of Siberia itself.

Some Siberian specialists have begun to question the prevailing strategies of settlements, based on large cities, on the one hand, and new towns plus temporary outposts scattered over the vast Northlands, on the other. (The problems of development planning via the outpost system will be examined in the following section.) They also criticize the reliance on huge new plants which, contrary to the conventional wisdom, are not always suitable to conditions east of the Urals. Scientists at the Far Eastern Research Institue, for example, claim that the inordinate growth of large cities in the eastern regions,

with their vast expanses is absurd. They maintain that
developing medium-size and small cities (i.e., up to
100,000 population) would make better sense economically
and would be more convenient for the people.[69] Other
specialists condemn the construction of gigantic forest-
processing complexes near hydrostations. Such large
conversion mills are encountering mounting difficulties in
raw material supplies, which must come from greater and
greater distances. They face the danger of steam and power
shortages as well, while middle-size plants could generate
them from their own wastes. Given the difficulties with
distances, tranportation, and the natural environment in
Siberia and the Far East, intermediate-size factories, two
to three times smaller than those of Bratsk and Ust'-
Ilimsk, would represent the appropriate scale. They
would also help correct distortions in the settlement
hierarchy.[70]

TEMPORARY VERSUS PERMANENT SETTLEMENTS: THE ROLE OF THE WORKSHIFT SYSTEM

The scale and complexity of regional development in
pioneer areas have long been vexing and debated issues in
Soviet literature.[71] Obviously, the more remote, unpopu-
lated, and environmentally rigorous a pioneer province may
be, the more difficult and expensive it becomes to strive
for a complex, multifaceted economic structure and the less
likely it is to succeed. Similarly, the more pressing the
nation's need for a given resource from a remote region may
be, the more likely is a crash attempt to make it available, a strategy which, by definition, must lead to an
extremely unbalanced kind of regional growth. Strategy, in
fact, may often be a misnomer in that case, amounting to a
series of emergency measures and frantic improvisation in
large part. It is in the West Siberian Northland,
producing over 60 percent of the nation's oil and gas,
where desperate urgency and harsh environment combined most
forcibly. That combination resulted in a pattern of
regional development characterized more by frenzied improvization than by carefully thought-out and implemented plans.
A partial answer to the mounting labor needs and the
corresponding shortage of housing, social infrastructure,
and amenities is provided by the "workshift" or "outpost"
system, which has become by now an indispensible component
of developing the West Siberian North. There are two
variants. The "tour-of-duty" (vakhtovyi) method involves

rotating teams of workers from base towns <u>within</u> West Siberia to makeshift settlements at the work sites. The "expedition" (<u>vakhtovo-ekspeditsionnyi</u>) method entails flying in specialized teams from outside the region altogether—mostly from old oil and gas fields in the European USSR. The latter, though more costly and physically demanding, reduces the influx into the base cities of Tiumen' Oblast, where the infrastructure and services are already strained beyond capacity.

The size of this rotating labor force has grown markedly since the early 1970s. By the end of 1983, some 200,000 persons were reportedly employed in Tiumen' Oblast under the two systems by all organizations engaged in the province. About 110,000 of these (55 percent) are said to work by the tour-of-duty method, living within the same region and flown to sites generally up to a few hundred kilometers only. The remainder rotate from much greater distances, mostly from outside Tiumen'.[72] Minneftegazstroi (Ministry of Construction of Petroleum and Gas Industry Enterprises) and the Ministry of Oil Industry alone flew in some 38,000 workers from elsewhere already at the end of the 1970s.[73] This number must be much larger by now. A full 40 percent of all drilling volume in Tiumen' Oblast today is accomplished by teams from ouside the province; the share of outsiders is roughly the same in the preparation and construction of drilling sites.[74] Large numbers of youths dispatched by the Komsomol (the communist youth organization) are also employed in the region on a temporary basis: some 40,000 of them for varying periods in the Tenth FYP (1976-1980) alone. Twenty-eight thousand students were also planned to be sent to Tiumen' construction projects after 1978.[74] (Significant overlap between these two categories, however, is probable.)

Gustafson has pointed out that local authorities are less than happy about the outpost system and lobby for permanent settlements with surprising vigor and enthusiasm. For many with an emotional stake in Siberia, "the fly-in system brings the wrong kind of workers, with the wrong attitudes" and results only in the grabbing of Siberian resources without real development—a short-sighted and, in the longer run, irrational policy. He quotes the Yamal-Nenets Autonomous District's first Party secretary castigating their "consumer-minded approach to the job and a plundering attitude towards nature." Local gas officials and Party personnel for the Yamal-Nenets District have succeeded in promoting permanent settlements. Farther south through the oil-bearing regions of Tiumen', despite

somewhat better environmental conditions, the growing
dependence on scattered smaller fields and the need for
vastly increased, more dispersed drilling have forced a
greater acceptance not only of the tour-of-duty but also of
the expedition systems.[76]
   Yet here too the method has come under sharp criticism
of late. The blunt statement of an official is worth
quoting: "The minuses of the [expedition] practice are too
obvious to speak of any superiority of the method in
principle. . . . The 'expedition' method is not an experiment, not the result of a search for rational ways of
developing the province but a grim necessity. There is
simply no place to settle oil workers in those regions
where they must work."[77] An interview with a specialist in
Novosibirsk also revealed contrasting attitudes and willingness among workers of different regions (and nationalities)
towards the workshift system. Oilmen and construction
crews from the Ukraine and Belorussia are claimed to work
much more willingly on such a system than those from the
Middle Volga and the Caucasus. To Tatars, Bashkirs,
Azeries, and Chechens, with close family ties, the shifts
away from home are unattractive despite the high pay, and
this attitude may also influence some Russians coming from
these regions.
   While the trend away from complex, multifaceted development towards the specialized, exploitative approach is
obvious throughout Siberia, the forces opposing blatant
Raubwirtschaft, the siphoning out of resources without any
long-term local benefits (and often at the cost of permanent damage to the local environment) still appear strong
enough to have some policy effects. Certainly permanent
cities like Surgut and Nizhnevartovsk (190,000 and 180,000
respectively) in an environment climatically analogous to
the Athabasca or Nelson River Valleys in Canada, though far
more marshy, or Noiabr'sk and Novo-Urengoi (each between
50,000 and 60,000), roughly corresponding to the environ-
ments of the Great Slave Lake and the Great Bear Lake, but
again much more marshy, cities that have increased in
population six to twelve times in fifteen years or (as in
the last two cases) were newly created, have no parallels
in other resource frontiers of the world.[78] The new
general plan for Novo-Urengoi projects a size of 160,000
inhabitants.[79] Since the beginning of the oil and gas
boom, ten new cities and over fifty large new worker settlements have been created in the West Siberian North.[80]
   It is well to bear in mind, however, Rumer's cogent
remarks concerning the deforming influence on Siberian

cities of the self-generating, expanding construction organizations (supra). We do not know to what degree the sizes of Surgut, Nizhnevartovsk, or even those cities in the 50,000-to-80,000 range would be inflated by such distortions. And one can certainly question whether the projected population of 160,000 for Novo-Urengoi in that physical environment is sensible and desirable even from the standpoint of local interest. The very north of Tiumen' Oblast (roughly the area of the Yamal-Nenets Autonomous District) is highly unlikely to prove economically viable once the gas reserves are depleted. It certainly will be unable to support more than a fraction of the current population (2,650,000 in January 1986), still less the peak population suggested by the projected size of Novo-Urengoi. The oil region of Tiumen' (roughly coterminous with the Khanty-Mansi Autonomous District) is environmentally more tolerable, though not very much so, and is capable of contributing only marginally to its food supply. Yet, here too, economic viability depend overwhelmingly on a depletable mineral resource, the life span of which is uncertain and whose known reserves are being extracted at an extremely rapid rate. Without the oil, the Khanty-Mansi District would be (and will be) unable to provide a livelihood for the one million people that inhabit it today.

It is also a fact that many of the "permanent" habitations in the West Siberian wilderness are not the result of planning or even the lobbying efforts of local officials, but are outposts turned into settlements by default. Even some of the cities and large settlements have grown in such a precipitous, improvised fashion that accommodations per capita actually worsened. In Noiabr'sk and Novo-Urengoi, for example, per capita housing space in 1980 amounted to 2.7 square meters and 2.3 square meters respectively, a sharp decline in a few years. A further deterioration is expected by an observer during the present decade,[81] especially since in the first five years alone both cities increased their population by five times.[82] Altogether Tiumen' Oblast has over 200 outposts at various stages of "permanency," and more are in the making.[83] Although a "Statute on Workers' Tour-of-Duty Outpost" states that these are intended for temporary residency, thus freeing the ministry and trust to which they belong from the obligation of providing a certain measure of amenities, one source claims the "the stipulations of the statute were nullified by practice a long time ago. Workers 'settle in,' hoping to receive an apartment in their organization's home city for their long-term service. Many raise families." Yet, the place is not officially listed as a "permanent settlement," keeping expenditures on housing and social services very low and shifting the burden to the worker. "Today there are 42 such unregistered settlements at various oil fields in Tiumen' Oblast."[84] (It is impossible to know for certain, but these are probably included in the 200 outposts mentioned above.) Another recent source states that, as of January 1982, a total of some 109,000 persons resided in those outposts, subordinated to construction organizations working in oil and gas projects in the province; of these, 22,000, or one-fifth, were dependent family members.[85] Some 9 percent of the total population of the oil-and-gas-producing districts of Tiumen' Oblast (Khanty-Mansi and Yamal-Nenets Autonomous Districts) lived in such settlements in the early 1980s. The share of these settlements in the total workers registered in the two districts, therefore excluding those who fly in from the outside, reached 13 to 14 percent of the total (Table 6.9).

Although, officially or unofficially, many of these outposts are turning into quasi-settlements, they still provide a means of saving on infrastructure and social consumption. One source claims about 14.5 million rubles were saved in the Arctic zone for every 1,000 persons employed under the expedition system.[86] This saving amounts to half the cost of providing accommodations and the required social services for a thousand new workers if they were to be settled in the Khanty-Mansi District and some 36 percent for the same number settled in the Yamal-Nenets District.[87] This is certainly not a comprehensive saving, for it excludes the wear and tear on the labor force and on their families, the effect of reduced labor productivity, and the cost of the high manpower turnover (every third worker migrates each year). Rather, it is a narrowly defined short-term gain even in strict monetary terms, accruing to ministries and trusts on their departmental ledger, governed chiefly by the dictates of short-term plan fulfillment. Therefore these temporary outposts and outposts turned into quasi-settlements by default exemplify the improvized, emergency nature of much of economic development in Tiumen' Oblast, as noted at the beginning of this secion.

The decline of Soviet petroleum output from 1983 through 1985 has only increased the pressure, bringing emergency measures and improvization evermore to the fore. Through a huge effort and new resources thrown into the breach, oil production in 1986 recovered again. Though further growth nationally is to be minimal, it seems Soviet leaders are determined to prevent a serious decline whatever the cost. This means Siberian oil output must continue to grow to compensate for the unremitting decrease of flows in mature petroleum provinces. Whether these plans are attainable remains to be seen. However, a prolonged reliance on a sizable temporary work force in the Siberian North, continued hasty improvization, and shturmovshchina (rush work) seem inevitable. Indeed, a recent Pravda article predicts that by the year 2000 up to 40 percent of all production personnel in the northern areas of West Siberia will consist of temporary labor on the workshift system.[88]

NOTES

1. Robert W. Campbell, The Economics of Soviet Oil and Gas (Baltimore: Johns Hopkins Press), p. 25 and Arthur Wright, "Environmental Disruption and Economic Systems," The ASTE Bulletin, Vol. 13, No. 1 (Spring), 1971, pp. 4 and 10.
2. I.S. Koropeckyj, "Industrial Location Policy in the USSR During the Postwar Period," in Economic Performance and the Military Burden in the Soviet Union. U.S. Congress, Joint Economic Committee (Washington, D.C.: Government Printing Office, 1970), p. 258.
3. V.F. Pavlenko, Planirovanie territorial'nogo razvitiia (Moscow: Ekonomika, 1984), pp. 24-25.
4. Ibid., pp. 53-54. Naturally, central control was also retained over defense and foreign trade.
5. Fyodor I. Kushnirsky, Soviet Economic Planning, 1965-1980 (Boulder, Colorado: Westview Press, 1982), p. 51 and 53-54.
6. In fact, the trend in budgetary control has been the other way. During each half of the 1970 decade, 49.3 to 49.4 percent of the state budgetary revenues were turned over to the fifteen republics. In 1983, the share of republics was only 39.1 percent and in 1986 44.5 percent. Only a little over one-third of the budget of republics is controlled by lower level administrative units (oblasts, krais, and ASSR) even in the vast Russian Republic, which contain seventy-one such units plus Moscow and Leningrad. V.G. Panskoi, ed., Gosudarstvennyi biudzhet SSSR i soiuz-

260

nykh respublik. 1976-1980 godakh (Moscow: Finansy i statistika, 1982), pp. 7 and 75-77; V.F. Garbuzov, O gosudarstvennom biudzhete SSSR na 1983 god (Moscow: Politizdat, 1982), pp. 5 and 23; V.F. Garbuzov, O gosudarstvennom biudzhete SSSR na 1984 god (Moscow: Politizdat, 1984), pp. 6 and 25; and Ekonomicheskaia gazeta, 1986, No. 48 (December), p. 16.

7. Kushnirsky, Soviet Economic Planning, 1965-1980, pp. 34 and 68.

8. Mason H. Soule and Robert N. Taaffe, "Mathematical Programming Approaches to the Planning of Siberian Regional Economic Development: A Nonmathematical Survey," Soviet Economy, Vol. 1, No. 1 (January-March), 1985, pp. 75 and 95.

9. Pavlenko, Planirovanie, pp. 195-196 and 200-202.

10. R.I. Shniper, "Planovaia rabota v regione: kontury budushchego," Ekonomika i organizatsiia promyshlennogo proizvodstva (EKO), 1981, No. 12, pp. 13-14 and B.M. Mochalova, ed., Territorial'no-otraslevoi printsip planirovaniia: teoriia i praktika (Moscow: Mysl', 1980), p. 84. The grave shortage of manpower for small-scale planning is shown by the fact that the average size of the labor force in raion planning commissions of the RSFSR was 1.7 person during the mid-1970s and that of city planning commissions 1.5 persons. Even on a higher level, the manpower shortage is severe. Only about 5 percent of the total planning bureaucracy of the RSFSR Gosplan is directly engaged in territorial planning. This does not, of course, include academic research institutes. A. Triakin, "Territorial'nyi aspekt planirovaniia," Planovoe khoziaistvo, 1977, No. 8.

11. Janice Giffen, "The Allocation of Investment in the Soviet Union: Criteria for the Efficiency of Investment," Soviet Studies, Vol. 23, No. 4 (October), 1981, especially p. 600.

12. I.L. Aparin and M.E. Krinitskaia, Industrial'naia baza stroitel'stva severnoi zony (Leningrad: Stroiizdat, 1979), p. 50; E.G. Egorov, Problemy regional'noi ekonomiki (Novosibirsk: Nauka, 1979), pp. 126-148 and Vsevolod Holubnychy, "Spatial Efficiency in the Soviet Economy," in V.N. Bandera and Z.L. Melnyk, The Soviet Economy in Regional Perspective (New York: Praeger, 1973), p. 26.

13. Pavlenko, Planirovanie, pp. 147-50; A. Makarov and A. Beschinskii, "Zamykaiushchie zatraty na toplivo i energiiu," Voprosy ekonomiki, 1982, No. 3, pp. 33-41; A.A. Makarov and L.A. Melent'ev, Metody issledovaniia i optimizatsii energeticheskogo khoziaistva (Novosibirsk: Nauka, 1973), pp. 194-215 and A.E. Probst, Voprosy razmeshcheniia

sotsialisticheskoi promyshlennosti (Moscow: Nauka, 1971), pp. 223-236.

14. In reality, West Siberia produced 1,657 million tons of oil equivalent, i.e., very close to target. Theodore Shabad, "News Notes," Soviet Geography. Various April issues of recent years.

15. A.G. Aganbegian, et al., ed., Sibir' v edinom narodnokhoziaistvennom komplekse (Novosibirsk: Nauka, 1980), pp. 15-16.

16. Pavlenko, Planirovanie, pp. 148-150 and Makarov and Beschinskii, "Zamykaiushchie zatraty," pp. 39-40.

17. Leslie Dienes, "The Development of Siberian Regions: Economic Profiles, Income Flows and Strategies for Growth," Soviet Geography, Vol. 23, No. 4 (April), 1982, p. 22.

18. M. Bakhrakh and G. Mil'ner, "Proizvodstvo chistogo produkta i ispol'zovanie natsional'nogo dokhoda po regionam v RSFSR," Vestnik statistiki, 1984, No. 6, pp. 14-23, especially pp. 20 and 22-23.

19. M.K. Bandman, Territorial'no-proizvodstvennye kompleksy: teoriia i praktika, predplanovykh issledovanii (Novosibirsk: Nauka, 1980), p. 27.

20. David S. Kamerling, "The Role of Territorial Production Complexes in Soviet Economy Policy," in U.S. Congress, Joint Economic Committee, Soviet Economy in the 1980's: Problems and Prospects, Part 1 (Washington, D.C.: U.S. Government Printing Office, 1981), p. 247. See also Peter de Souza, "The TPC Planning Strategy and Its Role in the Development of Siberia," in Institut du Monde Sovietique et de l'Europe Centrale et Orientale, Siberie 1. Economie, Ecologie, Strategie, edited by B. Chichlo (Paris: Institute d'Etudes Slaves, 1985), pp. 87-107. These two articles are probably the two most cogent studies on the TPCs in the Western literature.

21. Bandman, Territorial'no-proizvodstvennye kompleksy, pp. 29-33.

22. De Souza, "The TPC Planning Strategy," p. 100.

23. M.K. Bandman, "Sovershenstvovanie upravleniia programmno-tselevymi territorial'no-proizvodstvennymi kompleksami," AN SSSR, SO, Seriia obshchestvennykh nauk, Izvestiia, 1983, No. 6, pp. 3-5.

24. Kamerling, "The Role of Territorial Production Complexes," pp. 249-250.

25. Narodnoe khoziaistvo SSSR v 1982 godu, p. 110 and Narodnoe khoziaistvo SSSR v 1985 godu, p. 95.

26. A.G. Aganbegian, ed., Territorial'nye-proizvodstvennye kompleksy: planirovanie i upravlenie (Novosibirsk:

262

Nauka, 1984), p. 9 and M.K. Bandman, "Territorial'no-proizvodstvennye kompleksy kak forma organizatsii proizvoditel'-
nykh sil," in B.P. Kutyrev, ed., Razvitie regiona v sisteme
natsional'noi ekonomiki (Novosibirsk: AN SSSR, SO, IEOPP,
1985), pp. 89-90.
    27. V.A. Pertsik, "Pravovoe regulirovanie formiro-
vaniia i razvitiia territorial'no-proizvodstvennykh
kompleksov," AN SSSR, SO, Seriia obshchestvennykh nauk,
Izvestiia, 1983, No. 6, p. 20.
    28. V.P. Gukov and A.A. Beliaev, "Napravlenie dal'nei-
shego razvitiia Bratsko-Ust'-Ilimskogo TPC," in Modeliro-
vanie sotsial'no-ekonomicheskogo razvitiia territorial'nykh
sistem: opyt issledovaniia v sotsialisticheskikh stranakh
(Novosibirsk, 1983), pp. 237-255. Quoted in Referativnyi
zhurnal. Geografiia. 1983, No. 9, E150.
    29. S.N. Starovoitov, ed., Problemy razvitiia Zapadno-
Sibirskogo Neftegazovogo Kompleksa (Novosibirsk: Nauka,
1983), pp. 180 and 184; Pravda, May 22, 1978, p. 3 and
Theodore Shabad, "Population Trends of Soviet Cities, 1970-
84," Soviet Geography, Vol. 26, No. 2 (February), 1985, pp.
137-138. These small pygmies are wasteful of fuel, use
mostly petroleum products, and tie down a large share of
the labor force in this region with a critical manpower
shortage. In the settlements of Nadym and Novourengoi and
on the gas fields of northwest Tiumen' Oblast alone, these
pygmy plants employ 3,500 persons and produce electricity
at a cost of up to 20 kopeks per kwh. V.A. Dinkov,
"Neotlozhnye zadachi otrasli," Gazovaia promyshlennost',
1982, No. 1, p. 3 and V.I. Botvinnikov, ed., Problemy
razvitiia gazovoi promyshlennosti Sibiri (Novosibirsk:
Nauka, 1983), p. 78.
    30. Stroitel'naia gazeta, August 8, 1979, p. 1 and
Komsomolskaia pravda, January 18, 1977.
    31. Ekonomicheskaia gazeta, 1983, No. 37 (September),
p. 7; Izvestiia, January 5, 1984, p. 2 and January 15,
1984, p. 1.
    32. Leslie Dienes and Theodore Shabad, The Soviet
Energy System: Resource Use and Policies (Washington, D.C.:
Winston and Sons, 1979), p. 265 and Ekonomicheskaia gazeta,
1985, No. 23 (June), p. 5.
    33. Stroitel'naia gazeta, March 24, 1982, p. 2.
    34. Izvestiia, October 12, 1984, p. 2. and "Kak
upravliat' TPK." Roundtable Discussion. EKO, No. 4, 1985,
p. 61.
    35. Ekonomicheskaia gazeta, 1983, No. 35 (August),
p. 6.
    36. David A. Dyker, The Process of Investment in the

Soviet Union (Cambridge: Cambridge University Press, 1983), pp. 29-31. There were some important exceptions, however, such as the gas industry.

37. G.B. Poliak and B.N. Annenkov, "Finansovye aspekty formirovaniia territorial'no-proizvodstvennykh kompleksov," AN SSSR, SO, Seriia obshchestvennykh nauk, _Izvestiia_, 1983, No. 6, p. 26.

38. L.M. Kaplan and I.Iu. Murav'eva, _Ekonomicheskie problemy upravleniia stroitel'nym proizvodstvom na Severe_ (Leningrad: Stroiizdat, 1983), p. 16.

39. A. Anan'ev and A. Silin, "Obespechenie predpriiatii i stroek ZSNGK rabochei siloi," _Planovoe khoziaistvo_, 1984, No. 1, p. 96.

40. Shabad, "Population Trends," p. 137.

41. Boris Z. Rumer, _Investment and Reindustrialization in the Soviet Economy_ (Boulder, Colorado: Westview Press, 1984), pp. 131-132.

42. M.K. Bandman, ed., _Territorial'no-proizvodstvennye kompleksy: sovershenstvovanie protsessa formirovaniia_ (Novosibirsk: Nauka, 1986), pp. 154-67, esp. p. 165.

43. V.I. Sverchkov, "Internatsional'noe znachenie energeticheskogo stroitel'stva na Angare," in V.V. Alekseev, S.S. Bukin, A.A. Dolgoliuk and I.M. Savitskii, eds., _Sotsial'nye aspekty industrial'nogo razvitiia Sibiri_ (Novosibirsk: Nauka, 1983), p. 199.

44. Aganbegian, ed., _Territorial'nye-proizvodstvennye kompleksy_, pp. 90-92.

45. Ibid., pp. 90-91 and E.I. Pilipenko, "Formirovanie kadrov gazovoi promyshlennosti Zapadnoi Sibiri," in Alekseev, Bukin, Dolgoliuk and Savitskii, _Sotsial'nye aspekty_, p. 67.

46. Thane Gustafson, _The Soviet Gas Campaign_ (Santa Monica, California: Rand Corporation, 1983), p. 25.

47. Aganbegian, ed., _Territorial'nye-proizvodstvennye kompleksy_, pp. 56 and 58. Pliaskina holds a similar view. She wants to create a coordinating council, with full authority and responsibility, composed of representatives of major ministries and territorial organs involved in the development of the most important complexes. Her discussion focuses specifically on the West Siberian TPC. N.I. Pliaskina, "Problema soglasovaniia razvitiia gazovoi promyshlennosti i proizvodstvennoi infrastruktury," in Iu.I. Maksimov and G.M. Mkrtchan, eds., _Problemy i perspektivy razvitiia neftegazovykh kompleksov v Sibiri_ (Novosibirsk: AN SSSR, SO, IEOPP, 1984), pp. 18-19.

48. "Kak upravliat' TPK," pp. 56-89.

49. Gustafson, _The Soviet Gas Campaign_, pp. 24-25.

264

50. Aganbegian, ed., <u>Territorial'nye-proizvodstvennye</u> <u>kompleksy</u>, pp. 54 and 57.

51. Judith Pallot and Denis J. B. Shaw, <u>Planning in</u> <u>the Soviet Union</u> (Athens: The University of Georgia Press, 1981), pp. 246-247 and "Kak upravliat' TPK," pp. 71-72.

52. Pallot and Shaw, <u>Planning in the Soviet Union</u>, pp. 249-250.

53. M.K. Shishkov, "Vedomstvennaia razobshchennost' v raione: kak ee preodolet'," <u>EKO</u>, 1983, No. 11, p. 82 and Pavlenko, <u>Planirovanie</u>, p. 211.

54. <u>Ekonomicheskaia gazeta</u>, 1986, No. 52 (December), p. 16 and N. M. Dement'eva, "Finansovyi balans goroda, ego neobkhodimost' i znachenie," in Ministerstvo Vysshego i Srednego Spetsial'nogo Obrazovaniia RSFSR, Tiumenskii Gosudarstvennyi Universitet, <u>Trudy</u> (Tiumen', 1985), p. 89.

55. <u>Pravda</u>, December 24, 1986, p. 2.

56. Aganbegian, et al., <u>Sibir' v edinom narodnokhoziai-</u> <u>stvennom komplekse</u>, p. 88 and V.O. Rukavishnikov, <u>Naselenie</u> <u>goroda. Sotsial'nyi sostav. Rasselenie</u> (Moscow: Statistika, 1980), p. 20.

57. Aganbegian, ed., <u>Territorial'nye-proizvodstvennye</u> <u>kompleksy,</u>, p. 71 and Shishkov, "Vedomstvennaia razobshchennost'," p. 76.

58. Shniper, "Planovaia rabota v regione," p. 10.

59. Aganbegian, et al., <u>Sibir' v edinom narodnokhoziai-</u> <u>stvennom komplekse</u>, p. 89; G.F. Kutsev, <u>Novye goroda</u> (Moscow: Mysl', 1982), p. 132; Shniper, "Planovaia rabota v regione," p. 10; and personal observation on a field trip to Ust'-Ilimsk in August 1983 under a Soviet Academy of Sciences, Institute of Geography--Association of American Geographers exchange.

60. V.Z. Rogovin, "Raspredelitel'nye otnosheniia kak faktor intensifikatsii proizvodstva," <u>Sotsiologicheskie</u> <u>issledovaniia</u>, 1982, No. 1, p. 14.

61. Aganbegian, ed., <u>Territorial'nye-proizvodstvennye</u> <u>kompleksy</u>, p. 73.

62. B.I. Oglyi, <u>Stroitel'stvo gorodov Sibiri</u> (Leningrad, Stroiizdat, 1980), p. 201.

63. <u>Pravda</u>, April 6, 1984, p. 2; A.G. Granberg, ed., <u>Ekonomika Sibiri v razreze shirotnykh zon</u> (Novosibirsk: Nauka, 1985), p. 141 and <u>Narodnoe khoziaistvo SSSR v 1985</u> <u>godu</u>, p. 14 and 21.

64. M.B. Mazanova, ed., <u>Rasselenie naseleniia i</u> <u>razmeshchenie proizvodstva</u> (Moscow: Nauka, 1982), p. 143.

65. AN SSSR and Gosplan SSSR, SOPS, <u>Problemy rasse-</u> <u>leniia i urbanizatsii v razvitom sotsialisticheskom</u> <u>obshchestve</u> (Moscow: Nauka, 1980), p. 76.

66. Kutsev, Novye goroda, p. 68.

67. Aganbegain, ed., Sibir' v edinom narodnokhoziai-stvennom komplekse, p. 86.

68. Sotsial'naia i territorial'naia struktura goroda i sela: opyt tipologicheskogo analiza (Novosibirsk, 1982), pp. 76–94. Quoted in Referativnyi zhurnal. Geografiia, 1983, No. 9, E135.

69. Izvestiia, January 9, 1984, p. 2.

70. V.S. Sominskii, "Puti razvitiia tselliuiozno-bumazhnoi promyshlennosti," EKO, 1980, No. 11, p. 99.

71. For a comprehensive analysis see Robert N. North, "Soviet Northern Development: the Case of NW Siberia," Soviet Studies, Vol. 24, No. 2 (October), 1972, pp. 171–199.

72. Anan'ev and Silin, "Obespechenie predpriiatii i stroek," p. 96 and Sovetskaia Rossiia, December 9, 1983, p. 3.

73. Starovoitov, ed., Problemy razvitiia, pp. 202–203.

74. Pravda, April 3, 1984, p. 2 and Neftianik, 1983, No. 9 (September), pp. 9–12. The share of outside teams in the construction of drilling sites was 35 percent in 1981, according to the latter source, and increased 54.5 percent in that single year.

75. Tiumenskii meridian (No author) (Moscow: Izdatel'-stvo politicheskoi literatury, 1983), p. 225 and Alekseev, et al., Sotsial'nye aspekty, pp. 108–109.

76. Gustafson, The Soviet Gas Campaign, pp. 64–65.

77. Trud, April 18, 1980 quoted in Starovoitov, Problemy razvitiia, p. 203 and A.N. Filimonov, "Uroki Tiumenskogo Severa," EKO, 1986, No. 3, pp. 78–83.

78. Shabad, "Population Trends," p. 137 gives the 1984 population size of these four cities in order of appearance in the sentence above as 188,000, 178,000, 52,000 and 55,000.

79. Ekonomicheskaia gazeta, 1984, No. 9 (February), p. 6.

80. Ekonomicheskaia gazeta, 1984, No. 36 (September), p. 9.

81. Pilipenko, "Formirovanie kadrov," pp. 76 and 78.

82. Shabad, "Population Trends," p. 137.

83. Tiumenskii meridian, p. 54.

84. Izvestiia, January 30, 1984, p. 3

85. L.M. Kaplan and I.Iu. Murav'eva, Ekonomicheskie problemy upravleniia stroitel'nym proizvodstvom na Severe (Leningrad: Stroiizdat, 1983), p. 147.

86. Anan'ev and Silin, "Obespechenie predpriiatii i stroek," p. 96.

87. N.K. Gladina and V.K. Shirokov, "Trudoobespechen-nost' i uroven' zhizni v reshenii problem formirovaniia i razvitiia TPK v raionakh Severa," Problemy Severa, 1983, No. 21, pp. 32-33.

88. Pravda, December 24, 1986, pp. 1-2.

8

Conclusion

This work examined the geographic position of the Asian USSR in the spatial dimension of the Soviet economy. Furthermore, it analyzed the crucial impact of major national policy choices on the developmental prospect of Soviet Asia. Most of this hinterland is still weakly integrated into the country's economic mainstream, but the degree of that integration varies sharply, according to accessibility to the economic heartland, the nature of resource endowment, and the ethno–cultural composition of population. Because this landmass is so huge, its disparate regions play very dissimilar roles in the Soviet spatial system and are affected by different policy choices and issues on the national level. As shown, Central Asia–Southern Kazakhstan forms an entirely distinct geographic and cultural realm, with almost nothing in common with the rest of the Trans–Ural USSR, that vast frontier zone broadly referred to as Siberia. The latter, however, is far from a monolith. Physical geography, resource endowment, and perhaps most important, contrasting accessibility to the economic heartland of the European USSR and the world outside, have destined its macroregions to play radically different roles in the spatial economic system of the country. Not only are there striking developmental differences between the more settled southern belt and the far more inhospitable huge Northland, which plunges far to the south eastward of Lake Baikal, but the economic roles and prospects of Siberian regions contrast sharply according to their east–west positions.

In any country, the economic profiles and prospects of regions are a result of interaction between external and internal impulses. External forces, whether coming from the world at large or from the geographic locus of power within the same state, tend to dominate in the case of raw, pioneer areas with small population. In the centrally managed USSR, regional development is inexorably intertwined with major national policy choices and priorities. These almost totally determine the prospects of the different Siberian regions. The population of this vast land has remained too small and scattered even to cope with major projects of national importance without the influx of large numbers of temporary workers, let alone to be able to broaden local industries and social infrastructure essential for a more advanced and mature economic profile. The situation is somewhat different in Central Asia. National priorities have dominated the development of this non-Slavic and culturally non-European periphery as well, and the region is now more strongly tied to the controlling "metropolis" in a state of economic dependency than ever in its history. Yet external factors are not so totally overriding as in Siberia and may be still less so in the future. The regional market is large and manpower reserves are plentiful, if not yet adequately trained. The degree to which the vast cohort of mostly rural youth can acquire skills, enter, and integrate into the economy will be of fundamental importance to the region's future and, indeed, for the future of the USSR. However, investment from the Center (for which, at any rate, there are mounting claims from all over the country) alone will not solve the problem. Considerable reliance on local efforts and initiative and a combination of traditional skills and modern production methods will be necessary for development in the years ahead.

This book has shown that throughout Siberia the urgency and resource demand of major national policy decisions are making economic growth highly selective and distorted both in the sectoral and regional dimensions. The frenetic nature and unprecedented capital requirement of the current energy campaign have set the course for West and East Siberia and determined their industrial profile well into the future, but affect these regions and their subunits in contradictory fashion. West Siberia, but particularly Tiumen' Oblast, has become a quintessential energy colony of the European USSR, thanks to its oil and gas resources and the transportability of these fuels on a massive scale. Yet such pell-mell growth, focused almost exclusively on exploitation and outshipment of two commodities, leaves infrastructural and social development even further behind and forestalls any hope for a more balanced development. By contrast, East Siberia and even the Kuzbas-

Altai area of West Siberia have suffered because their vast energy riches (coal and hydropower) are far less mobile and must be utilized locally. The much greater use of Siberian energy resources within the region, however, is seriously hampered by the underdevelopment of machine building and the narrow, unbalanced industrial profile of the area. Even a strategy which stresses the fullest realization of Siberia's resource potential demands the more rapid development of machine building branches and the creation of a more complex industrial structure.

Such a shift in emphasis towards a more balanced development of the southern zone of Siberia seemed to have appeared briefly at the onset of the Gorbachev era. By now, however, it is fairly certain that very little of it will be accomplished over the next decade. The new leadership, with all its pressing problems and mounting fuel and material needs, simply lacks the resources to accelerate the more comprehensive development even of the better-located southern provinces east of the Urals. The first few years of that leadership also indicate that it lacks the desire to do so. Aside from a perfunctory statement about greater balance, Ryzhkov's latest (June 1986) report on the new Twelfth FYP shows an obvious reluctance to commit large volumes of investment to this end. Nor are the more detailed March 1986 Guidelines of the Plan any different in this regard.[1]

In fact, the mounting resource needs of the energy sector, so strongly focused on Tiumen' Oblast, and of the current campaign to modernize the capital stock in established industrial centers are lowering the rate of economic growth through most of the Trans-Ural territory. The 82 billion rubles of investment envisaged for Tiumen' and Tomsk Oblasts in the Twelfth FYP amounts to over 8.2 percent of all capital allocation in the USSR and should account for 40 to 45 percent (perhaps even more) of all outlays in the eighteen provinces of Siberia and the Far East.[2] Since the mid-1970s, industrial expansion here has already fallen below the Soviet mean, apart from oil and gas output and it has done so in all three macroregions (West Siberia, East Siberia, and the Far East) between the Urals and the Pacific. Similarly, growth lagged in neighboring Kazakhstan as well. The recent stagnation (in 1985, absolute decline) of Siberian oil production is bound to affect the prospect of the area still further, while the priority claim of the oil and gas region will siphon investment away from the other provinces.

The disappointing growth of the Soviet Far East is

also strongly linked to the evolution of foreign economic relations and national policy towards Japan. Because of that, major developments on the world market and the Japanese economy are almost as important as Soviet domestic constraints on labor and capital. Profound structural changes in Japan, highly successful conservation measures, and abundant alternative sources of raw materials have made Soviet resources essentially superfluous and increasingly unattractive to that economic giant. The BAM (Baikal-Amur Mainline) constructed at huge cost, has failed to improve the Soviet bargaining position significantly in the economic sphere, though it has strengthened the Soviet strategic position on the Pacific. Given no likelihood of massive foreign investment in the Far East, and especially not in the interior, and given priority efforts focused on regions west of the Enisei, Soviet economic policy in the Far East over the next decade must be essentially a holding action. Long-term prospects will remain hostage to the interplay of international relations, Soviet strategic concerns and aspirations on the Pacific, and of domestic capital and manpower needs of regions more accessible to the country's heartland.

National policy choices with respect to Central Asia are of an altogether different nature. They are inter-twined with fundamental political and ideological issues to a greater degree than elsewhere in the Asian USSR, since the extent and nature of investment allocation, transfer payments, population mobility, and elite participation cannot be separated from the nationality problem. Unlike in most of Siberia, where the incomplete integration into the national mainstream is essentially a question of physical obstacles, distance, and weak infrastructure, in Central Asia it is also linked to deep-seated cultural issues. Until the early 1980s, the regime had been quite successful in responding to the burgeoning population growth. Through active welfare measures and passive arrangements, such as a greater toleration of the second economy than elsewhere, it has forestalled the decline, even stagnation, of living standards. Since the early 1980s, however, certain signs of deteriorating conditions have appeared in the adequacy of welfare measures, just when Gorbachev's vigorous anticorruption campaign is also restricting gains from the second economy.

Economic expansion and active job creation, therefore, assume much greater importance for the rest of this century. A development strategy suitable for Central Asia requires dispersed investment in large numbers of small-

and medium-scale plants, particularly in small towns and rural areas. It also requires significant adjustments to the rhythm of rural life and to local cultural factors and preferences. In addition, dispersed industrialization in the Soviet context generally entails higher capital costs than the construction of a few large plants of the same capacity. Conflicting goals and criteria about efficiency, performance, and benefits, therefore, are all but inevitable between central ministries and local agencies.

So far, the regime's accomplishments in such flexible, dispersed industrialization have been relatively modest. Moderate success in Uzbekistan, the strongest republic, has been balanced by few results in the other three. At the same time, a significant expansion of agricultural employment is now possible only through grandiose irrigation projects requiring huge interbasin transfer of water from West Siberia. Plans for such water transfer have recently been shelved indefinitely. The project is clearly opposed by Gorbachev and is very unlikely to be revived under his leadership. For the next decade, perhaps longer, Central Asia also cannot count on more than very slowly rising volumes of capital allocation from Moscow planners. During the Twelfth FYP (1986–1990), for example, these four republics plus Southern Kazakhstan cannot count on much larger investment than Tiumen' and Tomsk Oblasts in West Siberia with one tenth as many people. The shortage of funds for economic expansion, combined with the decline in per capita transfer payments and restrictions on sub-rosa activities to support living standards, may upset the delicate social and political equilibrium established in that sensitive periphery.

Economic development through the vast expanse of the Asian USSR is linked to efforts of manpower, settlement, and regional planning in a more direct, straightforward fashion than west of the Urals. The resource-rich, pioneer hinterland, embracing Siberia, the Far East, and North Kazakhstan, have been historically short of labor and deficient in social (as well as economic) infrastructure and services. Even in Central Asia–Southern Kazakhstan, the overpopulated oases and valleys are separated from new mineral, hydropower, and agricultural development by large stretches of desert. As in Siberia, these new nodes of development struggle with manpower shortages and lack of infrastructure. Through most of the Asian USSR, therefore, working and living conditions, settlement structure and organization, and the planning and provisioning of services are integral components of the evolving regional profiles.

272

Manpower shortages in Siberia and the Far East have not led to an effective utilization of labor time. On the contrary, the harsh environment and lack of services and infrastructure, made worse by the perennial emphasis on "production activities" and plan fulfillment on the part of ministries and trusts, resulted in an extreme instability of the labor force. Not only is labor turnover much higher than elsewhere in the country, but the average time spent on the job is strikingly low both in industry and construction. At the same time, the uncommonly heavy workload on the agricultural population and its very unsatisfactory living conditions have accelerated rural flight all through the Asian Soviet Union, except Central Asia–Southern Kazakhstan. This is compounding the development problem for Siberia. The vast region is already grossly deficient in food and particularly so east of the Altai Mountains and throughout its huge Northlands.

Economic development takes place not in abstract space, but through a concrete settlement network. In Siberia, industrial growth and mineral exploitation tend to proceed through widely separate levels of the nonagricultural settlement hierarchy, a process that in many ways aggravates the problems of the region. On the one hand, industrial growth is concentrated in the largest established urban centers, on the other hand, in new towns and outpost settlements of mineral exploitation. Many of the latter, especially in the West Siberian North, rely on a temporary, rotating labor force (flown in from base towns or from outside Siberia altogether) to a significant degree in order to minimize infrastructural costs and speed up the opening of deposits. All this leads to enhanced spatial disparities, social problems, and still greater instability of the labor force. Successful mineral developments "family style" do exist in the Far North, but their costs are extremely high and they require long lead times. Given current economic pressures, very few additional large resource projects of that kind can be expected on the Siberian frontier in this century or even beyond.

A high share of temporary, though registered population (sailors, deep sea fishermen, and seasonal workers in the fish processing industry) also characterizes the cities of the Far Eastern littoral. Investment allocation for social–municipal services and infrastructure makes no allowance for them. The consequent pressure on the housing and tertiary sector, combined with a severe male–female imbalance (also aggravating the shortage of services, which depend overwhelmingly on female labor) here, too, results in social problems and exacerbates the labor turnover. All this complicates economic development along the Pacific coast, even along its southern sector, which probably represents the least objectionable physical environment for human occupancy east of Lake Baikal.

In Siberia and the Far East, the growth of both the large established cities and of the new towns is mostly fed not by immigration from west of the Urals, and certainly not from Central Asia, but by outmigration from small towns and villages within Siberia itself. The large rural outflow, of course, presents a severe problem for the Soviet regime throughout the Slavic republics. However, in Siberia, with its huge food deficit, continual rural outmigration imperils the entire development process. So far, the oft-repeated socialist goal of overcoming the socio-economic distance and differences in living level between city and village remains entirely unrealized anywhere in the USSR, with the partial exception of the Baltic republics. The very strong urban bias in the allocation of social and infrastructural investment (from 1918 through 1965, Soviet villages received a mere 9 percent of all such investment) has been challenged in recent years by influential scholars in Novosibirsk.[3] They press for the modernization of rural infrastructure and claim to have achieved an equitable allocation of "nonproductive" investment between villages and cities in West Siberia today.

The legacy of past neglect, however, cannot soon be overcome. In addition, the geographic obstacles to modernizing rural life and fully integrating the countryside into the nation's urbanized mainstream are greater in Siberia, the Far East, and most of Kazakhstan than west of the Urals, even though cultural and linguistic barriers affect only a small part of the population. The much greater isolation and far-flung nature of rural settlements east of the Urals more than counterweigh the generally lower proportion of villages with less than 200 persons. The huge expanse of cultivated area (and a still larger total agricultural area) per collective and state farm means the administrative dependence of six to seven outlying villages on the central settlement with the farm headquarters, where most social amenities and infrastructure, all economic and political power, and links to the outside world for such a farm are concentrated.

Current Soviet policy strives for the consolidation of rural settlements to facilitate the provision of amenities and infrastructure. Yet the farm leadership and rural planners face a dilemma, which is especially severe in

Siberia and Kazakhstan. The preservation of a network of smaller places is essential for the reasonably efficient functioning of agriculture, given the enormous size of the farms, the shortness of the growing season, and the poor road conditions. In fact, the fate of Soviet (and Siberian) agricultural production is inevitably decided in rural places of less than 500 persons, where most of those engaged directly in crop and stock raising live. Therefore, while the improvement of rural amenities can be most economically and rapidly effected in the nodal villages, the corresponding neglect, let alone liquidation, of outlying settlements, increases travel time, sharply raises the workload and, therefore, accelerates rural flight, which the very consolidation of settlements was intended to prevent.

In the USSR, the explicit involvement of planners with problems of regional development stem from both objective conditions and systemic factors. Immense size, strategic concerns, very uneven population and resource distribution, and a multinational population associated with specific geographic areas represent the most obvious objective conditions. The systemic factors relate to the problem of resource allocation in a centrally planned economy. In the latter, the vectors of principal resource flow (material and financial and, to a limited extent, even human) must be determined administratively ex ante as to quantity, mix, origin, and destination. And, because over the long haul, relative resource availablity and the production possibilities of an economy themselves change, long-term shifts in the spatial structure itself must become part of the planning process. Reality, of course, will diverge from the plan. Much improvisation will be the unavoidable consequence of imperfect knowledge and unforeseen emergencies even in the short run. The incorporation of the regional dimension, however, is a sine qua non of the planning process itself.

Yet, while the factors of geographic space and regional differences loom large in the Soviet planning process, this has not resulted in a comprehensive regional approach or in the increased power of regional authorities, except briefly during the Khrushchev period. The centralized, directive nature of Soviet planning, plus methodological and informational problems of using geographic areas as primary blocks for the construction of national plans, have relegated regional planning to minor importance behind branch planning through most of Soviet history. However, both of these obstacles to comprehensive regional planning

are reduced (at least in theory) for the huge pioneer
hinterland that makes up most of the Asian USSR. The early
stage of evolution and the relatively narrow profile of
economic activities compared to well-developed regions
lessen the data problem. At the same time, advances in
mathematical modeling interregional and regional programming permit the simulation and evaluation of a range of
possible choices.

Perhaps the most intense intellectural effort by
Soviet scholars to link branch and territorial management
of the economy has centered on the concept of the TPC
(territorial-production complex). In the old established
regions of the country, TPCs would mostly provide a framework for ex post analysis and, at best, for improving the
management of existing linkages. Through the sparsely
populated, pioneer hinterland of the Asian USSR however,
targeted-programming TPCs, consciously created, could
become the concrete areal organization for the realization
of specific regional problems of development. They would
provide the needed coherence and unity in decision making
for the development of new regions. They would operationalize that unity, on the one hand, by concentrating development spatially. On the other hand, they would help to
circumvent the autarchic, "empire-building" tendencies of
powerful ministries and compel the development of regionally associated linkages through the very task of problem
solving and by being defined around a specific target
program. Their former recognition as a planning unit is
indicated by the fact that, in 1979, Gosplan was instructed
to prepare for the development of individual TPCs. Since
1982, the Central Statistical Administration annually
reports the percentage growth of industry (relative to
1980) in the eight most important complexes. Seven of the
eight are found in sparsely populated pioneer areas, four
of them in Siberia and the Far East.

Recent developments in the Asian USSR show that the
TPCs have indeed promoted the geographic concentration of
investment in each of the major regions east of the Urals.
At the same time, however, they have not reduced organizational anarchy through the strengthening of economic
linkages among ministries and trusts operating in the TPCs.
Nor have they succeeded so far in forcing a better concentration and sharing of facilities, repair capacity, and
infrastructure among such ministries and other industrial
agencies. All the old sins of "departmentalism," such as
the duplication of facilities, chaotic, disjointed housing,
transport and service investments, and uncoordinated

manpower planning continue within the confines of the TPCs. Synchronized, coherent territorial development remains as elusive as ever.

Soviet scholars attribute such failures on the part of the TPCs to the lack of formal and informal power, to the absence of any legal status, and lack of a unified command. Intense debate on these issues so far has not resulted in any bold initiative or led to any significant improvement even in the Tiumen' TPC, where an interdepartmental commission under Gosplan was created. How Gorbachev's economic strategy which, among other things, apparently seeks to weaken the powerful branch ministries and to strengthen and enlarge interbranch production associations, will affect the role of the TPCs in economic and regional development is not yet clear. Severe restrictions on the power of ministries "to impose detailed targets on the enlarged production associations, a genuine devolution of decisions" could make the TPCs as a formal unit of planning unnecessary, but come alive in reality through enterprise self-interest.[4]

Whatever will be the outcome of Gorbachev's attempt to streamline the economy and improve the planning process, a more hard-nosed and less enthusiastic policy towards large projects in the Asian USSR is certain. A very few select areas, of course, will continue to receive priority. Current frenetic efforts in the West Siberian oil and gas regional will persist out of sheer necessity, the Kuzbas probably will be revitalized, the development of the Ekibastuz energy complex will proceed, and a handful of other nodes in Siberia and the Far East will probably grow at about the national rate. Basically, however, the development of all these select areas will be determined by immediate metropolitan priorities, among which fuel-energy needs are the single most important. The compelling role of energy priorities for the Trans-Ural regions is now further strengthened by the serious setback in the Soviet nuclear power program after the Chernobyl accident.

Enhanced metropolitan priorities, of course, mean that the Asian USSR, West Siberia, and select parts of Kazakhstan will be strongly favored (as they have been already in the past few years) against remote East Siberia, the Far East, and Central Asia, which has less additional resources to offer in the near future. As Theodore Shabad has put it, "if irreplaceable regional development programs, such as the oil and gas efforts in West Siberia, are taken out of the equation, the very essence of the Gorbachev economic policy, with its stress on improving the existing economic potential, implies a shift in orientation . . . from vast, undeveloped open spaces of the east to the great centers of economic activity in the west."[5] Indeed, a highly placed scholar from the Central Economic Research Institute under the RSFSR Gosplan was also decidedly negative on the prospect of Siberia recently, and at a major conference in Novosibirsk itself. He stated unequivocally that an economic growth rate for Siberia above the national mean in the near future is simply unfeasible.[6]

In Central Asia, the abundant labor reserves, in contrast to the general labor shortage in most other regions of the USSR, enabled three of the four republics to experience a gross industrial expansion somewhat above the Soviet average in each five-year period since 1970. Per capita, however, the region has fallen much farther behind the national mean. In addition, the growth of labor productivity here has been slower than anywhere else in the USSR. Since 1980, agricultural output also increased more slowly.[7] Significantly, the Guidelines of the Twelfth FYP project only a little faster growth rates for the region in industrial production than for the country as a whole (some 26 percent versus 24.3 percent) and virtually the same increase in agricultural output.[8] In the strongest republic, the Uzbek SSR, improvement in labor productivity is planned to contribute almost two-thirds of the growth in national income, four-fifths of the growth of industrial output, and all increase in the volume of construction. This appears wholly unrealistic. Labor productivity improvement in 1985 contributed only 23 percent to the rise of Uzbek national income and barely over a third to the rise of industrial production.[9] In the past, the theme of equalizing development among ethnic areas has tended to be emphasized or at least acknowledged in statements about regional policy. More recently, that goal has disappeared from among the explicitly declared objectives. Brezhnev, in 1972, declared the problem to be essentially solved.[10] A Soviet theoretician, echoing Brezhnev, stated a few years later that the reduction of such development gaps as do remain is to be subordinated to the common good of "building the material-technical basis for communism."[11]

Clearly, the subordination of regional equity considerations or of any economic "manifest destiny" in Siberia to efficiency, modernization, and national economic growth is even more central to Gorbachev's strategy. The new General Secretary also seems to display a hard-nosed, unapologetic attitude towards the country's far-flung periphery, both in the Slavic hinterland and still more in Moslem Central

Asia, though his commitment to its strategic security remains as firm as that of any of his predecessors. The remaining years of the twentieth century will not be favorable to development in the Asian USSR. The hypothesis suggested two decades ago applies even more today. In a political-economic atmosphere "of aggressive, optimistic expansiveness and/or comparative affluence, there is a tendency to invest more in some of the eastern regions, even though the expectation of return may be very long-term and the yield less than might be obtained from similar investment in places closer to 'home.'" The converse applies in periods of capital stringency,[12] which today is made more severe by the unanticipated huge hard currency shortfall and isaccompanied by domestic social and international pressures. Putting Siberia, especially its regions east of the Enisei, "into mothballs" will not affect the stability and cohesion of the Soviet state. Only time will tell how long Central Asia, with its booming population (almost 70 percent of which is under thirty years of age[13]) and with its articulate native elite can remain "mothballed" economically while subject to political control by Moscow.

NOTES

1. Pravda, June 19, 1986, p. 4 and Osnovnye napravleniia ekonomicheskogo i sotsial'nogo razvitiia SSSR na 1986-1990 gody i na period do 2000 goda (Moscow: Izdatel'stvo politicheskoi literatury, 1986), pp. 74-75.
2. Chapter 3, footnote 11 and Pravda, June 19, 1986, p. 3.
3. Chapter 6, footnote 24.
4. Philip Hanson, "Gorbachev's Economic Strategy: A comment," Soviet Economy, Vol. 1, No. 4 (October-December), 1985, p. 307.
5. Theodore Shabad, "The Gorbachev Economic Policy: Is the USSR Turning Away from Siberian Development?" Paper presented at the Second International Conference on Siberia, University of London, England, April, 1986.
6. L.A. Kozlov in V.E. Seliverstov, "Razvitie Sibiri v narodnokhoziaistvennom komplekse SSSR," AN SSSR, SO, Seriia ekonomiki i prikladnoi sotsiologii, Izvestiia, 1986, No. 1, p. 50.
7. Narodnoe khoziaistvo SSSR v 1975 godu, pp. 203,

215-16; Narodnoe khoziaistvo SSSR v 1985 godu, pp. 102-105, 113-14 and 188.

8. Pravda, June 19, 1986, pp. 1-4; Narodnoe khoziaistvo SSSR v 1985 godu, p. 61 and Materialy XXVII S'ezda Kommunisticheskoi Partii Sovetskogo Soiuza (Moscow: Izdatel'stvo politicheskoi literatury, 1986), pp. 322-37.

9. A. Korneev, "Chto na poverkhnosti i chto v glubine," Ekonomika i zhizn', 1986, No. 9 (September), p. 6.

10. Pravda, December 22, 1972, p. 5.

11. Quoted by Gertrude E. Schroeder from Istoriia SSSR, 1976, No. 3 (March), pp. 3-21 in "Soviet Regional Development Policies in Perspective." NATO Colloquium, The USSR in the 1980s: Economic Growth and the Role of Foreign Trade. Brussels, 1978.

12. David Hooson, "Industrial Growth—Where Next?" Survey, 1965, No. 57 (October), p. 123.

13. The source refers to Uzbekistan which, in 1985, accounted for 61 percent of the population of the four Central Asian republics. The age structure of the other three is very similar to that of Uzbekistan. R.A. Ubaidullaeva, ed., Sotsial'no-ekonomicheskie problemy ispol'zovaniia truda molodezhi v Uzbekistane (Tashkent: Fan, 1982), p. 12.

Index

Aganbegian, Abel, 236-237, 247-248
Agriculture:
  cotton production, harvesting, 123, 130. See also Cotton "complex"
  employment share in material production, Siberian provinces, 191-193
  in the Northlands, 191, 195, 203
  mechanization in Siberia, 173-174
  private, subsidiary in Central Asia, 141-142
  state and collective farm employment in Central Asia, 127-132
  workload in North Kazakhstan, 174, 175
  workload in Siberia and and Far East, 174, 175
Aldan (iron ore), 105, 108
Altai Krai, 64, 68, 106, 174, 185, 197.
Altai Mountains, 27, 28, 55
Amur Oblast, 24, 93-94, 96, 107, 195, 198

Amur Valley, 24, 30, 93, 111
Angara-Enisei region, 33-34
Andizhan, garment production, 145
Andizhan Oblast, 36, 146
Angara, Lower Angara TPC, 241, 242
Apparel, production in Central Asia, 123
Arable land:
  Central Asia, 22
  North Kazakhstan, 24, 28-29, 177
  Siberia, including Far East, 24, 30, 93, 173
Aral Sea-Lake Balkhash, as boundary between hinterlands, 7, 21
Autarchy, departmental, problem of, 52, 54, 200, 242-249
AYAM (Amur-Yakutsk Mainline), 110
BAM (Baikal-Amur Mainline), 25, 29, 30, 32, 94, 98, 99
  military significance of, 110-112
BAM Program, 104-110
Birth-rate of Moslem population, 23
Bond, Andrew, 213, 214